Glenn McGrath

Line and Strength

Glenn McGrath

Line and Strength

The Complete Story
Glenn McGrath with Daniel Lane

YELLOW JERSEY PRESS
LONDON

First published in Australia by Random House Australia in 2008
Published by Yellow Jersey Press 2009

2 4 6 8 10 9 7 5 3 1

First published in Great Britain in 2009 by
Yellow Jersey Press
Random House, 20 Vauxhall Bridge Road,
London SW1V 2SA

www.rbooks.co.uk

Addresses for companies within The Random House Group Limited can be found at:
www.randomhouse.co.uk/offices.htm

The Random House Group Limited Reg. No. 954009

A CIP catalogue record for this book
is available from the British Library

ISBN 9780224082877

The Random House Group Limited makes every effort to ensure that the papers used
in its books are made from trees that have been legally sourced from well-managed and
credibly certified forests. Our paper procurement policy can be found at:
www.rbooks.co.uk/environment

Mixed Sources
Product group from well-managed
forests and other controlled sources
www.fsc.org Cert no. TT-COC-2139
FSC © 1996 Forest Stewardship Council

Printed and bound in the UK by
CPI Mackays, Chatham, ME5 8TD

For Jane, James and Holly

Contents

PART TWO

PART THREE

Foreword

by Dennis Lillee

A lot of things may come between a 10-year-old's dream to play for his country and a 20-year-old actually getting to the stage where he might. He would, however, have a far greater chance of making it if he really believed he could . . .

I wrote that in my book *The Art of Fast Bowling* way back in 1977. I have no idea if Glenn McGrath ever read that passage, but by representing Australia in 124 Tests and 250 One Day Internationals, he's proof that I told the truth all those years ago.

Glenn didn't really start to play cricket until he was in his mid-teens – and that's quite late. In this book he tells the story of how he worked to fulfil his secret dream of representing Australia by practising religiously, bowling at a 44-gallon drum behind his father's machinery shed.

McGrath did that even though few people at his junior club thought he had any ability as a bowler. I think it says a lot about his drive and his determination that he single-mindedly pursued a dream many thought was way beyond his reach.

But the people of the Backwater Cricket Club in outback

New South Wales needn't punish themselves for not seeing anything special in their most famous player. You see, when I first laid eyes on him 17 or 18 years ago, I definitely didn't earmark him as a Test bowler in the making – let alone as one of the game's greatest. Glenn was raw – red raw – when I watched him in the Sydney Cricket Ground's practice nets. He was in a NSW fast bowlers' squad that had been formed as part of a national initiative to identify up-and-comers with potential.

In my role as the head consultant, I travelled around Australia to cast my eyes over the young bowlers. I'd either change inefficient or injury-prone actions or techniques, finetune individual actions, or offer bowlers advice when, and if, it was needed. My first reaction, watching Glenn bowl, was not that he was a champion in the making. He bowled *okay*, but to be brutally honest, I saw nothing to write home about.

I thought he'd need to develop his core strength if he was to have any hope of even surviving the fast bowler's game. He was wiry, and indeed back then he was painfully thin. However, no-one realised he was doing it so tough financially that he often ate a Mars Bar for dinner because it was all he could afford.

Glenn couldn't have been any older than 19 when he was in that squad, but what his progression to international cricketer highlighted was that a player can change from his late teenage years to his early twenties. Glenn's confidence, strength, ability and skills changed dramatically in the space of those few short years; and another thing I've noted is that each body responds differently.

The ties that bind cricket's great fast bowlers are their tremendous work ethic along with a level of determination and desire that borders on a form of madness.

You need the madness. McGrath definitely has it.

People who watch cricket on the television might think fast bowlers have an easy gig – my goodness, they're wrong. A fast bowler's lot is tough. They're often performing in temperatures well above the 30-degree mark, and even when their body aches and their feet blister and bleed, they must push on and try to get the breakthrough wicket the team is sweating on.

It's those demands that sort the strong-willed from the rest. Fast bowling is a pursuit where blokes with weak tickers fall by the wayside and perish. One or two might sneak through and last for a short time, but in my view, Glenn McGrath – a bowler who has endured the test of time – is one of a unique breed of athlete. They're big-hearted, they're tough and they're special. And they deserve our admiration.

McGrath's longevity alone is something that must be admired. He competed at the highest level for 14 years and his career spanned 124 Tests – at the time of his retirement it was the greatest number by a fast bowler.

I attribute Glenn's ability to play that many Tests to several factors, including:

- his pain threshold;
- his strength and conditioning, which were excellent; and
- his action – McGrath had a machine-like action that was economical *and* easy on his body.

I took a genuine interest in Glenn's career. I worked with him on a number of occasions, firstly with the NSW development squad at the SCG nets, then at the Cricket Academy in Adelaide, and after that in numerous private sessions. Over the years I found him to be likeable, respectful, professional and willing to take advice on board. McGrath was a model student – and now he has plenty to offer the next generation of pacemen as a teacher and mentor.

Glenn McGrath will be remembered as one of cricket's greatest fast bowlers, and for good reason – he took 563 Test wickets and created all sorts of records and milestones along the way.

He has long been compared to bowlers from other eras, but I don't like doing that because it's a pointless and fruitless exercise. It's impossible to compare players from different eras because no matter how hard you try or how well you think it'll work, it just doesn't. I know people will continue to make comparisons but I think that's unfair, because all you can go by is a player's statistics – and they don't always tell the true story.

I would prefer to celebrate Glenn's career – and everyone else's, for that matter – by remembering how good he was during his own time. Compare him to his peers. Glenn is in good company – Waqar Younis, Wasim Akram, Shaun Pollock, Courtney Walsh, Allan Donald and Curtly Ambrose, to name but a few.

I am thrilled and honoured to have been invited to write the foreword for *Glenn McGrath – Line and Strength*. Glenn has a great and powerful story to tell. He proves that hard work and sheer determination can be rewarded. After all, he rose from obscurity in the New South Wales outback to become one of cricket's great fast bowlers.

Away from the field, Glenn joined his wife Jane in meeting head-on the challenge of breast cancer. The dignified way they've conducted their battle has helped the public gain a greater awareness of an insidious disease, and their actions and fundraising feats through the McGrath Foundation have given hope to thousands upon thousands of people.

There is no doubt Jane is a wonderful, special human being – her courage has moved me. Yet Glenn has also impressed me.

I am certain many others in his position would have wilted; they would have given up the ghost. A few might have said 'I don't have the guts for this' or 'Life's unfair', but while he made it clear that Jane and their kids, James and Holly, were (and still are) his priority, Glenn soldiered along quietly on the cricket field.

In any era, in any team, Glenn McGrath is – in my view – one of life's true champions.

Dennis Lillee
Perth, January 2008

Preface

by Glenn McGrath

In January 2007 I retired from the Australian Test team feeling happy because I knew nothing could be better than bowing out after regaining the Ashes from England in a 5–0 whitewash. There was an incredible sense of emotion and elation as I walked around the Sydney Cricket Ground with my team-mates, holding hands with my children, James and Holly. I didn't feel the slightest sense of sadness about retiring. I knew I'd reached the end; my body told me that. And even more importantly, I'd realised that those special moments I was missing in the life and times of my family were too great . . . the moments had become weeks at a time, and I didn't like it.

Before working on *Line and Strength*, I hadn't sat back and thought too much about my journey – from bowling at an old 44-gallon drum when there were doubts about my ability, to fulfilling my dream of opening the attack for Australia. Now I've gone through that process, I feel humbled – and I feel blessed. I have benefited greatly from the goodwill and generosity of so many people that I could never begin to thank them all in this preface. What I will say is that their examples and thoughtfulness made an impact on me, and I have attempted to display the same level of kindness to young fast bowlers looking to me for help and guidance.

Having a book written about my life has been strange because I have never seen myself as anything more than an ordinary person. It is a bit daunting to realise my innermost thoughts are there for others to read. I have been honest and I have addressed a few matters I would really rather forget.

My life's greatest reward has been my marriage to Jane and having our children. I dedicate all I have achieved to her, and I want Jane to know the love, strength and pride I have drawn from having her as my soul mate. To James and Holly – you gave me an extra motivation and reason to push on during those days it would have been all too easy just to give up. My mum, dad, sister Donna and little brother Dale were often in my thoughts during this project, and it is my hope they realise how special they are to me.

I offer a big thanks to those people who cheered me through thick and thin, and I hope you realise I never took your support for granted. It was generous of you and I valued it.

I write this message from Delhi, India, where I am playing in the Indian Premier League Twenty20 competition – and it is amazing. Had anyone told me 16 months ago that I'd be playing in India, I'd have laughed and called them crazy. It simply proves that life truly is a surprise packet and that we have to make the most of it. If anyone is to take anything away from this book, I hope it is that they make the most of their opportunities and never, ever listen to those people who say they can't do something.

Glenn McGrath
Delhi, May 2008

Part One

1

The Boy Who Couldn't Bowl

Glenn was just too erratic.

Backwater under-16s bowler Mark Munro
on Glenn McGrath's bowling

The sun was deep into its descent over the horizon of western New South Wales, its long rays streaked across the outback sky, lighting it with colours that looked to the boy like smears of drizzled honey, burnt orange, molten gold and bronze. Normally Glenn McGrath would have paused to admire the view. Although he was only 16 years old, he knew enough to realise that appreciating nature's wonders – sunsets, sunrises, lightning storms – is nutritious for the soul. But on this particular evening, McGrath didn't have time to spare. He turned his back on God's grandeur, determined to finish his final 'job' of the day before his mum called him in for dinner.

McGrath was bone-tired and weary. He and Dale, his 14-year-old brother, had spent yet another day toiling in the back paddock of the family's Narromine property, sowing as many as they could of its 1000 acres for the next season's wheat crop. In years to come, McGrath would say that not even the unforgiving heat and humidity of Pakistan or India were as exhausting as the time he had replaced his father as the man of the family. Glenn and Dale were boys doing men's work, thanks to the age-old farmer's curse: crippling bills and scarce income. The account book for the 1987 season looked grim and the boys' father, Kevin, was working as a road-train driver, transporting livestock from the Northern Territory and central Queensland to the abattoir at nearby Dubbo.

As McGrath remembers, working the family property was a big responsibility: the family's livelihood depended on the brothers doing a good job, and the task was one that could quite easily have frightened him, had he allowed it to. But his younger brother was born to work the land. Dale would lighten the mood by waiting for Glenn to lift a heavy sack of grain from the ute – then he'd leap from the vehicle onto his brother's back. The extra weight would crumple Glenn's skinny legs and he'd crash to the ground in an angry cloud of dust. Dale would laugh loudly before running for his life as his brother picked himself up and hurled abuse, calling him 'a bloody pest'.

'It was a tough time,' Dale agrees. 'But we got through it. I liked to stir him up. But Glenn could always find something – a bit of rock, some fibro or a golf ball – and nine times out of ten he'd hit me.'

The weight of responsibility McGrath carried for those few weeks as the man of the house was heavy, like the sack of grain, but he steadied himself by accepting that he had to deal with the situation as best as he could; it was the responsibility he had inherited as the elder son. What he felt, but couldn't then properly articulate, was the need to worry only about controlling the controllable. This was a mantra that would serve him well in later life: McGrath would call upon it regularly, when he'd challenge the world to do its worst while he tried to do his best as a cricketer and a devoted husband.

And yet there were times when he was out in the paddock

that the boy wished that Kevin would offer some fatherly advice. McGrath was not to know that out on the road, as the kilometres rolled by, Kevin's thoughts were always with his boys and how they were going.

'I knew they'd do a good job,' Kevin says. 'I knew they'd work well together.' Although the boys planned their time so that one worked for an hour while the other took off on the motorbike, somehow they got the work done. 'Glenn handled the job very well, though Dale was more farm-minded – even as a little kid he would run into the sheep yard, get knocked over, and get straight back on his feet. Glenn was more into playing his sport.'

Against the setting sun McGrath prepared to push himself one last time before calling it a day. The dirt from the back paddock was still on his hands and in his boots. This last job of the day wasn't a chore like feeding the chickens or tending the lambs – and it was as much a passion as an escape. He picked up the scuffed, red leather cricket ball from the ground and prepared to bowl at the 44-gallon drum that bore, like belly wounds, the numerous dings and dents from deliveries that had found their mark over the years. When Glenn's mother, Beverley – better known as Bev – heard the regular bang of leather ball thumping into steel drum, she knew exactly where he was – behind the shed that housed her husband's machinery. She accepted as a healthy obsession her son's afternoon ritual of perfecting what the respected television commentator Richie Benaud would one day call a 'nagging line and length'. 'He's not hurting anyone or himself,' she'd say.

McGrath was a child of Australian cricket's last great depression. In the summer of 1986/87, the Australian Test team was still recovering from the void left by the retirements of Greg Chappell, Rod Marsh and Dennis Lillee two years earlier.

In the absence of these great players, the Australians were bullied, particularly by the West Indies, whose fearsome four-pronged pace attack was cricket's answer to the Four Horsemen of the Apocalypse: War, Famine, Pestilence and Death. They'd starve the Aussie batsmen of runs before leaving them battered and bloodied, humbled and humiliated. So desperate was their plight that after Test player David Hookes had captained Joel 'Big Bird' Garner for South Australia (when Garner played there in 1982/83), Hookes urged the Australian Cricket Board (ACB) to consider tempting young West Indian pace aces to pledge their allegiance to the baggy green cap, the most sought-after prize for an Aussie cricketer. But as it turned out, the ACB didn't need to look that far, because the answer to Australian cricket's numerous prayers was in the wheat belt of western New South Wales, bowling his heart out at an old fuel drum.

McGrath remembers the ascendancy of the West Indies during the 1980s, but it was the grit of the opposing Australian captain that inspired him. 'The Windies was an awesome team, and while I remember the '80s as a tough time for Australian cricket, I also remember listening to the radio as we'd drive along and Allan Border was batting,' says McGrath. 'He was brave. Border stood up to numerous challenges and my dream was to play alongside him. So I trained and I dreamed.'

Bev was her son's greatest supporter, but there were others who believed he should concentrate on basketball. He was certainly built for it – skinny as a garden rake, he already stood well over six feet. Very few people in Narromine thought the lad had much ability, if any, as a bowler. Indeed, his summer Saturdays playing cricket were whiled away deep in the outfield, well away from the action. Shane Horsburgh, McGrath's first captain at the Backwater Cricket Club under-16s, joked that a broomstick had more talent than Glenn. McGrath had a strong throwing arm and an ability to slog the ball, but the boy's main role in the side seemed to be simply to make up the numbers. Almost 21 years later, Mark Munro, the star bowler from that under-16s team, reminisced over a cold drink about the nature of those long-gone games and McGrath's wayward bowling. 'Glenn was just too erratic,' he says.

Glenn McGrath, the boy who couldn't bowl. But the boy learned to bowl, improving his accuracy during his lonely training sessions, never bothering to tell anyone – Bev included – that the reason he spent those hours finetuning his style was that he *knew* one day he'd play for Australia. It was as certain for him as the fact that the sunrise would bring the promise of even more back-breaking labour. His long hours were inspired by some words of wisdom the South African golfer Gary Player once offered a supporter who wished he could hit the ball like Player. 'Go hit a thousand balls a day and you will,' was the champion's reply.

'It's about dedication,' McGrath says. 'When you know what you want to do, where you want to go, it's up to you to put it all in place.'

On that distant evening, the 16-year-old McGrath limbered up in the near-darkness. While his every muscle screeched in agony at the prospect of more physical activity, the boy walked towards the mark from where he'd start his long run-up. Many thoughts swirled through his head, including the jobs that were still ahead of him and his brother, and, more despairingly, the ever-widening cracks in his parents' marriage. There was little he could do to change the course in which his mother and father were headed. Donna, McGrath's younger sister, says their parents' eventual divorce made the three children stronger. 'And it makes you stronger in many ways because you have to live with it.'

When McGrath finally turned to face the 44-gallon drum, he entered a world in which he was dressed in pristine cricket whites and standing on the hallowed Sydney Cricket Ground (SCG) with the likes of his hero, Dennis Lillee, and champion wicketkeeper Rodney Marsh. He had only ever seen the SCG on television, but it was there before him in the Narromine paddock; his mind's eye marvelled at the large, Aussie-flag-waving crowd in the stands. McGrath imagined that he gripped not a war-weary ball but a shiny red Kookaburra six-stitcher. The order from Allan Border to get an early breakthrough against the West Indies rang in his ears. As he commenced his run from the Bradman Stand end, his head buzzed with commentary by Richie Benaud.

'The debutant prepares for his first delivery in Test cricket. Desmond Haynes on strike; the rookie from the Australian outback versus the West Indian master. I must say, the newcomer looks confident. He was known as 'the boy who couldn't bowl' when he lived in outback Narromine . . . Let's see what he's got . . .'

McGrath was oblivious to the dust blasts his feet kicked up with each strong and measured step that carried him towards the popping crease. He didn't see the remnants of the wheat crop bow in the breeze or the kangaroos in the top paddock. He didn't even hear the screeches of the cockatoos as they scrambled back to their trees, the cicadas' chant or the bull belching and bellowing. His focus was fixed firmly on the target 22 yards away. But as was always the case, the boy didn't see a simple drum: instead Haynes stood before him, sleek and elegant as he tapped his bat on the pitch in anticipation of that first delivery. Soon it would be the great Viv Richards on strike, and then the frightening fast bowler Michael Holding would be trying to keep the Windies' tail alive in the face of the boy's one-man assault on the 'Calypso Kings'.

Benaud's commentary continued. *'He bowls a beautifully pitched delivery. It's bang on target . . . BOWLED HIM! My goodness, the middle stump is cartwheeling back towards the wicketkeeper. I haven't seen that since the days of the great Wes Hall. A wicket with his first delivery – welcome to Test cricket, Glenn McGrath!'*

Destiny dictated that, in time, Glenn McGrath *would* single-handedly take the fight to the great West Indians; he *would* become the game's most successful fast bowler; his name *would* be revered in Australian sport and at cricket grounds around the globe; and he *would* one day destroy England at Lord's, the home of the noble game. But in the meantime, he continued to dream and prepare himself for the day opportunity knocked.

And on this particular evening, Australia's latest backyard cricketing hero was snapped back to reality by the sound of his mother calling out for the umpteenth time that dinner was on the table. It was dark but he picked up the ball for one last delivery. 'The Master Blaster' Viv Richards was on strike. It was up to him – the boy who couldn't bowl – to tame him before tea.

2

A Skinned Rabbit

My, he looks like a skinned rabbit!

Poppy Don Watts on first seeing his
grandson, Glenn, in 1970

On Monday 9 February 1970, Glenn Donald McGrath, destined to be cricket's most successful fast bowler, arrived in the world. It was a time of insufferable heat in the New South Wales outback, and a time of darkness for Bill Lawry's Australian team, which was touring South Africa. The future pace bowler should probably have been kicking and wailing. Instead Bev noted her son – born with his head resting upon his arm – appeared to be at peace with the world. In later years McGrath would joke that his arm being positioned behind his head at birth was a sign he was born ready to bowl.

'He was a good baby, all my three children were, so I was pretty lucky in that respect,' Bev says. 'I was only 20-and-a-half when I had Glenn and while I was fairly young, I never regretted it because Glenn was the only one of my three kids my father, Don, saw before he died, so that was special. He was a proud grandfather, too. My dad loved cricket and while he didn't see what Glenn grew up to become because he died before Glenn turned two, it was really good he got to spend that time with him.'

11

Kevin McGrath, a hard-working 24-year-old share farmer, was sweating as he paced up and down the waiting room at the Dubbo Base Hospital. He wasn't perspiring from nerves at the prospect of the new responsibilities that awaited him. He was excited about becoming a father. Instead he was sweating buckets because the state's far west was gripped by a fierce heatwave, and even though the hospital's ceiling fans were at full bore, they couldn't shift the heat that hung over the room like a thermal blanket. The unrelenting nature of the heat forced many in Dubbo to desert their homes at night to try to find some relief – and sleep – on their front lawns.

But Bev defied the heat to remain relaxed through the final stages of her pregnancy. Indeed, before going to the hospital at midnight for the birth, she'd whiled away the hours by playing a game of quoits against Don in the back yard of his house in town.

Kevin and Don were filled with anticipation when they laid their eyes on the baby boy for the very first time.

'It wasn't like it is today because fathers weren't allowed in the delivery room,' says Kevin. 'So I waited outside with Bev's father and I remember feeling very excited about what was happening. We saw all the babies lined up in the nursery and Don and I looked at them lying in their cribs and not knowing which one was Glenn. We were saying, "Oh that's a nice baby. There's a nice baby." We knew the nurse in there and she waved to us and showed us where Glenn was. He was on his own away from the rest. Who knows, he must've been annoying the other babies just like he used to do the other cricketers!

'The nurse wheeled him over to the window, Bev's father and I looked at the little fella, then we looked at each other, then we looked back at the little baby, and I can still remember Don saying, "My, he looks like a skinned rabbit!" His legs and arms were that skinny! As it turned out he grew into "Pigeon" as a cricketer because of those skinny legs.'

While their son's arrival was the most significant event to have occurred in the couple's young lives, the world didn't stop that day, as the local paper – *The Daily Liberal* – duly noted. McGrath was born as a total fire ban was enforced throughout the region. As if to emphasise the stupidity of ignoring the warning, the paper ran on its front page a photograph of a Jubilee Street housing commission house that was razed in the early hours of the previous Saturday morning. FAMILY LOSES POSSESSIONS IN HOUSE – TWO HURT, screamed the headline.

The *Liberal* also reported that a major retail company planned to open a store in Tralbagar Street, and the editorial welcomed the promise of more jobs and added prosperity in the area. A local grazier was bound for India as a member of a three-man team to develop a sheep-breeding program there. Two 18-year-olds hooked a 45-pound cod while drifting down the Macquarie River in their small boat. The battle that was described could have been lifted from the pages of Ernest Hemingway's *The Old Man and the Sea*. A local identity declared the whopper to be the biggest he'd seen in his 40-odd years of fishing the local rivers and estuaries.

There was plenty for *The Daily Liberal* to say about the Far West Cricket Council's competition: Dubbo pace bowler Bruce Warwick had been selected to play for Country Firsts against City at the SCG; minor premiers Nyngan had been bundled out of the finals series by Gilgandra; and the Rugby Union XI had been hammered by Paramount. Kevin McGrath's cousins Graham and Eric Shanks were mentioned after Graham belted 81 for South Dubbo against Coalbaggie and Eric scored 60 before being run out.

While Bev lovingly nursed her newborn child, Bill Lawry's

Australians were reeling after the third day of the Second Test against the Springboks in South Africa. The AAP-Reuters cable, published in *The Daily Liberal*, pulled no punches:

'Humiliated and humbled, Australia can only look to Durban's cloudy skies to save them from an innings defeat at the hands of the Springboks today. The Australians lost their last six wickets for the addition of only 109 and were all out for 157. It was the fifth successive time that they had failed to top 200 in the first innings of a Test against South Africa.'

The Australians, ordered to follow on, languished 365 runs behind the home team's massive total of 9 (declared) for 622, thanks to local heroes Graeme Pollock and Barry Richards, who belted 274 and 140 respectively. All hope of restoring pride in Australia's baggy green cap rested upon the shoulders – and nerve – of Keith Stackpole (who'd compiled 55 runs) and Doug Walters (8) before rain stopped play. A chance meeting with Walters 18 years later would be life-changing for McGrath, but meanwhile *The Daily Liberal*'s correspondent wasn't at all confident of a rousing, backs-to-the-wall victory. He finished his report on an ominous note: 'Unless the rain gods answer the Australian prayers it may well be over before tea.'

Glenn McGrath, the skinned rabbit, was the latest of a proud line of Australian pioneers, soldiers, farmers and athletes. The McGrath roots stretched back to Francis McGrath, who farewelled his native Ireland 118 years before Glenn's birth to migrate to the new world – New South Wales – aboard the ship *Irene*. A free settler, Francis paid £3 10s for his family to make the long journey. On his disembarkment at Port Jackson on 16 October 1852, a customs officer noted that Francis was 38, a Catholic, literate and had worked previously as a butler.

Rather than remain in Sydney, Francis and his family

headed west, travelling across the Blue Mountains in search of opportunity. In 1864 he was made postmaster of Merendee, a flyspeck on the map between the bigger settlements of Mudgee and Wellington. Francis held that respected position until his retirement in 1882, when he endorsed his granddaughter to look after the Royal Mail. The founding father of the McGrath clan in the New South Wales outback died a year later after 'falling over a precipice'.

One of Francis' grandsons, known as Jim, married Rose McLauchlan and bought a property named *Stanhope* near Cooyal, a bumpy 22-kilometre horse-and-buggy ride from Mudgee. While isolated, Cooyal had a grocery store, a hotel, a post office, two churches, a dance hall, a cheese factory and a butcher's shop. Here Jim and Rose raised crops and three children, including Glenn's grandfather, Carlyle, born in 1915 and known as Lyle. The family grew fruit and Jim built himself a blacksmith's shed at the back of the house. (Jim's niece Muriel M. Marks recalls his forge and bellows in her 1987 book *Cooyal Stories*.)

The family was devastated in 1921 when Jim died of Spanish Flu during a trip to Sydney aged only 37. He was one of millions of people worldwide to die from the strain of influenza which had been brought to Australia by soldiers returning from the battlefields of World War One.

Jim McGrath was buried in Sydney's Rookwood Cemetery, the world's largest cemetery in the nineteenth century. The final resting place for over 600,000 souls, it covers 300 hectares, the size of modern Sydney's central business district. Not long after his retirement from Test cricket in 2007, McGrath made a pilgrimage to Rookwood to search for his great-grandfather Jim's burial site. While he found the area, it was overgrown with thick weeds and ancient shrubs. There were no headstones, making it impossible to identify his ancestor's final resting place.

For McGrath, finding the exact position of his great-grandfather's burial is important. 'I want to find the plot,' he says. 'It's important because it's to do with my roots, my sense of belonging and my heritage. That is becoming even more important to me as I get older.'

With the help of relatives, Rose McGrath continued to run the property. But the pile of rocks Jim had intended to use for the foundations of a new home on the sunny side of their property became her stones of sadness. The widow eventually found it too difficult to live alone and, after selling *Stanhope* to a relative, she relocated to Dubbo to be closer to her sister and to provide her three children with a high-school education. In 1943, Rose's son Lyle joined the Australian army as part of the 209 Light Aid detachment. Lance Corporal McGrath saw action against the Japanese in the south-west Pacific theatre of war. The only Anzac Day story Glenn ever heard his quietly spoken grandfather recall was of the time he was at sea and the ship he was on took a direct hit from a torpedo. Lyle married Vera Griffiths in 1944 and they had two sons, Kevin and Malcolm (known as Malc).

Glenn always remembers 'Grandad McGrath' out on the farm. 'He was a kindly man who liked to smoke his pipe. When I was little I tried to help him do things,' he says. 'There's a photo of me as a toddler trying to change a tyre. He died in 2000 when I was playing English county cricket for Worcester.'

Lyle's wife, Vera, was the boss of the family – 'a real matriarch', as her eldest grandson recalls. Now aged 93, she unfortunately suffers from Alzheimer's.

Bev's family, the Watts, were 'good breeders'. Glenn's great-grandfather James fathered 17 children. His grandmother Marjorie Hawke was one of 16. Bev's father was christened Baden Powell Watts, but later changed his name to Albert

Donald Watts – incorporating the name of his idol, Donald Bradman – after copping too much stick from his army buddies for being named after the bloke who founded the Boy Scout movement. Don volunteered for active service during World War Two and endured horrific conditions in Papua New Guinea, transporting supplies and ammunition as a member of the 3 Australian Pack (Horse) Transport Company. After suffering repeated bouts of dengue fever and malaria, which was reputed to have killed more diggers in the tropics than the enemy's bombs and bullets, he gained an honourable discharge in 1944.

'He'd suffer from bouts of malaria when we were kids, because it comes back,' Bev remembers. 'We really didn't know how bad it was for him until after he died. One thing about Dad was he didn't complain much.'

One of Bev's lasting memories of her father is of his passion for gardening. His tomato plants grew close to 20 feet high. 'You'd have to climb up on a ladder to get them and one slice was big enough to fill a dinner plate. I've never seen anything like them,' says Bev proudly. (She thinks her father's secret to growing the best tomatoes in the Western Districts might have been the thick trail of sugar he'd pile in the furrow as he planted the seeds.)

When Glenn was ten, his grandmother Marjorie suffered a stroke. He vividly recalls how this event dramatically altered the family structure in the course of a single school day: 'I was in Year 5 and I remember walking out of the classroom and getting picked up. My grandmother had suffered a stroke and I remember how upset everyone was. She lived for another 23 years and it wasn't easy for her. That kind of thing makes an impression on you, especially when you're only a kid.'

Back at Dubbo Hospital that hot February day in 1970,

Kevin looked on proudly as Bev cradled her newborn son in her arms. The only promises they could make Glenn on that first, special day were simple: he'd be loved and he'd be well cared for. These were promises they kept, but McGrath knows it wasn't always easy for them. He was a farmer's son, and that meant struggle and hardship were as certain as drought and flood.

3

Narromine Boy

We don't respect the clouds up there, they fill us
with disgust,
They mostly bring a Bogan shower – three rain-
drops and some dust.

'The City of the Dreadful Thirst',
A. B. 'Banjo' Paterson

Four hundred and fifty-eight long and lonely kilometres separate Narromine from the traffic snarls and ceaseless tramp of feet in Sydney. The township of 3500 people nestled on the eastern fringe of New South Wales' Western Plains was named 'Narramine' by the area's original inhabitants, the Wiradjuri. One translation suggests it means 'place of honey', while another insists it's 'place of lizards'. The only irrefutable fact concerning the town's name is that a simple error by the local newspaper's first editor changed the spelling to Narromine.

John Oxley, the Surveyor General of New South Wales, and the members of his 15-man expedition were the first whites to view the district's open, sunlit plains during their 1818 exploration of the Macquarie River. While Oxley searched in vain for an inland sea, he noted the region's fertile land and the potential for crops and livestock to thrive there. Narromine's first white settlers were squatters who followed Oxley's trail in the 1830s. William Charles Wentworth, a member of the first group of Europeans to cross the Blue Mountains in 1813, became a celebrated resident of the district when he counted 'Narramine Station' among his vast landholdings in 1835. The Main West railway linked the outpost to Sydney in 1883; the district's first school opened that same year and the population started to grow.

In 1973 Kevin McGrath bought the 1140-acre property *Lagoona*, which lay about 14 kilometres south-east of Narromine. He hoped to God that Narromine would be a place of milk *and* honey, because he was staking his family's future on the move being a success. He had reason to be optimistic; after all, in the good times the district was renowned for producing wheat, citrus, fruit, vegetables, lambs, wool and even cotton. He was aware, too, of the risk that nature could turn on him. When drought bites, Narromine shares the same postcode as Hades: the ground blisters, the air feels like the Devil's breath and symbols of desolation – sheep skulls, limp crops and skeletal cattle – dominate the landscape. But as Kevin packed up his young family – which now included two-year-old Dale – to make the 40-kilometre trip from Dubbo to *Lagoona*, he was buoyed by a genuine belief he could kick a goal. His family was, after all, leaving behind a successful enterprise in Dubbo.

'We owned our own place. Dad had acreage on a small farm on the edge of Dubbo,' Kevin recalls. 'When Malc and I each got married, Dad surveyed 100 acres off for me and the same for my brother.' The brothers also owned a poultry and pig farm, with over 4000 chooks and 20 or 30 sows, and share-farmed on a couple of well-known properties near Dubbo.

When Glenn was almost three, the McGrath clan found what Bev and Kev agreed was the perfect spot to drop anchor and raise their family. There were two adjoining properties for sale at Narromine; Kevin bought one and Malcolm bought the other. Lyle felt it was important to remain close to his sons, so he and Vera also moved, leaving the chicken and pig farm for a property just a few kilometres down the dirt road from the boys. Bev describes the move as 'long and difficult'. It was a logistical nightmare by any stretch of the imagination, with lots of machinery and the contents of three houses to move.

The 4000 chickens that remained at Dubbo were probably glad to see the back of Glenn and his cousin Craig, older by four months. The pair had terrorised the chooks almost from the first day they could walk, screaming at the top of their lungs as they chased them around the barnyard.

'They were like twins,' says Bev of the two boys. 'They grew up and did everything together, be it playing cricket or kicking a football. They were that close many people actually thought they were brothers.'

Despite hitting Narromine in a convoy of heavily laden trucks, the McGraths' arrival at *Lagoona* went seemingly unnoticed. If anyone had a thought for the newcomers, it may have been simply to wish them good luck for having a go. However, the eventual rise and rise of Glenn McGrath from battling bush cricketer to international sporting superstar would become entrenched in the town's rich folklore, which included 'The City of the Dreadful Thirst', a poem about the dust-bitten place by the famed bush balladeer Banjo Paterson. Another noted moment, one of the proudest in the town's history, occurred in 1944 when a Royal Australian Air Force twin-engined Beaufort Bomber – christened *Narromine* because it was paid for by the townsfolk – taxied all the way down Dandaloo Street to the local airstrip before seeing action in the south-west Pacific campaign.

Narromine has also produced many sporting champions, including rugby league player David Gillespie, who played for the Canterbury-Bankstown Bulldogs and Australia; sprinter Melinda Gainsford-Taylor, who held the 200-metre indoor track world record and competed at the 1996 and 2000 Olympic Games; David Jansen, the world's top glider pilot in the 1990s; world champion clay pigeon shooter Kevin Heywood; and champion archer Jody Webb. And then, of course, there is Glenn McGrath. Enough to entitle Narromine to proclaim itself 'The Town of Champions'.

'Narromine was a great place to grow up,' says Gillespie. 'While it was only a small town, sport played a really important part in the everyday activities. It was a release. And one thing you have out there is the time to work on your game.'

McGrath agrees. 'People joke about there being something in the water in Narromine, but I reckon the town's success comes back to the number of sporting facilities the kids have available to them,' he says. 'When I grew up, you couldn't escape competing in some sort of sport because there was a basketball court, tennis courts, an indoor cricket centre, a rollerskating rink, golf course, footy and cricket fields, and even a gymnastics centre. It was great, but without wanting to sound like an old man, that was also pre-PlayStation days. Sport was one way we kids remained occupied.'

Kevin McGrath believes the wide open plains encouraged kids to roam, allowing them to breathe and develop.

'When I've been to Sydney or the other big towns around Australia, the kids don't seem to have big enough back yards to play . . . we needed binoculars to see what Glenn, Dale and Donna were up to. The bush is a healthy lifestyle. The country creates strong people, too. If you see some of those men in the back country, they're very fit, very strong.'

The McGraths took to life at *Lagoona*, although the first big rains brought floods. While the levee bank stood true and protected the house from being submerged, the deep water that isolated the sheds and back paddock made an impression on Glenn's young mind. The water that ran down the back of the McGraths' property gave his first cricket club its name: Backwater.

'The water ran down the back of our property and it made its way to a big lake nearby that was a bird sanctuary. I don't ever remember actually seeing the sanctuary, but I do know the area was teeming with rabbits and foxes.'

In 1974 Beverley and Kevin celebrated the arrival of their third child, Donna, who grew into a sure-footed and talented athlete and followed Glenn into basketball and volleyball.

At Narromine, the annual harvest break was a two-week period when all organised sport was put on hold so the farmers could harvest their crops. As a frustrated park cricketer who couldn't ever get a bowl, Glenn loved the harvest break. After a hard day's work in the paddock, he would usually end up with Dale, Donna, his cousins Craig and Nettie, and uncle Malc playing a 'Test' behind the machinery shed. The pitch would be pockmarked with pebbles and deep divots, and although this made it dangerous, McGrath enjoyed the opportunity to pretend he was playing for Australia. It was tough cricket which required quick reflexes: if a delivery kicked up off a stone it'd rear at the batsman with the speed – and venom – of a tiger snake.

'The pitch was a shocker,' chuckles McGrath. 'I can't remember anyone ever scoring a half-century in any of our games. The pitch just wasn't batsman-friendly – not that there was anything wrong with that.'

Dale remembers the matches best for the preview they offered of the famous Glenn McGrath 'stare and verbal' – the look and abuse the world's best batsmen would become all too familiar with if ever they managed to connect the bat with one of McGrath's fireballs.

'You'd hit him back over his head and he'd go off like a firecracker – he'd abuse you,' laughs the younger brother. 'He didn't like it as a Test player, but he *hated* it at *Lagoona*.'

While Dale was more interested in becoming a farmer like his father than pursuing sport like his older brother, he did enjoy playing tennis once a week with the family. Families would take plates of sandwiches to the local tennis courts, and after their matches finished the adults would sit in the pavilion and discuss the latest events and the town gossip. Glenn, however, preferred to spend as much time as possible out on the floodlit court. He'd started playing tennis aged seven and had the genes to serve, volley and chase the ball well enough to be a competitive player in local tournaments.

In the 1930s a distant relative, Vivian McGrath, had been ranked alongside fellow Australians Jack Crawford, Harry Hopman and Adrian Quist as one of the world's leading tennis players. Quist, a winner of two Wimbledon doubles titles, wrote of McGrath in his book *Tennis Greats 1920–60*:

'Vivian McGrath was the original wonder boy of Australian tennis. Aged 17 he defeated both Wilmer Allison [ranked fourth in the world] and Ellsworth Vines [Wimbledon champion]. His two handed backhand was then a unique stroke in tennis, and it was his great strength. No-one had seen a shot like that backhand before and the players of that time did not know how to handle it. During the 1930s I consider there was no better single shot in tennis than Vivian McGrath's two handed backhand. [He was] one of the most likeable people ever to play the game but he never trained seriously. If he had done he might have been an even better player.'

Not training seriously, however, was an accusation no-one could ever level at Vivian McGrath's distant relative, because if Glenn McGrath was to prove anything as an athlete, it was the value of hard work, incessant training and bloody-minded persistence.

As the McGrath kids grew older, so their responsibilities around the property increased. After school Glenn would drive the tractor or help Kevin with the lambs. And he and Dale grew seeds behind the chook sheds – wheat, barley, lucerne, soy beans, sunflowers.

'There was lots of responsibility for all three of us,' says Glenn. 'But when I think back to those days, I really loved growing up in the bush. There was a sense of freedom and there were opportunities I don't think the city kids ever had.'

But there was one chore that never failed to leave McGrath in a cold, clammy sweat – feeding the chickens late at night.

'It didn't matter what time of night it was, even midnight, one of us had to take the food scraps to the chooks,' he recalls. 'The hairs on the back of my neck would be on end from the moment I left the house, because whenever I shone the torch into the darkness it would catch the eyes of so many feral cats . . . they were big, and they were everywhere.' Once Glenn reached the chickens, he'd throw the scraps at them and flee straight back to the house.

'I'd feel the eyes trained on me and then there'd be this awful feeling that something was bearing down on me. It terrified me, so I'd sprint twice as fast as I'd normally run and slam the back door behind me when I made it to the house.'

But the fear he sprinted from at night didn't stop McGrath from exploring the bush that surrounded the property on his own.

'You hear some people say the bush frightens them, but I never felt that, not even as a kid,' he says. 'I like the solitude . . . I find a real sense of serenity when I'm out there. I'm not religious but I am spiritual, and I feel very peaceful when I'm out among nature. Always have.'

During those treks McGrath not only fostered his deep love and appreciation for the bush, but he also developed a strong arm from throwing rocks at the rabbits and foxes that infested the area.

'I could throw a cricket ball from one side of the field and clear the fence on the other,' says McGrath. 'It weakened considerably when I dislocated my shoulder when I was at TAFE. Before that, if Dale did something to annoy me he'd run down the back to escape on his motorbike. As he bolted, I'd look on the ground and pick up a stick or a rock, whatever was handy, and even if he was on the motorbike, I'd still get him. I remember hitting him in the leg with a stone one time when he was flying on the motorbike 60 or 70 metres away! I'd also have a go at the feral cats, foxes and rabbits – Donna too, when she deserved it!'

Donna has painful memories of her brother's throwing arm. 'As I said – he was always throwing things. I remember him once throwing a piece of fibro at Dale as he tried to escape from Glenn after he did something to annoy him on his motorbike. He threw the fibro and it curved and hit him square on the head. It was quite amazing, really.

'But he was always doing things like that; he'd get a golf ball and point with his driver at the shed he was aiming to hit. They were a few hundred metres away, he'd hit the ball and you'd wait a few seconds. When we heard the bang of the ball hitting the tin roof or the side wall, Glenn would raise his arms in triumph!'

So for the Narromine boy, the bush was a place of both peace and violence – a contrast that would continue in his lifelong passion for guns and accompanying respect for the creatures he hunted.

4

The Straight Shooter

After Glenn took his 500th Test wicket, Jane bought him an S-2 Blaster .500 Nitro Express with an interchangeable .375 Barrel and walnut stock, and had it personally engraved.

Australian Shooter magazine, 2006

The sound of gunfire in the bush that surrounded *Lagoona* kept ten-year-old Glenn McGrath awake until the early hours of the morning. It was exactly as it sounded – a battle: the latest engagement in the age-old war between farmers and the vermin that stalked and mutilated their newly born lambs. Like Dale, Glenn lay in his bed wide-eyed and excited by the action. He could hear the engines of the gunmen's souped-up utes rev and groan as they chased the prey. Sometimes the spotlights – 'spotties' – would briefly illuminate his room as the men scoured the scrub for another fox or feral cat.

Glenn and Dale heard their father describe foxes as 'bastards' whenever he came across lambs that had been butchered in the night. The foxes normally killed with a single bite to a lamb's neck and, as if to add salt to the farmers' wounds, they ate only the tongue and tail – it was, as any man of the land would swear, an infuriating waste. '*Bastards*,' Kevin McGrath would curse.

The McGrath boys witnessed firsthand that foxes are surplus killers – they slaughter more creatures than they can possibly eat. The lambing season – when the scent of the ewes' afterbirth lures foxes from their dens deep within the bush – was the annual call to arms for neighbours to try to eradicate their common foe.

Glenn and Dale lay wondering how anything could survive as they listened to volley after volley of shotgun blasts. Glenn, while buzzing at the action going on just a few hundred metres from his window, was disappointed to have been confined to the barracks by his father. But he was far too young to be exposed to the many dangers that came with being among a troupe of armed men shooting in the dark.

In time, the boys realised their father did not like guns. He hadn't fired a shot until he was in his twenties and had to defend his livestock from the predators that would raid the paddocks and the chicken coops. The only reason Kevin owned a rifle at all was to keep at bay the foxes and feral cats that threatened his family's livelihood. Unlike the other members of his posse, he wasn't attached to the weapon and he dreaded that his boys would one day want to become shooters.

'I didn't hate guns, but like a lot of parents I was nervy about the kids using them,' says Kevin. 'The boys' mother was more concerned about it than me, but I just wanted them to realise to be careful and to appreciate they were dangerous. I didn't want them to use the gun until they were old enough to take responsibility and to take notice of what I had to say on the subject.'

While McGrath knew the men spent the darkened hours shooting and killing foxes, he was still shocked by the scene that confronted him before breakfast one morning when he opened the door to his father's workshop. The sight of three animals sprawled on the grease-stained concrete floor made him recoil in horror. While McGrath had seen dead stock before, this was different – not only because their bullet wounds were still fresh, but also because they'd been killed by his father's hand. For the first time in his life, McGrath felt scared at being so close to death.

'The rifle fire sounded exciting,' he says. 'However, when I saw those three dead foxes on the workshop floor that morning I felt a bit . . . well, I felt a bit scared of them . . . of their being dead.'

Despite the fear he felt for those three foxes, Glenn and his brother were eventually called upon to join the men in the firing line.

McGrath's first night shooting was during the lambing season. When they shone the spotlight into the darkness, the boy could see what looked like hundreds of foxes surrounding the sheep and their lambs. And then everyone started shooting.

'Someone would flick the spotty on, I'd sight the fox, shoot, kill it and reload,' he recalls. 'The light would go on again and I'd shoot again. Sometimes they'd bolt and we'd chase them. It was my first shoot and I still remember the adrenaline rush. It wasn't the thrill of the kill; it was the idea I was helping to save the lambs.

'We covered about 5000 acres over the three nights and we killed a total of 99 foxes, which gives you an idea of how rampant the foxes are out there. Like the pigs, they were an introduced species and they're doing terrible damage to the environment. I know people have varying ideas on shooting, but the feral animals are doing lots of damage out in the bush.'

Despite Kevin's loathing for shooting, the McGrath family is steeped in the traditions of the sport. In the early 1900s, his grandfather Jim and four uncles formed the McGrath

Brothers Rifle Team in the Hargraves District near Mudgee. For competitions the fab five wore military tunics and slouch hats of the style favoured by Australia's colonial troops during the Boer War. When they moved en masse to Cooyal, the New South Wales National Rifle Association granted them permission to form a new club, for which the lads were careful to select the safest spot possible – the paddock of local farmer Andrew Baker. As Muriel Marks notes in *Cooyal Stories*, 'It is an ideal site for a rifle range, with the high mountain in the background where there is no danger of stray bullets doing any harm.'

Glenn remembers his grandfather Lyle McGrath's many shooting trophies. 'But my dad didn't share his father's love for the sport. He was anti-guns and would get very angry whenever he found out Dale and I had sneaked his .22 rifle out of the house to shoot at some targets in the back paddock. It was a rubbish gun. The firing pin was worn out and it was a bit like playing Russian roulette in that it'd only fire every 20 shots. We'd take it in turns to take aim at the target and squeeze the trigger, only for it to go click, click, click, *bang*!'

Despite Kevin's best attempts to steer Glenn and Dale away from shooting, they embraced it.

'Glenn was absolutely mad on it from the start,' Kevin says. 'I noticed when he went overseas on cricket tours, he would always be photographed or filmed talking to the guards in places like India or South Africa and asking about a submachine gun. He has a photo album of wild pigs that he has shot . . . That's a bit different.'

The brothers became accurate shots and sure-footed hunters, and made good money from selling fox and feral cat skins to the wool traders. Skinning the animals was messy work, but it was much more profitable than their alternate means of making extra cash – collecting aluminium cans to trade for one cent each.

McGrath soon set his sights on wild pigs, which he grew to admire for their intelligence and heartiness. But that did not spare them from the bullet, for they massacre lambs. Wild pigs are said to kill and eat up to 40 per cent of the lambs born in some areas.

'They crunch through the lambs like we do toast,' says Dale about the old enemy. They also damage crops and fences, and can carry diseases like foot-and-mouth disease as well as a variety of parasites, including the screw-worm fly.

As he matured as a hunter, McGrath would challenge himself not only to stalk the wild pigs, but to sit in their midst and observe them.

'That to me is the thrill of the hunt,' he enthuses. 'If I'm hunting something that is 400 metres away, I'd rather stalk it than take it out with a long-range shot. That's when skills come into play. It's then a matter of tracking the prey, studying it, observing its actions and then making my move. It's a process, a calculated one at that, and when I make my decision to take the shot – it's the only thing that matters in that split second, and I do everything to ensure it is a clean shot. Sometimes I don't fire. If the pig is a mother with babies that can't fend for themselves, I won't take it. There are some blokes who shoot everything they can, but I don't.'

For McGrath, hunting is as much about mateship as anything else. Some of his best friends are hunters. 'They're not rednecks that go around shooting anything that moves,' he says. 'They're actually responsible, community-based people and environmentally conscious. They're some of the best people you could ever hope to meet.'

In 2005, Glenn McGrath and two cricket mates, Brett Lee and Jason Gillespie – the cream of Australia's fast bowling talent – were sitting around a campfire in outback New South Wales discussing everything from their sport to the day's hunting. They were at McGrath's 34,000-acre property outside Bourke, one of the trappings of his success as the world's leading strike bowler. Divided by the Cuttaburra River and reaching the Queensland border in some parts, the property was where McGrath would go to reinvigorate his body and spirit after a gruelling cricket campaign. On this particular night, with the smell of ash in the air and a billy of tea boiling on a low flame, the trio marvelled at 'the wond'rous glory of the everlasting stars', as Banjo Paterson had described the night sky over a century earlier in his poem 'Clancy of the Overflow'.

For Gillespie, hunting with McGrath had been a tough experience. He was more comfortable targeting batsmen's wickets than feral pigs, but he was happy to be with two of his mates from the Fast Bowlers' Cartel (the team within the Australian team whose membership was restricted to individuals who could hurl a ball from one end of a wicket to the other at speed in baking heat, when they were bone-weary and mentally hammered).

'I think I shot the gun twice in the four days I was there,' says Gillespie. 'I'd never really been around guns before; the first time was when we were in Zimbabwe and I went with Glenn to a couple's place in the middle of nowhere – it was Tarzan territory. But going to his property was brilliant.'

Lee – a self-proclaimed country boy from Wollongong, south of Sydney – understands McGrath's passion for pitting his tracking and shooting skills against the beasts.

'It's not the hunting,' Lee says. 'For me, it's being out there in the open and camping . . . getting away from the cricket world for a while. I'm definitely a country boy at heart – any chance I get to go out to the wilderness and sleep in a tent, do some fishing, and be in a place that's without electricity, well, it's great fun. Glenn loves it. It seems to me to be where he's most relaxed.'

For the teenage McGrath, stalking and hunting vermin was a lot more enjoyable pursuit than attending school. Shyness made the blackboard jungle a place of absolute terror.

5

Harsh Lessons

As One We Succeed

Narromine High School's motto

For all his gun-slinging boldness at *Lagoona*, when it came to school Glenn McGrath was crippled with shyness. Bev was happy to hear her elder son's Year Five teacher comment at the annual parent–teacher night on his good manners, quiet nature and the steady progress he was making in class. However, in the same breath he mentioned an action he had taken to help Glenn overcome his acute shyness, which disturbed her. As was the way of the era, Bev kept her thoughts to herself for fear of offending the teacher.

The teacher told Bev that Glenn didn't mix well with the girls in his class, so he sat Glenn next to a girl. But Bev didn't agree with this approach.

'I didn't think it was the teacher's place to do that because Glenn was just a normal boy, shy, but he was like most of the other boys who hung around with each other, just like the girls would stick together.'

The experience didn't scar McGrath, but his acute shyness made school a challenge. 'I was an A-student, but I was painfully shy and I allowed it to build into something it should never have been,' he says. 'I struggled to speak in front of people; I would have done just about anything to get out of it. Even when I knew the answer or might have had something worthwhile to add to the class, I couldn't express what was on my mind. It was awful, but I was like a lot of teenagers and conscious of what the others thought of me. Stupid really.'

Narromine High School's Year Ten English teacher couldn't possibly have realised the torment she put McGrath through whenever she'd ask him to read a passage from a novel or answer a question about a sonnet by Shakespeare – or she'd have left him in peace. While McGrath was both a clever and good student, he would be overwhelmed by what he described as a 'dread' whenever he was forced to participate in the lesson. McGrath would hope against all hope not to be called upon to speak in front of his peers because he'd choke with nervousness at the thought of how his classmates might judge him. As he stammered his way through the latest task, McGrath thought he could read their thoughts: He *sounds* stupid; What does *he* know?

The shyness that plagued McGrath in the classroom would remain a problem for years to come. It would even prevent him from making the most of some early opportunities he had to gain a media profile as an aspiring fast bowler at Adelaide's Australian Cricket Academy, where he'd run and hide from a camera crew or avoid journalists as if they had a contagious disease. When McGrath eventually overcame his shyness, he realised the last thing that would have been on his classmates' minds as he mumbled his way through John Steinbeck's *Of Mice and Men* would have been thoughts of him – let alone judgements about him.

Even so, McGrath's fear of talking in front of people was so deep-seated it had a bearing on his decision to leave school after Year Ten. He was spooked – not by the increased study and workload required to obtain the Higher School Certificate (HSC), but by the graduation ceremony. The mere thought of having to attend the Year Twelve leaving ceremony terrified him. Year after year McGrath would watch the HSC students stand on the stage in front of an auditorium crammed with other pupils, parents, extended families, local politicians and anyone else who cared to applaud them and wish them well for the future. He'd squirm miserably in his seat at the mere prospect of one day being among them.

'I couldn't think of anything worse than having to speak in front of the crowd – put me in front of a firing squad instead,' McGrath confesses. 'One very real reason I left school in Year Ten was to avoid all of that.'

However, his school days in Narromine were mostly enjoyable. He made some firm friendships, gained good grades and was in the A class every year of high school, but perhaps the greatest legacy of McGrath's state-school education was his love of reading.

'When I was on the farm I'd read a lot because I found it a great escape from reality. I still read quite a lot of fiction.' McGrath's favourite authors include Wilbur Smith and Jack Higgins, and Australian authors Matthew Reilly and Tony Park, who has written a number of books set in Africa. 'On the 1999 tour of the West Indies I ploughed through 12 books because of the amount of free time we had,' McGrath recalls.

Melinda Gainsford-Taylor, a year behind McGrath at Narromine High, remembers him simply as a 'quiet boy'. He *was* a quiet kid, happy to keep his nose clean. While McGrath was popular enough, he didn't have what he would call a 'best mate' in the playground. His cousin Craig had been his best friend, but he was sent to boarding school at Bathurst, which left McGrath feeling a sense of loss.

'That was tough,' says Bev of Craig's departure. 'They did everything together and then he was gone.'

'I was one of those guys who moved about groups,' says McGrath. 'We had a tremendous bunch of blokes in my year. I could name my entire class.'

McGrath's physical education teacher Chris Harding (who once played rugby league for the famous English team Featherstone Rovers) remembers his school's most famous student for being, well, remarkably unremarkable.

'Glenn was a nice kid,' Harding recalls. 'He was well behaved, never in trouble. He came from a good family and was good at all the sports he played. Back then it was golf, volleyball and basketball. However, he was very, very shy. I always thought Glenn would make a better basketballer than cricketer. I think I'm right in saying he was never picked in a schoolboy cricket team, but I remember he was quite a good bowler. He blossomed later and we are proud of what he has achieved.'

Bev was always pleased to read Glenn's school reports because the teacher's comments simply reinforced what she knew: her elder son was growing into a mature, well-mannered and rounded young man.

Photographs in McGrath's old school magazines show he was a gangly, enthusiastic member of the school's basketball and golf teams. He also ran in Narromine High's cross-country team. While he had no trouble running kilometre after kilometre around flat-as-a-tack Narromine, McGrath was 'cooked' early in the inter-district meet at Oberon, where the hills took a heavy toll on his skinny legs.

The school rarely played his favourite sport, cricket, because there weren't enough teams in the district to compete against.

McGrath's height and natural hand–eye coordination

allowed him to adapt easily to life on the basketball court, and his talent was recognised early when he was picked to compete in the then-burgeoning State League. One trip that made an impression on him was when the Far West representative team competed in Sydney and was based at Kings Cross, the notorious centre of sleaze and spice.

'It was a shock for a group of kids from the bush,' McGrath recalls with a laugh. 'We'd never seen anything like it. There were plenty of what I guess you'd call "colourful characters" hustling out on the street. There were also, um, working girls, but none of our parents needed to worry about our moral fibre because I think we were all scared of them. I know I was. Anyway, I was safe because my mum drove the team mini-van – there was no way she was going to let me misbehave in any way during our time in Sydney.'

In the summer of 1986, McGrath had to make a decision about his future: he wanted to leave school after his Year Ten exams but he wasn't sure of his career path. That year was also significant because, after 16 years of his parents' favourite country and western songs, he heard rock music for the first time on a compilation tape. He was hooked after hearing the first few notes of 'Manic Monday' by the Bangles. It was a new world, but he had to make a decision about his future. McGrath realised that despite his great love for the land, his heart wasn't in farming. Four of his classmates were joining the police force but that didn't appeal to him either.

'I toyed with the idea of joining the force, but it was only fleeting,' he says. 'What turned me off that as a job was the prospect of having to deal with things like domestic violence and telling a parent their kid had been killed in an accident.'

Instead McGrath enrolled in a carpentry course at the local TAFE. As he threw himself into the theory and practice of the course, he became excited by the prospect of one day becoming a builder. When he couldn't obtain an apprenticeship, however, he got work as a labourer on a cotton farm. Toiling under the blazing sun was hard yakka. As his hands blistered and his back became sore, opening the bowling for Australia from the Paddington end of the SCG seemed a much better career option.

6

The Heart-to-Heart

We just enjoyed our cricket, had no grand plans
of playing for Australia or whatever. We didn't
have grand plans for anything, most of us. But,
yeah, Glenn wanted to play for Australia. Kept it
a secret and, to his credit, every opportunity that
was given to him, he took it with both hands and
literally ran with it.

Narromine cricketer Mark Munro,
ABC TV 2007

O ne more Saturday afternoon spent roaming the boundary
for the Rugby Union XI cricket side frustrated McGrath
to the point that he went against his notoriously shy nature and
approached Brian Gainsford for a 'chat' about cricket. Or, more
to the point, to ask Gainsford (Melinda Gainsford-Taylor's
father) whether he should even bother to keep playing. After
sweltering under the sun and waiting for the batsman to hit the
ball in his direction – or for the call that rarely came from his
captain to roll his arm over – McGrath had spent most of the
afternoon wondering whether it would be wiser to listen to
the people who suggested he focus his attention on shooting
hoops in the burgeoning bush basketball league.

'It seemed as if everyone thought I was wasting my time playing cricket,' McGrath says. 'Basketball had just started to become popular in Australia, so there were opportunities starting to open up. The National Basketball League was up and running, it was getting good airplay on television and the Kings enjoyed a huge following in Sydney.

'But there was a "but". I *really* wanted to make it in cricket. There were times when it would've been easy just to give up; I mean, I didn't even get a bowl! But I didn't want to quit. I think that was the reason I wanted to speak to Brian. I just wanted to hear someone say to keep going.'

McGrath couldn't have sought out a more supportive person. Brian 'Gamy' Gainsford enjoyed widespread respect beyond the Western Districts because he was a hard-working delegate to the NSW Cricket Association who ensured bush players of all standards received support. His son David played first-grade for Manly in the Sydney grade cricket competition and his daughter Melinda was a champion 200-metre sprinter. Gainsford himself boasted a distinguished playing career and had been selected in the Western NSW Country XI that played the West Indies in 1975. While Gainsford didn't get the opportunity to bat against Michael Holding, he did catch the Windies' reserve wicketkeeper David Murray.

At the time of his heart-to-heart with McGrath, despite being in his mid-forties Gainsford was still a prolific run-getter as an opener for Backwater in the Far West competition. As McGrath discussed his frustrations, Gainsford could see the 17-year-old genuinely wanted some direction, so he thought about why he loved cricket and used that to speak to the boy openly and from the heart.

'Everyone knew Glenn was a talented basketballer,' says Gainsford. 'But he'd been lured to cricket by his mates and it was obvious to me he enjoyed the game. He started off by playing in the under-16s at our club, Backwater, and I knew him to be a good, quiet kid who was very respectful and very well mannered.

'When we sat down, I talked to Glenn about the merits of cricket over basketball. I'd never played basketball, but I could tell him about the camaraderie players share on and off the cricket field. I told him that regardless of whether he played in the bush or went all the way to become an international cricketer, he'd make great friends – and I thought that was a worthwhile reward for doing something you loved.

'While he bowled a bit erratic back then, Glenn was quick. It was also obvious, just by looking at him, he had all the requirements a fast bowler needed. All Glenn needed was time to develop, and I told him that. However, I also warned him that cricket was a sport where you could be on a high one day but be brought back to earth very quickly the next.'

By the time the hour-long conversation had finished, McGrath had decided to retire his basketball singlet. He was committed to becoming a fast bowler and he wanted to do whatever was necessary to fulfil his dream to play for Australia.

Yet try as he might, there was always a voice of treason that questioned his ability.

'Shocking, absolutely shocking,' recalled Mark Munro when asked about McGrath's early days the night before his farewell Test. 'Didn't have a clue where a batsman was, let alone the stumps or a good length.'

And yet, McGrath continued to believe he *could* bowl – every afternoon when he'd measure his run-up and launch delivery after delivery at the old drum.

'It was just something I loved doing,' he says. 'As far back as I can remember, it didn't matter whether I was playing in my grandparents' back yard or watching the Aussie team play on television – they weren't all that successful back then and did it tough – I wanted to play for Australia. It was just something I had a passion for. I'd watch the guys bowl on television and, while I never tried to copy any of them, I looked closely at what they did and it helped me develop my own style.'

McGrath's apparent lack of talent was a blessing in disguise: because his coaches didn't have the time to waste on someone who was never going to be a strike bowler in their attack, it meant they didn't tinker with his style.

'It actually worked in my favour that no-one thought to coach me when I started out,' he says. 'So my bowling in the early days was all about fun, which is probably the way it should be. Through that approach, my body found its most natural way to bowl and I'm sure that is what allowed me to enjoy longevity. Later on, when I first worked with Dennis Lillee at the Academy, his priority was refinement and working with what I had rather than changing it. I had developed what he called a "sound action", because my hips and shoulders were aligned and that was what I needed. I think even as a kid with no guidance I knew how to get the most out of myself.'

Bush cricket was, as Gainsford had promised, a source of good friendships and great memories. McGrath has played in World Cup victories, Ashes triumphs and tense matches on the Subcontinent, but he always remembers his time in bush cricket with a smile. Like the time a team-mate was accused of not putting in when a hare-like sprint after the ball towards the boundary suddenly became an uncertain trot. The fielder was mercilessly bagged for not trying, even when McGrath and his mates saw that the ball had stopped next to a deadly brown snake. And the way walking out to bat at the Narromine Racecourse was like retracing the steps of the early explorers Burke and Wills.

'The racecourse had a cricket field inside the track. To bat, you had to leave the stand, cross the racecourse and then make your way through knee-length grass just to make the outfield and then you'd make it out to the middle of the field,' McGrath recalls. 'The only other place that was nearly as tough to get out to was Lord's, because you need to walk down two flights of stairs before an attendant swings open the door that leads to the famous Long Room.'

After absorbing Gainsford's words of wisdom, McGrath trained even harder and bowled longer sessions behind the machinery shed. The toil paid off when he was picked for the Narromine representative side after showing rapid improvement for the Rugby Union XI. McGrath's selection in that team allowed Gainsford an insight into the depth of McGrath's mental strength, a trait that in the years to come would astound his Aussie team-mates and international opponents.

'I think ability is a 10 to 20 per cent requirement,' says Gainsford of the 'right stuff' needed to make it in cricket. 'You need 80 to 90 per cent mental strength. You need that mental strength – and if Glenn's proved anything at all, he has proved that. He wasn't overly aggressive, but my goodness he was determined. He came from a farming family and that life was certain to instil toughness into him, as it does any kid. When Glenn was given his shot, there was no way he was going to let it slip through his fingers.'

But even when McGrath gained his representative spurs for the Narromine XI, doubts remained as to whether he would cut the mustard. In one game at Bourke he finished footsore and disappointed after an unrewarding day in the field. He then suffered a body blow when he was overlooked for the Country under-21s squad after he played in the annual Colts' Carnival.

'There were always question marks over whether he would make it,' says Gainsford. 'Glenn was different to Adam Gilchrist, in the sense that when I saw him play for the North Coast under-17s, I could tell Gilchrist was going to be a superstar cricketer. It was the same with Michael Slater – when he played for the Riverina team, it was obvious he had it. That instant recognition wasn't the case with Glenn.

'I've always believed you could tell within 12 months if a kid was going to make it, but I've also always been open-minded, to make sure people don't get too carried away with a young player. Glenn achieved a lot through hard work, whereas there have been many players who were blessed with so much natural ability but they fell by the wayside for whatever reason. Glenn just kept working and there is a lesson in that for anyone.'

In 2003 Gainsford stood on stage alongside twins Steve and Mark Waugh and Michael Bevan to receive his life membership from the NSW Cricket Association. It acknowledged over 40 years of blood, sweat and tears which Gainsford had given to help improve the game and foster young talent. When McGrath heard of Gainsford's accolade, he spared a special thought for the old Backwater opener whose words of wisdom 'pumped up his tyres' at a time when he needed it.

'A lot of people helped me make it in cricket,' he says. 'However, Brian will never be able to understand how much his conversation meant to me. He was not only generous with his time – because it had been a long day for everyone in the sun – but he gave me encouragement when I needed it. And just as importantly, he gave me a bit of hope.'

Gainsford describes the role he played in the rise and rise of Glenn McGrath as brief but humbling. However, he says it reinforces the power of words and the importance of giving someone – even a kid who couldn't get a bowl – some time and advice.

'I have to say, not for a minute did I finish our chat and think it would have an impact on his life, because it was basically about the enjoyment of playing cricket and I'll talk to anyone about that,' Gainsford says. 'But it obviously struck a chord with Glenn.'

7

Dougie's Tormentor

I vividly recall it. Everyone was lined up in the
dressing-room trying to sign him up – Greg
Matthews, Doug Walters and, I think, Steve
Rixon.

Dubbo guest captain and former
Australian all-rounder Greg Matthews

In October 1988, seven years after Doug Walters had retired
from top-class cricket, he was back at the crease batting
for the Parkes representative XI in their annual grudge match
against Dubbo. A tall, reed-thin fast bowler with the same
haircut Walters had sported during his days as a National
Serviceman in the 1960s tormented him with a constant
nagging line and length, making it a tough grind to overhaul
Dubbo's 218. As Walters played and missed – again – a bunch
of children added to his frustration as the ball thudded into
the wicketkeeper's gloves by yelling 'C'mon, Reidy!' – acknow-
ledging that his torturer bore a resemblance to the Test bowler
Bruce Reid.

Walters was going on 43, and while the old eyes weren't as
sharp as they'd been in the 1974/75 Ashes series (when he'd
brought up his hundred by hooking for six the last ball of the

day from Bob Willis), they could spot talent – even under the dodgy floodlights that left dark patches of shadow over Parkes' Pioneer Oval. As the veteran of 74 Test matches faced up for the next delivery, he wondered why no-one had uttered a word about this lanky kid the previous night at the Coachman's Hotel, where he'd spent hours autographing beer-stained coasters and shaking hands with old fans and new friends at the official pre-match function. Walters had heard everything he could possibly need to know about the pride of Parkes playing under him: Graeme Tanswell, Alan Day and Ken Keith. It had even been pointed out to him that Dubbo's Stuart Border was related to the Test captain Allan Border. But for the life of him, Walters couldn't remember a single damn word – of warning or otherwise – about McGrath.

Walters was back in the firing line as the face of the Toohey's Country Cup Challenge, a competition started in 1977 by former Test skipper Bob Simpson. The aim of the contest was to send members of the NSW Sheffield Shield squad out bush to play alongside country cricketers in a series of inter-district representative games. Simpson hoped the initiative would help to reinvigorate the game in areas neglected by the game's administrators, and also that it might unearth a few gems, like the McGrath boy from Narromine.

The Dubbo side was bolstered for that October night's battle by the inclusion of Steve Smith, Greg Matthews and Mark Taylor, while Parkes boasted Walters, Mark Waugh and Graham Smith. McGrath's shyness ensured that he was seen and not heard as he sat in the dressing-room alongside the big shots, but he absorbed everything he could when they spoke cricket.

'It didn't matter to me when we were out on the field playing that I was up against first-class cricketers, or that Dougie had played for Australia,' he says. 'I just loved bowling, and it was a great challenge. But I was a little bit in awe of them while we sat in the rooms before the game. I didn't say much – I was just enjoying it, and I listened to everything they said. In terms of playing that day, I didn't put extra pressure on myself. I never worried about how I was going to go in a game – I was more concerned with what I hoped to achieve in the game.'

When Matthews tossed McGrath the ball to begin his spell, he could see Dubbo's first-change bowler was dead keen to prove himself against elite company. However, it was no secret that Walters' best days were long gone, and Matthews urged McGrath to show 'the great Dougie' the respect to which he was entitled. McGrath was surprised – Matthews' reverence for the old warrior seemed to contradict his reputation as a party boy with a penchant for rattling the cage of his conservative sport. At the peak of his career Matthews was considered the hippest cricketer about, with his super-cool lingo and daring earring. His image ensured he gained a cult following – but it didn't endear him to the starched-collared members of the Australian Cricket Board, who branded him a maverick.

Although Matthews didn't want to see Walters' hard-earned reputation tarnished by a young punk with a point to prove, he need not have wasted his breath on McGrath. While McGrath certainly wanted Walters' scalp – and Waugh's and Smith's, for that matter – his plan was to bowl a tight line and length. He was well aware of Dougie's place in folklore: that he'd smashed 250 against the Kiwis; that three of his 15 Test centuries were scored within a session; that he'd amassed 5357 runs against his nation's foes at an average of 48.26 and had taken 49 wickets as a bowler. It was a career to be proud of and McGrath had no intention of taking any cheap shots. He was also mindful that Doug was his mother's favourite cricketer and she probably wouldn't appreciate watching him ducking and weaving against short-pitched deliveries from her son.

'Greg talked about it being an honour for me to bowl at someone of his standing, and that was all fine,' says McGrath of Matthews' direction. 'I had no intention of bouncing Doug because I respected everything he'd achieved. I was more interested in seeing how I went bowling a good length at him – and, while I didn't dismiss him, I was pretty happy with how I went. I'd played some representative cricket in the 12 months leading up to that game – for Narromine, Far West and Western Districts – but it was exciting to get picked to play for Dubbo. I saw it as a vote of confidence, a sign I was doing the right things. A talent scout from the Penrith grade club had apparently been sent out to watch me play in a game before the Toohey's Cup match – I knew nothing about it – but I guess the long drive must've seemed like a great waste of time to him because I didn't receive a phone call. He probably marked me down as just another bush player.'

As his eyes focused on the 18-year-old running in to bowl again, Walters might have wondered how that talent scout could have kept his title. The ball rocketed off the pitch much quicker than he had anticipated; the speed and sudden bounce forced him to cramp up and he popped up a catch, but it was too hot for the fielder at gully to handle.

Wiping the beads of sweat from his forehead, Walters shrugged his shoulders and grinned to himself. This McGrath kid was the reason many of his old Test team-mates refused to play in exhibition games. They didn't fancy being the prey for young turks desperate to make a name at their expense by removing either their middle stump – or their head.

But ego was never a problem for Walters. He'd done more than enough at the top level to feel the need to prove himself to anyone. His aim as the face of the Toohey's Country Cup Carnival – at the crease or at the bar afterwards – was to entertain the locals who'd paid their three bucks to watch the limited-overs action.

'I had finished my career long ago,' says Walters of playing in the scrub. 'The young blokes thought it was nice to get me out, but that never worried me too much. I was a country boy myself, so I knew how important things like the Toohey's Cup are to the bush, and I was happy to play and to participate. My view on that sort of thing remains the same as it was then: the more we do to help the talent out in the bush – and there's plenty of it – the better it is for everyone.'

Indeed, Walters had himself benefited from such a spirit in 1962, when at the age of 16 he represented Maitland against the legendary Jack Chegwyn XI, a cavalier team that consisted of state players and top Sydney first-graders who made annual tours to the bush. Young Doug didn't miss his chance to shine, smashing an unbeaten 51 and bagging four wickets. On the strength of that performance he was picked for the NSW Colts, where he scored 140. A few weeks later, having turned 17, he was at the SCG representing NSW against a Queensland attack that contained the great West Indies pace ace Wes Hall. He scored 1 in the first dig and a half-century in the second, and he never looked back. Now it was his turn to put something back, and he was happy to see a farmer's son step up to the plate in Parkes that night.

McGrath was the player who excited those in the 2000-strong crowd who really knew the game.

'Glenn McGrath bowled very well that night,' recalls Matthews two decades later. 'I remember it well. He wanted to get in there and stick it to 'em . . . but he was also cool and controlled. What I noticed about Glenn early on – and it was to become his greatness – you only had to tell him something once. I liked him the first time I saw him – he's a beautiful man. He owns that man in the mirror. A very special dude.'

Mark Taylor, who learned his cricket in Wagga Wagga – a country town near the Victorian border, home to many elite athletes including cricket's Michael Slater and Geoff Lawson and the famous rugby league Mortimer family – says one of the joys of playing in competitions like the Country Cup was unearthing the occasional rough diamond like McGrath.

'Some blokes stood out and Glenn was one of them,' says Taylor. 'He was a tall, lanky guy for a start – a beanpole of a kid, actually. He had good bounce and pace, and while you'd never have imagined he'd one day take 500 Test wickets, I wondered how he'd go in Sydney. I'm glad he came down.'

As one of the selectors who'd picked McGrath for the Dubbo XI, Brian Gainsford was ecstatic at the way the boy who had started out at the Backwater club handled the step up in class.

'Glenn had played some representative matches and I thought it was time to throw him in headfirst, to see if he would sink or swim,' says Gainsford. 'It was an exhibition match – and he'd shown enough that year to justify selection and he made the most of his opportunity. We all knew he would.'

McGrath's effort was no mean feat – he was bowling on a pitch that could be described as, at best, a cur of a thing.

'The pitches we played the Toohey's Cup matches on had an aluminium base with a strip of synthetic stretched over it,' Walters says. 'We'd put them down in places that didn't have a turf wicket, like Pioneer Oval at Parkes. The way they played depended really on how they were put down: if it was done properly the pitch would be okay, but because most grounds have little ridges on them it was sometimes impossible to lay them dead flat. A consequence of that was we had little ripples up and down the pitch, so if the ball hit the down slope it didn't bounce. However, if it hit the up zone it took off – and if I remember correctly, Glenn was hitting that up zone quite regularly when Parkes played Dubbo! But what I most vividly recall thinking to myself was that if this bloke could bowl so well on an aluminium wicket, imagine what he could do on a good pitch.'

McGrath's main memory of the aluminium pitch is that he couldn't wear spikes. He was also denied a hat-trick through sloppy fielding, and it surprises him to think that Mark Taylor, who is remembered as one of Australia's great slips fieldsmen, dropped a sitter.

'It went straight to him, too,' rues McGrath. 'I had four dropped that night.'

While Taylor remembers spilling the chance, he says McGrath has forgotten the Pioneer Oval lights – they were so dodgy the fieldsmen should have had coalminers' helmets with lamps so they could see.

Beverley McGrath felt great pride and emotion as she and Donna sat in the grandstand and watched Glenn play in a game involving such big names. Watching Walters in action made Bev think of her cricket-loving father, who'd often told her how he'd played cricket against Walters' dad and uncles before World War Two. In 1965 she'd sat beside him and watched the family's black-and-white television as Walters, then a fresh-faced kid of 19, nailed a Test century on debut against England.

'As I watched Glenn bowl at Doug, it struck me as being special that my dad knew his people,' Bev says. 'It was a great experience, because apart from being happy that Glenn was playing, having Doug Walters out on the field gave me a connection to Dad as well. Donna and I had a great night, and we were so proud of Glenn.'

Walters was eventually dismissed for a scratchy 20, though he fared a little better than Parkes' other guest stars. Mark Waugh was dismissed for 8 and Graham Smith was sent packing for a duck. *The Parkes Champion Post* was disappointed to report that after falling 40 runs short, their team had lost the grudge match to Dubbo for the second consecutive summer. 'Parkes were never in the hunt,' was the *Post*'s unnamed correspondent's matter-of-fact view.

After the game Walters peppered the Far West officials with questions about McGrath. He also requested a contact number because he knew his old team-mate Steve 'Stumper' Rixon, then the NSW coach, would want to make a call to Narromine after they'd spoken. Rixon, a former Test player, was always on the lookout for fast bowlers. He had maintained strong ties to Sutherland, his old club, and had a good reputation for knowing how to foster talent.

Many years later, when McGrath retired with the mantle of Test cricket's most successful fast bowler, it was suggested to Doug Walters that he take a bow for unearthing this gem. While most people would be keen to wear such praise as a badge of honour, Walters shook his head slowly and deliberately as he recalled that line and length which had almost driven him to despair two decades earlier.

'Make no mistake about it, Glenn McGrath would have been discovered,' he insisted. 'I take no credit for discovering him because he had more talent than the average guy. If anything, I may have helped him get to where he was headed that little bit quicker, but make no bones about it, he was definitely headed there.'

Toohey's Country Cup Challenge
Dubbo vs Parkes
Pioneer Oval, Parkes
3 October 1988

Dubbo: Mark Taylor*, Steve Smith*, Greg Matthews (captain)*, Steve Wheeler, Luke Morrish, Cameron Humphries, Tony Campbell, Andrew Grant [all from Dubbo], Mark Pope [Wellington], Stuart Border [Gilgandra], Glenn McGrath [Narromine], Mark Heffion (12th man) [Dubbo]

Parkes: Doug Walters (captain)*, Graham Smith*, Mark Waugh*, Alan Day, Graeme Tanswell, Ken Keith [all from Parkes], Tony Beasley [Grenfell], Graeme Newcombe, Scott Gilmour [both from Cowra], James Dargan [Condobolin], Andrew Chapman [Forbes]

Umpires: Kevin Pye and David Davis

Dubbo 218 (Smith 85, Pope 50, Taylor 20. Day 2 for 41, Tanswell 1 for 12) defeated Parkes 178 (Beasley 40, Walters 20, Dargan 20. Grant 4 for 48, McGrath 3 for 44)

* Denotes guest player

8

The Narromine Express

In all honesty, Glenn didn't really stand out.

> Sutherland's chairman of selectors,
> Tom Iceton, after Glenn McGrath's
> first net session

In southern Sydney, the Sutherland Cricket Club's selection committee stood in a small group near the Caringbah Oval practice nets to cast a critical eye over their latest recruit, who'd been signed – sight unseen – for the 1989/90 Sydney grade season on the recommendation of Doug Walters and at the invitation of Steve Rixon. Perhaps they'd expected too much because he'd been anointed by Walters as 'something special'. However, after watching Glenn McGrath bang down a number of deliveries to the likes of John Dyson – the first-grade captain and former Test opener – the committee wasn't overly impressed. No-one was prepared to describe McGrath as anything more than just another fast bowler.

Twenty years later, Tom Iceton, who'd been chairman of selectors at the time, maintains there was nothing to indicate that he and his peers had witnessed the unveiling of a future champion who'd rewrite the game's record books and set standards very few could ever hope to attain.

'But you have to realise Glenn came to Sutherland with quite a raw style – it was nowhere near as refined as the one people saw when he played for Australia,' Iceton insists. 'I thought he was all right . . . but in all honesty, Glenn didn't really stand out.'

At the end of the session McGrath was told he'd start his grade career in Sutherland's third XI. 'I never thought I was much of a net bowler, so I had no idea of what the selection committee thought about me when I bowled in front of them that first time,' he says. 'They picked me in the thirds, and that was fine by me because I just wanted to play. Though, after our preseason trip to Nowra I was promoted to seconds because I took 3 for 1. I was young and impressionable, and while I listened and learned at the net sessions, I was happiest when I was out on the field and playing.'

The fact that Iceton and the boys didn't roll out the red carpet for their new player didn't faze Rixon, but he insisted McGrath be given a fair go. Rixon believes that a player with skill can be nurtured. For instance, it matters not to Rixon if a young spin bowler struggles to get the ball on the pitch, because if the kid can *really* spin it, he has a foundation to build on. It was the same with McGrath. Rixon knew the so-called 'Narromine Express' would be raw, because after fielding the tip from Walters to take a look at this bush player who bowled a rare line and length, Rixon had done his research. He'd phoned former first-class player Stuart 'Webby' Webster for his local knowledge. Webby played for NSW in the mid-1970s and lived in Dubbo.

'I called Stuart to ask for his thoughts on McGrath,' says Rixon. 'Stuart was honest, saying all he knew about Glenn was he came from Narromine, he played basketball and he was relatively new to cricket. It wasn't enough information, so I pressed him and asked what he actually saw in McGrath as a bowler. It turned out Webby liked the look of Glenn because he was tall and skinny, but he added that he'd need plenty of work if he was to develop.'

After watching McGrath bowl, Rixon listed the advantages he thought the 19-year-old possessed. First, he was 1.95 metres tall (six foot five), which to Rixon meant that when McGrath delivered the ball it would rain down at the batsman from close to eight feet.

Another positive was McGrath's simple action: 'When you look at some fast bowlers you think to yourself, yeah, he can bowl. But you can also see he is going to have some problems down the track. That was never the case with Glenn.' Rixon could see that McGrath released the ball well and had a natural ease in his approach to the crease.

'I needed Glenn to understand early on that, over and above everything else, his simplicity was his strength. I found that the more we talked about that, the more he started to believe it. Glenn had a nice open mind when it came to his bowling, but he also knew when to say, "Thanks very much but I don't need that."'

When Rixon invited Glenn to try his luck with Sutherland in 1989/90, it generated what Bev admits was some much-needed cheer in the McGrath household after her marriage to Kevin had ended in divorce and *Lagoona* had been sold. Apart from providing Glenn with the opportunity to play a much higher standard of cricket, Bev believed Rixon's offer would also expose her eldest child to greater opportunities than those available in the far west. There was nothing wrong with life in the country, but her mother's intuition suggested Glenn wanted more. Playing for Sutherland would provide him with some direction.

But his move to Sydney also added to the family's financial burden, made heavier by the divorce.

'When Glenn joined Sutherland we had to buy his cricket gear – there was no sponsor – and to get the boots and the whites and the bat and pads was expensive. We paid for it all on a credit card,' Bev recalls. 'Glenn was working but he wasn't making much as a bank teller. But we always managed to get by somehow, though it was a real struggle.'

Bev helped to prepare Glenn for the next step in his development as a cricketer – and as an adult. McGrath bought a caravan to live in because it would be much cheaper than renting an apartment, and Bev hit the telephone to find the most affordable caravan park near Caringbah Oval. They eventually chose the Grand Pines Tourist Park at Ramsgate, a 15-minute drive over the Captain Cook Bridge from Sutherland's home ground and about the same distance from the Hurstville branch of the State Bank, where McGrath would be working. The plot cost $18 a night, cheap by Sydney standards, but it stretched McGrath's meagre budget. Caroline Weir, who'd taken Bev's call, sealed the deal when she assured Bev that the caravan park's ablution block was always kept in immaculate order.

'We also did some training before he left home,' says Bev. 'He'd never really done any fitness training before, so we'd get on our pushbikes and ride for miles around town. Glenn would push on after I'd stop. He'd ride along the highway because he wanted to go to Sydney fitter and stronger.'

McGrath felt very little nostalgia about leaving his home town. He welcomed the opportunity for a different life and new challenge.

'I think I was ready for a change,' he says. 'I was working in the bank and playing sport of a weekend – there was no real big picture of where I wanted to go, I was drifting along a bit.

So when the cricket took off it gave me something. Thinking back on it now, part of me always thought I would play for Australia – but it is easy to say that now – but I'd experienced what playing representative sport was about and I loved it.'

McGrath spent his last week at the Narromine branch of the State Bank quietly telling the customers he was headed for Sydney, where he'd give cricket 'a real go'. The overwhelming mood among the locals was extremely supportive and positive. The few prophets of doom who suggested he was setting himself up only to be knocked down did nothing to dampen his enthusiasm or quest for adventure.

'I never even thought about failing,' he says. 'But I didn't think about succeeding either. All I wanted to do was have a go and to see what could happen. I was off.'

Donna remembers little of her elder brother's departure for his new adventure, but she does remember his determination to make it.

Bev volunteered to tow Glenn's Millard caravan (after which he would be given the nickname 'Millard') to Sydney, while he followed in his prized Commodore, a car he bought after saving his money from labouring in the cotton fields and working on properties in the district. It rained almost every kilometre of the journey and the dangerous conditions caused the trip to drag out for seven long hours.

'I got lost when we reached Hurstville,' McGrath recalls with a laugh. 'I arrived at the caravan park about half an hour after Mum and she pretty much had everything set up, so it was good timing! I remember we were both so tired after the drive, it didn't take too long to fall asleep.'

Bev realised a world of opportunity – and adventure – was opening for her son, but saying goodbye to him the following morning was one of the toughest things she'd ever done. She and Glenn shared a strong bond and the sight of him standing alone on the quiet side road and waving farewell brought tears to her eyes. All she could do was to trust everything would work out, hope he'd be safe and believe he would be happy. However, long after she'd crossed the sandstone curtain – the Blue Mountains – that divides Sydney from the western plains, Bev found herself fighting the urge to turn back and make sure her son was okay.

The realisation he was all alone hit McGrath soon after his mum left. He was standing on the outskirts of a city where he knew nobody. McGrath returned to his caravan and, as he surveyed what was to be his home for the next 13 months while he established himself with the Sutherland Sharks, a few home truths hit him. He'd now have to cook for himself, wash and iron his clothes, and keep the caravan clean.

Lying down on one of the two single beds, he imagined he must have looked like a comedy skit character because his long legs dangled hopelessly over the edge of the bed. In a few days' time he'd rectify that by extending the base with a large piece of masonite and adding a chunk of thick foam as a mattress. And only when he stood up did he realise how low the caravan's ceiling was – he was forced to hunch over so as not to bang his head. Indeed, the only way he could stand square-shouldered and at his full height was to put his head through the vent in the ceiling.

The clock revealed his mum had been gone for eight whole minutes. He didn't feel like watching the small television set perched on the counter that doubled as his dining table. Ever the practical son of the bush, McGrath told himself he was in Sydney to fulfil his dream to play cricket for Australia, so he decided *then* was as good a time as any to start. McGrath took a single stump and a cricket ball from his kit, and made his way to the nets he'd noticed in the park across the road. He measured his run-up and was soon in full stride.

'I don't mind admitting that the 13 months I spent in that caravan was a pretty lonely existence, but I never minded my own company,' he says. 'The isolation was probably good, in the sense it made me think a lot about why I was in Sydney. I wasn't there to party or to attend social events, or even climb my way up the bank's management chain. I was there to play cricket, to make the Australian team, though even at that stage I still hadn't told anyone that. I made some good mates through Sutherland, but I was a loner. The funny thing is I never felt homesick for Narromine in that first year, though I missed my family terribly – Mum especially.'

Rixon knew only too well the problems McGrath faced. He had also moved to Sydney from the country to play grade cricket as a teenager. Although he had an aunt in the Harbour City, he remembers his first 12 months as the hardest year of his life.

'I hated it,' he says emphatically. 'There were a number of times when I could quite easily have jumped on a train and returned to Albury. However, the reality was that, like Glenn, I was in Sydney for a reason. He had a dream and his desire to achieve it was strong enough to overcome a lot of issues that would certainly have challenged him.'

A few weeks after moving into the caravan, McGrath woke up one Sunday and realised he had absolutely *nothing* to do, so he went for a long walk, just as he sometimes did at *Lagoona*. He began to walk the 15 kilometres to the city, following the Princes Highway, passing through suburbs overcrowded with shoeboxes that passed as units and apartments. He stopped only to drink water from taps in reserves. There was no point to his walk except to escape the regimented lifestyle that had become like a form of solitary confinement.

'I didn't need to keep a diary when I settled in Sydney because I had my daily routine down to a tee: I'd wake up; shower; eat breakfast; brush my teeth; make my lunch; go to work at the bank; have lunch; either train with the Sutherland boys or practise alone at the local nets; go for a walk along Ramsgate Beach; eat dinner; iron my work clothes for the next day; brush my teeth and hit the sack. Day in, day out, that was it! So on this day I went for a walk, a long walk, and what struck me when I walked around the city was that even though there were a lot of people there, it was still a lonely place – at first. I walked back because I didn't know how the train system worked but I caught a cab from the airport because I was too tired.

After 13 months, McGrath left the caravan to move into a two-bedroom flat in Cronulla with his Sutherland team-mate Tony Clark. 'A terrific bloke,' says McGrath of Clark. 'We hung around with a few of the other Sutho boys – Evan Atkins, Justin Kenny, Phil Wetherall and Mark Chapman – and while I was a bit younger than them, they helped open a new world to me. It was one of having fun in between the hard work. It was so different to the lonely life of the caravan.'

However, McGrath has no doubt that the challenging times he endured in the tin box on wheels gave him an edge over many other cricketers with greater natural ability and similar aspirations to reach the top.

'What kept me going during the hard times was that I'd tell myself I was here to play cricket and I had that dream to play for Australia. That was my focus. I also never lost sight of the fact that thanks to Doug Walters, Steve Rixon and Sutherland, I had an opportunity some people might have thought I wasn't really entitled to. I wasn't prepared to blow it, even on those days when I missed my family.'

9

Making the Grade

'Millard' has arrived! What a debut season! If
only we had a photograph of Tony Fort's face as
G. McGrath's first delivery thudded into his chest.
It was great to add firepower to an already proven
seam and spin attack, and with some carefully
placed muscle bulk and strength, Glenn will only
get better. His approach and attitude to the game
are an example for anyone to take note of.

Sutherland captain John Dyson in the club's
1989/90 annual report

On the notoriously flat Waitara Oval at Hornsby, Northern
District's opening batsman Tony Fort took guard and
tapped his bat patiently as he waited for Sutherland's rookie
opening bowler to steam in. Like a prize-fighter eyeing an
opponent for the first time, he made a quick mental note about
his adversary, some kid from the sticks named McGrath who
looked 'tall and lean'. But McGrath's first ball would place the
batsman on his back foot. It was pitched at a good length then
reared suddenly like a cobra, and before Fort realised what
was happening it struck him. The ball crashed into his chest
and shocked him, because while his home ground's pitch was

considered fair, it was by no means a bowler's paradise. Fort waited until the aftershock of the blow settled down before again taking strike. This time he was more wary.

Like McGrath, Fort was a country boy. He hailed from Maitland in the Hunter Valley and, although a few years older than the man making the ball whistle around his ears, he'd heard some whispers via the bush telegraph about a McGrath from Narromine who was a cricketer with promise. That first ball, however, said a great deal more than anything he'd heard. Fort kept his head down for the over's remaining deliveries – and couldn't help but be impressed by McGrath's demeanour. It was only his second game in first-grade and yet the teenager didn't appear at all nervous.

'I just saw him out,' says Fort. 'He had the ball jumping up at a length and I saw that as a major positive for a fast bowler. It didn't take him long to settle into a good line and length. Five out of six from the over would hit the same spot with a small variance.'

One ball, however, was a hand grenade of a delivery and exploded into Fort's glove. 'I took a look and saw the bugger had split the thumb cap,' he says. 'So that suggested he bowled with a bit of force.'

While McGrath tattooed the stylish opener with a bruise and ruined his glove, it was his opening partner, Phil Wetherall, who finally sent Fort packing, caught and bowled. As Fort showed his team-mates what McGrath had done to his glove's thumb cap, he couldn't help but feel he'd just faced a bowler who not only had a future, but a future well worth following.

While McGrath didn't dismiss Fort, his first innings' haul of 5 for 36 earned him tremendous praise from his skipper, John Dyson, and coach, Len Pascoe, a former Test bowler. Pascoe had forged a reputation in the 1970s and '80s as an aggressive type who bowled fire and brimstone.

The coach nodded with approval as McGrath and Wetherall (who claimed 3 for 60) skittled Northern District for 156 to lay the foundations for Sutherland to enjoy its fifth win in six games. The Shire had started to prepare for their top team's first semi-finals appearance since 1978/79, and there was a sense of excitement about the club. Pascoe was especially pleased with himself for having taken the punt to promote McGrath after only a handful of second-grade games.

'I wanted to fast-track him,' says Pascoe. 'When I first saw Glenn there wasn't a great deal of pace, but what I liked was when you told him something he absorbed it and applied what was necessary to his bowling. He didn't need to be told twice.

'A good coach doesn't need to say a lot. The players should take a lot in with their eyes and ears. I fast-tracked him, I wanted to give him a taste and, to his credit, Glenn didn't let go.'

Word quickly spread about Sydney's latest paceman of promise. Australian opening bowler Geoff Lawson was motivated enough by the hype to make a special trip to the Village Green to watch McGrath bowl at his University of NSW team. His main memory of that first glimpse of greatness was to think how unremarkable the Narromine Express appeared.

'I went to watch Glenn because Steve Rixon told me he had a young kid down from the country, and because I was once a young kid down from the country I had extra interest in watching him,' says Lawson. 'Rixon said he was tall and skinny and he was going to be good. But he was unremarkable. He was tall, he had a pretty good action, he wasn't particularly quick but he was steady. The Village Green had a pretty good batting wicket and it was tough for all the bowlers, but I thought, "Oh yeah, he might develop into something." It was a different reaction to when I saw Brett Lee for the first time. He was a 17-year-old – I thought, "Wow!" Because he bowled *fast*.'

McGrath was a member of the Sutherland team that played Balmain in the 1989/90 semi-final at Drummoyne Oval. But unfortunately for Pascoe, Dyson and the boys, the game was decided when Balmain won the toss and elected to bat. Balmain needed only to draw to make the grand final, and rain hampered Sutherland's attempt to overhaul the home team's score. But McGrath still remembers Dyson's determination to go down swinging. 'There was a belief we were building something, and I was happy to be a part of it.'

McGrath finished his eight first-grade games in the summer of 1989/90 with 28 wickets at an average of 13.2. During an interview with *The St George Leader*'s cricket writer Jacquelin Magnay, retiring batsman Paul Bourke credited McGrath with providing a much-needed X-factor for the Sharks.

McGrath was hungry – not just as a fast bowler, but as a growing boy. It wasn't until the end of the season that his mother discovered he'd been so short of money he could often only afford to have a chocolate bar or instant noodles for dinner. McGrath was well aware his mother had struggles of her own, so he'd told her nothing.

'It hurt to learn that,' says Bev. 'He was painfully thin, but I didn't realise he was only having a Mars Bar for dinner. My kids always ate well at home – breakfast, morning tea, lunch, afternoon tea and dinner – and for Glenn to go from that to a chocolate bar at dinner must have been so terribly hard for him. However, he never once complained in all that time he was there. He had a dream, and he was going to do whatever it took.'

McGrath started the 1990 season a 'marked man', with *The St George Leader* reporting: 'Sutherland is brimming with fast bowlers with Glen [sic] McGrath tipped to join [Rod] Davison in the NSW Sheffield Shield side this year.'

McGrath started his second season in outstanding form, taking 5 for 33 against Hawkesbury off 18 overs. As Sutherland spin bowler Mark Chapman noted, Dyson used McGrath wisely: 'Glenn McGrath was used in short spells, but every time he came on he took a wicket.'

McGrath also took no prisoners. In a match against University of NSW, he battered the students with such a fearsome spell the openers had to head straight for the first-aid kit.

His second season in the top grade was also a reality check for the 20-year-old paceman. He took 29 wickets at a respectable 22.21, but as captain Dyson stressed in his end-of-season remarks, there were other areas of McGrath's game that needed sharpening up, including his fielding and batting. He also discovered the variability of wickets: 'Millard discovered this season that Sydney wickets are not all bounce and seam at pace, but can be somewhat Hume Highway-like at times. He is now a known quick around the competition and, as such, will have to generate real pace and control at all times.'

But Dyson concluded his review of McGrath's second season with high hopes for the bush bowler: 'I expect big things.'

10

The Academy

What are you feeding this bloke? Raw meat?

NSW opener Steve Small to Len Pascoe
after facing a McGrath bouncer at
Caringbah Oval

When he accepted a scholarship to the Australian Institute of Sport (AIS) Cricket Academy in Adelaide, Ricky Ponting was only 15 and hailed by Rod Marsh, who ran the Academy, as the best teenage batsman he'd ever laid eyes upon. Ponting enjoyed mixing with the older blokes at the Academy and he accepted that everyone was different – but he viewed the fast bowler named Glenn McGrath as one of the more 'interesting' cadets. This McGrath was more like Crocodile Dundee than Dennis Lillee.

Although they were friends, Ponting realised that the bloke from the outback was someone not to mess with the day he walked into McGrath's room and watched his handiwork with a knife.

'We were given these big boxes of cereal at the Academy by the official breakfast sponsor, and I remember wandering into Glenn's room for a chat one day and I saw he had them all lined up along the counter,' Ponting says. 'And then I saw why.

He was armed with a small sharp knife and as he rolled across his bed like a soldier out of the commandos, he threw the knife and – BANG – it stuck into the cereal box! Maybe he thought he was hunting pigs in the bush.'

Another teenager, Brad Hodge, whose Test career would be crowned by a majestic double-century against South Africa in 2005/06, also remembers McGrath's stint at the Academy for gorier things than his short, sharp bowling at the indoor nets.

'I was just an 18-year-old kid from suburban Melbourne and Glenn would have been the eldest at the Academy,' Hodge says. 'I got to know him, but the first time I saw him watching a video on how to skin pigs and deers was a bit . . . confronting. I'd never seen anything like it before. How do you think I felt when I then saw him throw his knives at the boxes of cereal? I believe he still has those skills.'

In 1992, Len Pascoe applied for scholarships to the Australian Cricket Academy for McGrath and 17-year-old Stuart Clark. They accepted only McGrath, because Rod Marsh believed the older player needed immediate help to build his frame up. Marsh ran the Academy in the manner of a drill sergeant. He demanded discipline and punctuality – and he'd go to extremes to enforce them, as McGrath heard on his first day when a cadet brought him up to speed on what to expect.

'We discovered Rod didn't tolerate slackers,' McGrath says. 'Apparently one guy didn't wake up in time to go to training because he'd had a big night on the tiles. Rod is said to have literally dragged the bloke out of bed to do some *extra* training. The story went that even though it was the middle of winter, Marshy made him go to the beach and run in waist-deep water until his lips turned blue. It sounds harsh but – if it's true – it was that kind of expectation that made the Academy so successful.'

When McGrath was given the scholarship to the Academy,

he vowed to make the most of his time there and not to waste the opportunity. He found the calibre of the lecturers who gave their insights into the game made it impossible for him to give them anything but his total attention. And unlike his days at Narromine High, at the Academy McGrath threw himself into class discussions and wasn't scared to ask questions.

'I was always learning,' he says. 'One of my great thrills was the fact Dennis Lillee was there as a lecturer, and he was also on hand to oversee our net sessions. I listened to everything. I took in what the other cadets asked, I threw up heaps of my own questions and I absorbed the answers. I'd then go and try whatever sounded interesting. If it worked I'd finetune it, but if it did nothing I'd discard it and move on to other things.

'But Dennis helped me in many different areas. He pointed out that the follow-through is just as important as bowling the ball itself. Dennis told me that if you have a good follow-through and slowly run down the wicket, it reduces the risk of injury from pulling up too quickly.'

Rod Marsh aimed to produce national or state representative players, which he achieved by enforcing discipline, hard work and responsibility. This regime produced players like McGrath, Ponting, Hodge, Adam Gilchrist, Peter McIntyre and Paul Wilson, who all represented Australia. As McGrath notes, other countries have copied the program, 'and I think they took on board Rod's old-school style'.

The Academy was established in 1987 with the intention of encouraging the cadets in its college-like setup to eat, sleep and breathe cricket. Marsh considered that teaching the young players about discipline and commitment was a crucial part of the curriculum.

When asked about the cadet he made run into the winter

surf, Marsh says that he was probably a few minutes late for training. 'I've always prided myself on being punctual,' he says. 'I mean, what happens if you turn up late to bat? You don't turn up late for anything.

'I believed that if I could instil discipline in their private lives, it would help them as cricketers as well. I never stopped them from celebrating if there was a cause to, but when the hard work was there to be done, we did it together.'

McGrath revelled in Marsh's approach to cricket because it was in synch with his own philosophies and beliefs. 'Rod and the Academy staff were great to work with because they believed cricket was a simple game complicated by too many people,' he says. 'Marsh also liked his students to have an uncomplicated style because he thought it was easier to add finesse to an individual rather than spend time undoing poor technique or rectifying sloppy habits.'

McGrath also learned a lot about nutrition and fitness at the Academy. He did strength-training at Adelaide University's state-of-the-art gymnasium and swam laps at the state's best aquatic centre. Having eaten chocolate bars for dinner because they were all he could afford as a bank teller in Sydney, he kept the kitchen staff at the Academy busy by eating as much food as he could wrap his mouth around.

'We wanted him to pack some extra weight on,' says Marsh. 'He was also taking a food supplement, and rather than doing an aerobics class with the rest of the guys, he was assigned to do extra weight sessions. He was such a skinny bugger who just needed more beef.'

Marsh and his crew also prepared the Academy's cadets for the mental and physical rigours required to succeed at state level by having them play four-day games. Although Marsh demanded the rookies give nothing but their best, McGrath discovered he was not unreasonable: Marsh accepted that a player could have a bad day.

'What I liked about Rod's approach was the fact he wasn't driven by an individual's stats – he liked flair and initiative,' he says. 'When I played against the Tasmanian second XI at Launceston, I was smashed in the first innings and finished with 0 for 100, and while I was disappointed, I didn't drop my chin. I sat down and thought about where I went wrong and came back to take 4 for 50 in the second innings. And that pleased Rod because he could tell I'd learned from my mistakes.'

Marsh is adamant McGrath marked himself far too harshly during that first innings in Launceston, because his memory of the match is of a kid who showed plenty of ticker in tough conditions.

'He was a tall kid that ran in pretty straight,' Marsh says. 'He looked as if he had control over what he was doing, too. If I recall correctly, it was a good batting pitch; you don't look at figures in a situation like that and think one outing makes a career. If he'd have taken eight-for in that first innings it wouldn't have changed my opinion. He was a prospect, and you always look at fast bowling prospects. And the beauty of that, in my position, was if you make a mistake, well, you find the next one. But with Glenn, we didn't make a mistake.'

On the back of McGrath's effort in Launceston, former Test player Kerry O'Keeffe – now an ABC radio commentator with a cult following – urged cricket fans to jot down the name 'G. McGrath' as a player of the future. He wrote in his popular *St George Leader* column, 'Come In Spinner': 'The mention of Sutherland's Glenn McGrath as a potential NSW fast bowler is sure to raise a few eyebrows. Why I don't know! This lad from Narrabri [sic] is very impressive.

'Already he is under the notice of the state selectors; he set up the AIS Academy win over Tasmania's second XI in Launceston last week.

'For some time John Dyson has hailed McGrath's virtues; his spells in Launceston suggested a growing maturity and a capacity to learn by mistakes. Jot the name G. McGrath down because you will hear more of him!'

In 1992 McGrath was selected to tour South Africa with the Australian Cricket Academy squad, along with Adam Gilchrist – who was the squad's captain – and Ricky Ponting. Marsh told *The Australian* that the trip would provide both an invaluable learning curve for the players and a chance for him to assess the depth of South African cricket ahead of the Aussie team's tour there in 1994.

'I just think it is a wonderful opportunity, because at some stage these guys are going over to play Test cricket in South Africa, there's no doubt about that,' Marsh said. 'That's the whole idea of the [Academy program], to go and play in these places before [the players] represent Australia in senior cricket.'

Marsh, assistant coach Richard Done and the Academy students also conducted a series of multiracial coaching clinics and visited numerous black townships.

'That was an experience,' McGrath says. 'What stood out was the Africans had nothing, but they were happy a group of strangers took an interest in them. We were cricketers – it wasn't as if we were superstars – yet they made each of us feel welcome. The kids loved it and I noticed there was a lot of natural cricket ability. But I was impressed most of all by their enthusiasm – it was infectious – and visiting the townships was one of the real highlights of the trip.'

McGrath found the South African cricket conditions to

his liking. He sent the Northern Transvaal team reeling in the opening 55-over game by taking 3 for 12 from four overs. His effort helped the Academy XI blast the home team out for 136 to give them a 115-run victory. The Australians finished their eight-match tour undefeated. And there was one South African opponent whom McGrath, Ponting and Gilchrist would get to know extremely well in the ensuing years – Natal under-23s all-rounder Shaun Pollock, a gifted cricketer and future South African skipper.

Back in the Sutherland Shire, if McGrath expected Pascoe to treat him any differently after his return from the Republic following a successful wicket-taking safari, he was badly mistaken. Sure, Pascoe was pleased to learn that from 75 overs McGrath had bowled 21 maidens and taken 12 wickets for 200 runs at an average of 16.67, but he refused to allow the up-and-comer to rest on his laurels.

'After spending time at the Academy, Glenn took an hour to warm up, an hour to warm down, but he hardly played,' says Pascoe. 'I remember saying to him it was okay to play for the Academy against the Mullumbimby XI, but if he wanted to get noticed by the state selectors he had to take wickets in grade. It was as simple as that.

'As luck had it, we were playing Bankstown that weekend and they were known as "The World" then, because they had superstars like Steve and Mark Waugh, Steve Small, Wayne Holdsworth – you name them, they were there. I said to Glenn if he could take five wickets he'd be noticed. But I also told him if he could "helmet" someone – hit their helmet with the ball – he'd *really* be noticed.'

Len Pascoe and Jeff Thomson had formed a terrifying opening bowling partnership for Bankstown in the 1970s, so when state opener Steve Small recognised more than just a little of Pascoe's brand of bowling in McGrath's bombardment, he turned towards the pavilion and directed some choice words at his old team-mate.

'Steve yelled at me I was feeding raw meat to my bowlers,' laughs Pascoe. 'But that was good. It meant Glenn was being recognised as a bowler to respect – and when he proved that day that he was good enough to helmet Mark Waugh, everyone was talking about his ability and his potential.'

Small recalls a fiery spell that made him and a few others take notice. 'Mark was hit on the helmet and it seemed a good idea to stay down the other end for as long as possible,' he laughs. 'It was very hostile, but it was also very good.'

Mark Waugh recalled the delivery for *The Sydney Morning Herald* on the eve of McGrath's Test debut in 1993, telling how the ball almost went for six after it deflected off his helmet: 'He almost took my head off. I didn't know who he was, all I knew was he was quick.'

His brother Steve, who was clean-bowled by McGrath for just 6, trudged slowly back to the pavilion certain he'd just faced a player he'd see a lot more of.

'It was a flat, slow pitch and there was nothing in it for the pacemen,' he says. 'This lanky kid with a very short haircut and short long pants had an ungainly style. However, I remember thinking, "He's got something about him, this bloke; he's got a bit of get up and go." He seemed pretty focused and his body language was pretty good. He came across as a simple and uncomplicated bowler who just went about his business in a quiet, productive way. It didn't take much to see there was something more than the average about him.

'I think Glenn was only getting used to his body. He was only young, and while he didn't look uncoordinated, he was just *ungainly.* He had a simple, economical action as well. I think it just took him time to get to know his body because once he did, Glenn developed more pace.'

McGrath had found his feet. His time with Marsh had added an extra dimension both to his game and to his confidence. It made for a formidable combination, and the state selectors started to pay closer attention to Sutherland's young fast bowler.

11

False Start

> He's a typical country lad – hard as nails inside and shows no emotion. He's physically a lot stronger since he's been with Rod Marsh at the AIS.
>
> Len Pascoe introducing McGrath,
> *The Sunday Telegraph*, 25 October 1992

If Lenny Pascoe proved just one thing during his time as McGrath's coach, it was that he understood what excited the selectors – and in some people's reckoning, that should elevate him to the rank of 'genius' because few involved in cricket really know what makes selectors tick. Sure, plenty have questioned their decisions – Marvan Attapatu called those responsible for picking the Sri Lankan team that toured Australia in 2007 'Muppets', and former Australian chairman of national selectors Trevor Hohns received hate mail when he dropped Steve Waugh from the one-day team in 2002 – but no-one understood their thought processes quite like Lenny.

McGrath took 3 for 64 from 24 overs that day against Bankstown – with Waugh and Steve Small among his victims – but Pascoe's theory about a bowler standing out from the crowd by whacking a batsman on the head proved correct.

The newspapers, which rarely devote much space to grade cricket, even considered the little-known Glenn McGrath hitting Mark Waugh's helmet was worthy of newspaper ink.

When McGrath turned up to Sutherland training the Tuesday after their win over 'The World', his mobile phone rang and for a few seconds he wasn't sure if the voice at the other end of the phone was a Sutherland team-mate having a belly laugh at his expense – or the selector he purported to be. The caller introduced himself as a state selector and congratulated McGrath on being named 12th man for the NSW team to play Western Australia in the Mercantile Mutual Cup one-dayer in Perth the next Sunday.

'Once I realised it was serious I was really excited,' McGrath says. 'I was on my own so I did a bit of a jump in the air and hoped no-one was watching. I rang home to let everyone know the good news. The Sutherland guys were great, they were so happy for me.'

The *Leader*, which had documented McGrath's rise and rise, reacted positively to the news with the headline GLEN GRABS STATE SPOT (it would be another year before the media realised his Christian name ended with a double 'n'), and reporter Brad Forrest captured the optimism that accompanied McGrath's breakthrough to the big time: 'His 83 first-grade wickets at 18.8 suggests he can pressure the other fast bowlers, including Bankstown's Wayne Holdsworth and St George's Phil Alley, for a spot in the Sheffield Shield side this season.

'Originally selectors were happy to allow McGrath to master his trade at the AIS Academy in Adelaide and carry on his learning with Sutherland this season. But McGrath has taken the bit between his teeth and forced the selectors' hand.'

McGrath was replaced in the Sutherland side by Stuart Clark. Like McGrath, Clark's spirit was tested when people doubted his ability and he was dropped from fifth-grade.*

McGrath was given the task of carrying the drinks tray and realised he was being 'blooded'. He'd already gained a welcome insight into the NSW team's culture courtesy of Steve Rixon, who had included him in the training squad midway through the previous summer. McGrath remembers the side as a good group of blokes: 'What was great about that era in New South Wales, and the ones that followed it for that matter, was that everyone was respected,' he says. 'I was told that it wasn't so pleasant a few years before that – backstabbing, that kind of stuff – so I was very fortunate to come in at a good time.

'What struck me was how everyone seemed to be happy to enjoy each other's success. Even when I was named 12th man for the Perth trip, it was treated as something to celebrate. The guys were great. Greg Matthews said he remembered me from Parkes and called me a "cool cat". He made it known from the outset he's different. Mike Whitney was there and, while he's ultra-competitive by nature, he was tremendous in giving advice, and Steve Small – well, he was like a rugby league player; he just wanted to get out and do the job, and I liked that.'

Although NSW's tour to the Western Australian Cricket Association ground (the WACA) wasn't successful – after being dismissed for 206, the home team breezed to an eight-wicket victory, with Mark Veletta, Justin Langer, Damien Martyn and Tom Moody all making solid starts – at least McGrath didn't spill the drinks. He is convinced his push for state selection was due as much to his hours of hard work in the gym and the pool during his stint at the Academy as to his 'dinging' Mark Waugh.

'Before going to Adelaide I really didn't know much about

---

* In 2007 Clark would again replace McGrath as the workhorse of the Australian Test XI.

fitness training. I relied a lot on training in the nets for my fitness,' McGrath says. 'It wasn't enough. I had my eyes opened by the likes of Rod Marsh at the Academy to what was really needed and, apart from whacking on four kilos of muscle, the extra fitness gave me a good base when the season started. My strength and fitness allowed me to bowl a few yards quicker than I had the previous summer. I was able to bowl spells of sustained pace. In my first game for Sutherland in 1992 I bowled 25 overs at the one pace. It gave me tremendous confidence.'

The one thing McGrath couldn't have been prepared for was pulling a side muscle when he played in Mike Whitney's testimonial match at North Sydney Oval. The injury came just days after he was named to play for NSW against Queensland in a one-dayer. There was a suggestion his body was struggling to cope with the workload. But all McGrath knew was that it was a terrible setback, and he did all he could to remain upbeat.

'It hurt to be so close, only to have selection in a rep team taken away,' he says. 'There was no point getting down in the dumps. I did my physio and recovery and hoped to hell it would be a quick recovery. Shane Lee was given his chance to play for the state.'

New South Wales' long-term physiotherapist Pat Farhart – a big-hearted Lebanese-Aussie who for years has been the players' confidant, healer and trusted mate – remembers the severity of the muscle injury that sidelined McGrath. Few people understood its gravity. According to Farhart, the injury to the side muscle was so bad that it took a bit of the bone off McGrath's iliac crest, which is part of the pelvis. As Farhart says: 'That should give an indication of how bad it was. That, and the fact he needed eight weeks to recover. Yet rather than mope around, Glenn turned it into a positive and took it as a message he had to do even more strength and conditioning work.'

The talk of Glenn McGrath being raw, unrefined and ungainly was long gone. People started to believe he would make the cut. Among them was Jock Campbell, a lower-grade cricketer with Sydney University and Sutherland who became the Australian team's fitness conditioner. He remembers the nights he'd hit the Caringbah Inn with mates and point to the lanky bloke busy making some much-needed extra income by picking up glasses, pulling beers or doing some handyman work around the place.

'A group of us would go to Coyotes nightclub inside the Inn and I'd point out Glenn and tell whoever I was with, "See that guy there? He's going to be a star." They'd look at me strange, but I knew. Though it wasn't a scoop – a lot of people had started saying it.'

At last, McGrath was handed his chance to prove the likes of Campbell right when the selectors picked him to wear the baggy blue cap for NSW in a Sheffield Shield match against Tasmania at the SCG in January 1993.*

Few could have imagined the significance the game would have for Australian cricket. In that match, three of the modern game's greatest players would stride onto centre stage.

---

* The Sheffield Shield was Australia's domestic first-class cricket competition. It started in 1892/93 after Lord Sheffield from England donated £150 towards the development of Australian cricket. From 1999 it became known as the Pura Milk Cup, and until the end of the 2007/08 season it was called the Pura Cup.

12

First Blood

His direction is pretty good; the only thing that concerns me a little is his length. He's fast, though – that's the important thing . . .

Rod Marsh on the eve of
McGrath's debut for NSW

The catch off the debutant's bowling screamed towards Greg Matthews at pace – and he took it easily. Matthews felt a sense of delight for the new kid, who he thought had a unique sense of cool, with his Victor Trumper-style haircut and his daggy short long pants that didn't quite cover his ankles. The kid, he thought, had talent.

'I turned to whoever it was standing next to me in slips and said, "This guy will get a hundred Test wickets,"' says Matthews. 'Dude – how wrong was I?'

Injuries to Mike Whitney and Phil Alley fast-tracked McGrath's entry into the NSW team. Aged 22, he was picked to open the bowling with Wayne Holdsworth against a Tasmanian XI which was – as its opener Dene Hills remembers – 'building towards something'. He recalls the game as the unveiling of the cornerstones of Australian cricket's most prosperous reign: Glenn McGrath, Adam Gilchrist and Ricky Ponting.

While Tasmania had enjoyed a confidence-boosting win over competition pacesetters Queensland the week before, their line-up lacked the edge of NSW. Even without Test players Mark Taylor and the Waugh brothers, NSW still boasted the likes of Matthews, Holdsworth, Phil Emery, Steve Small, David Freedman and talented up-and-comers Michael Slater and Michael Bevan. On the Tasmanian side, Ponting arrived in the Harbour City with huge raps.

Before being handed his spurs, McGrath was put to the test in a series of gruelling fitness sessions in the week leading up to the match. Coach Steve Rixon wanted absolute proof the paceman had overcome the side strain that had benched him for two months. He had planned to make McGrath work up a sweat against a Shoalhaven Invitational XI at Nowra on the New South Wales south coast two days before the Shield match, but a deluge foiled that. After being put through his paces in a tough net session overseen by Rixon and Dennis Lillee, McGrath told the media he was ready to seize the moment:

'It was the best workout I've had this season,' he told *The Sydney Morning Herald* the day before he took the new ball. 'I probably would have bowled 20 overs all up, almost at top pace. I didn't feel at all sore afterwards and nothing when I woke up the next day. I saw the physio yesterday and he's really happy with the way I'm progressing.'

What McGrath failed to mention was how his thigh had tightened during that bowling session. The twinge he felt as he cooled down would ultimately take some of the gloss off an outstanding debut, which finished with his name being etched in gold on the SCG's historic honour board.

On 27 January 1993, McGrath arrived at the ground for the first day of play almost an hour before any of his new team-mates. Even though the clouds threatened a day interrupted by rain, he didn't dare run the risk of being late – Marsh had drummed into him the importance of punctuality.

As he waited for a ground attendant to open the home team's dressing-room, he and Bev sat in the seats outside the then 107-year-old members' stand and soaked up the scene. Bev had made the trip from the bush and, while she was bursting with pride, neither said much. She instead marvelled at the confident man her son had grown into.

The boy whose Year Five teacher had forced him to sit next to a girl because he was so shy of girls now stood tall. He looked people in the eye when he spoke and he seemed relaxed as strangers offered him their best wishes. He was still the same old Glenn, but he had a spark, and Bev offered Rod Marsh silent thanks for that.

'Rod took Glenn under his wing in Adelaide,' says Bev. 'He assigned him to work in the office with him. But he also invited him to his house to eat dinner with his family on a few occasions and it seemed to help bring him out of his shell. It was pleasing to see.'

Marsh took young cricketers and helped turn them into men by instilling discipline and thrusting responsibilities upon them, but he says taking an interest in the cadets was one of his most important duties.

'My job was to make them feel at home,' he says. 'I remember Glenn came around to our home to do a bit of gardening. One stage he fixed the fence to keep our bloody dog in – I figured he would be better at that kind of thing, coming from the bush. But I'm not at all surprised by what Glenn achieved. I always welcomed his achievements but I was never surprised.'

McGrath wasn't nervous about the challenge ahead of him at the SCG that day; he was lost in deep thought as he gazed at what had been his field of dreams during those countless afternoons at *Lagoona* when he'd bowl ball after ball at the 44-gallon drum behind his father's machinery shed. He'd always thought playing on the SCG would be a special event, but as he sat there that morning he didn't see the ghosts of the greats who'd played there before him, nor did he feel tingles of excitement run up and down his spine. Instead, he experienced what some might call a revelation.

'I was surprised,' he says. 'I was about to play on the SCG – the hallowed turf – but I didn't feel at all overwhelmed. I always imagined I'd treat playing there as a great moment in my life. And while it *was* a great moment, I found I didn't get caught up in sentiment or a sense of achievement when the time came. It wasn't until that hour before I made my debut for NSW that I realised playing at the SCG *wasn't* my dream – the dream was to play for Australia, and fulfilling that had nothing to do with the ground; it was about playing cricket.'

McGrath didn't have to wait long to play cricket that day, because Tasmania won the toss and elected to bat. When he was tossed the new ball to bowl at Dene Hills and his fellow opener Nick Courtney, McGrath simply gripped the seam hard and committed himself to rip 'n tear.

'It was the most basic process,' he says. 'I hadn't seen Dene bat before, so there was no firsthand knowledge of how I should take him on. He was a left-hander; I was told he was particularly strong on the off side. That was it. So I bowled a regulation length going across him. Hills nicked the ball and it went straight to Greg Matthews at second slip – it was my first wicket for the state and I was ecstatic. I didn't think it could get any better; I felt on top of the world.'

At the time, Hills had no reason to appreciate the significance of entering the scorebook as McGrath's first 'kill' in top-class cricket. But he was definitely annoyed with himself as he trudged slowly back towards the visitors' dressing-room with the scoreboard reading 1 for 11 – of which he'd contributed only 3 during his 23 minutes at the crease. While Hills was eventually to follow McGrath's career keenly, albeit from afar (although he would become Australia's assistant coach in 2007), he has only fuzzy memories of that inaugural encounter.

'He was six foot five, young and bowled at a rate of knots,' Hills recalls. 'I knew nothing about him except he'd been through the Academy, so I realised he'd be well trained, well drilled. It was a case of batting against someone sight unseen. As a batsman in that situation, you just play balls on their merit. But I don't remember much about that particular innings except he got me out. Glenn went on to be a great bowler and I loved everything about the guy because he had a very simple action, his theory was simple and he received his just rewards.'

McGrath next dismissed Courtney for 20 when Bevan took a good catch at cover. He finished his first eight-over spell with 2 wickets for a miserly 11 runs, impressing one of his fellow Academy cadets, Adam Gilchrist, a hard hitter from the north coast via Sydney's Gordon club. Gilchrist was also making his debut that day in the first of his ten games for NSW before he transferred to Western Australia, where he'd become arguably the game's greatest wicketkeeper–batsman.

'Glenn was somewhat of an unknown to everyone because he hadn't graduated through the junior ranks, like the NSW under-17s and under-19s,' Gilchrist says. 'He had a tremendous first innings, taking five wickets, and in that time he gave an indication of what he would soon become – a bowler who'd terrorise the batsmen with his consistency and patience.'

Tasmania finished a rain-interrupted first day at 6 for 200. Ponting remained unconquered on 98 after being stuck in the so-called 'nervous nineties' for 54 painstaking minutes, while the all-rounder Shaun Young was yet to score when the umpire called stumps.

McGrath finished his baptism of fire with an impressive 2 for 55 from 21 overs. *The Sydney Morning Herald*'s Greg Growden noted: 'McGrath, 22, has several elements in his favour. He is fast. He has a marvellous bowling action. He's smooth in all areas of his run-up. He is prepared to attack the stumps. And he does not get sucked into trying to show batsmen how high he can bounce a ball over their heads.

'The early Tasmanian batsmen seemed surprised by the amount of pace McGrath could extract from the most innocent of actions. His early overs in his first match were his best, first producing the required off-cutter to have Dene Hills caught at slip, before confusing Nick Courtney who tried to flick him through the on-side only to get caught in the covers.

'McGrath was not as effective when used as a stock bowler, but a damp ball did not help his cause . . .'

From the hours they had spent together finetuning his technique in the nets, Marsh could picture exactly how McGrath would have approached his state debut – and he insisted that even for a greenhorn, it was a sure-fire formula for success.

'I know I said it to him – and I'm sure other coaches would have said it to him – if you continue to bowl 80- to 90-mile-an-hour outswingers over the top of off stump at a good length, you'll get a few wickets. I think he basically tried to do that. And if it wasn't swinging, he would still get the ball bouncing over the top of the off stump – whether it be in Australia, India, South Africa or Pakistan, he still tried to do the same thing. The only time Glenn ever bowled badly was when he went away from those plans, when he lost his temper and tried to do different things. Even in the early days, Glenn was smart enough to realise that it's not rocket science.'

Bev watched the action from the back row of the members' stand. She was delirious with pride – and sharing her joy was a woman she befriended that day, Dot French. Dot had been a member of the SCG for over 40 years. She would go on to become a great friend of Bev's and, over the years, they would watch as McGrath imposed his authority on the game. The pair were also treated that day in January with Ponting's emergence as a future superstar.

A few minutes into the second day of play, at 18 years and 40 days, Ricky Ponting knocked the champion Tasmanian batsman Jack Badcock out of the record books to become the youngest Tasmanian to score a first-class century. Badcock – once described as an 'infant prodigy' – played his first game for Tasmania in 1929 at just 15 years old. Ponting also entered the record books that day as the sixth-youngest Australian to make a century at the elite level. That list of baby-faced assassins included the likes of Ian Craig, Archie Jackson, Doug Walters, Clem Hill, Neil Harvey, Greg Chappell, Keith Miller, Arthur Morris and Bobby Simpson. Ponting compiled an accomplished 125 runs before being caught by Small off Holdsworth's bowling.

While the media hailed Ponting's success as a positive sign for Australia's cricket future, his strokeplay didn't surprise McGrath. He'd had enough duels with Ponting in the indoor nets at Adelaide Oval to realise the extent of his class.

'One thing I quickly learned about Ricky when we were at the Academy in Adelaide was that he'd murder anything short,' says McGrath. 'He was so strong and he'd smash anything just short of a length. He did it to me a few times in that game, but I found I was soon hitting good areas and keeping the ball up there at him.'

While Ponting's century only enhanced the so-called 'talented teen's' reputation as a star in the making, the Tasmanian was equally impressed by the pace McGrath generated on what was generally regarded as a spin-friendly SCG wicket.

'I had a fair idea of what to expect from Glenn and he didn't let me down,' says Ponting. 'I'd faced a countless amount of balls from him in Adelaide. Believe me, the indoor nets at the Adelaide Oval are the worst place in the world to bat against tall guys armed with brand-new cricket balls . . . and Glenn *was* quick back then. I remember playing for the Academy team when we toured South Africa. We played at Johannesburg, and when I fielded at second slip I stood 30 metres away from the batsman because McGrath was that fast! The height made it hard. When someone is bowling from Glenn's height – 1.95 metres – it feels as if the wicket is 18 yards long, not 22, because of how big and tall they are. It's really hard work. It's bounce that gets good batsmen out, not pace. Pace rarely gets good batsmen out; pace *and* swing might, but bounce will bring more batsmen undone any time.'

McGrath measured out his run-up on that second day of the match with captain and wicketkeeper Phil Emery's demand ringing in his ears – take wickets with the second new ball. He responded by snaring three more scalps: Shaun Young, Michael Farrell and Mark Atkinson. McGrath's final wicket – Atkinson – ensured his name would appear on the honour board that acknowledges those players who either score a century or take five wickets or more in a first-class innings at the SCG. McGrath finished the match with 5 for 79, and – as was the case in the Toohey's Cup match four years earlier at Parkes – he walked from the field feeling as if he'd proven he was up to the big league.

'One thing about my career was that the higher the level I played, the better I performed,' he says. 'In grade I did okay in seconds, but I bowled much better in firsts. I just loved competing – and with five wickets in my debut, I walked off the SCG feeling very pleased with myself. The memory that stands out most of all is how much I loved every minute I spent out there. I don't remember feeling any nerves. I am still not sure if I could believe I was there . . . it was amazing and I loved it.'

He also sauntered off the SCG with a new nickname – 'Pigeon' – which was to become one of the best known in Australian sport.

'Our all-rounder Brad McNamara saw a pigeon in the outfield,' recalls Rixon. 'It had legs like pipe-cleaners, not dissimilar to Glenn's. So Brad said, "Look, there's Glenn McGrath!" And it stuck.'

Unfortunately, the inaugural flight of the Pigeon was a short one. As he ran into bowl midway through his 14th over in Tasmania's second innings, he experienced so acute a pain it felt as if he'd been shot through the thigh.

'It felt tight,' he says, grimacing at the mere memory. 'I'd thought to myself, "That feels a bit sore," earlier on, but I thought it was nothing to worry about so I kept bowling. When I lifted my leg up to bowl what was to be my last delivery of the match, it felt strange. I'd torn a thigh muscle – I'd never had a muscle go like that before. It crept up on me and I was well and truly gone. At training before the game my thigh was a little bit sore and I worried at the time it might go on me again. I gambled a bit by not saying anything. I told everyone I felt fine, but it all went wrong in the second innings. I still have a hole in my thigh muscle.'

As McGrath received treatment in the back room Pat Farhart used as his studio, the Tasmanians were condemned by the media for their go-slow tactics in the second innings. The visitors made it clear they were intent on denying the Blues an innings victory and, in the process, bored the pants off the 900 enthusiasts who'd turned out. Courtney took 45 deliveries to get off the mark and the usually flamboyant Danny Buckingham stayed perched on 0 for 31 painstaking minutes.

'If this is the way Shield captains carry on, the competition's survival is doubtful,' said *The Sunday Telegraph*, blasting captain Rod Tucker's stonewall tactics.

'Even though the wicket held no dangers for the batsmen and the bowling was hardly threatening, Tasmania played as if they were facing a ten-pronged West Indian pace attack, where basic survival was imperative,' added *The Sun-Herald.*

McGrath would have given anything to return to the fray to liven up proceedings with some pace, but he was prone on a massage table hoping to hell his injury hadn't hurt his chances of being picked for the state again.

'I remember lying on a bench while Pat Farhart treated me,' he says. 'I was looking up and counting the little squares on the ceiling. I just couldn't believe it. I'd just taken five wickets and I was on my back injured. Later on, the NSW boys laughed at me – they thought it was hilarious I'd got my chance only to blow it badly. I'm not sure what I thought at the time, but I don't remember it being negative at all.'

Farhart couldn't help but feel amazed by how McGrath retained his composure after suffering yet another setback so soon after his side muscle trauma.

'He handled it with a minimum of fuss,' he says. 'It impressed me because he seemed to take it all in his stride. I was to learn over the years that it was exactly how Glenn handled most things in his life – he just got on with it. I remember thinking he handled it a lot better than a lot of other blokes in the same boat.'

However, it's a sad fact that tall, skinny fast bowlers don't have a great reputation for cricketing longevity, and while Adam Gilchrist hoped his fellow debutant would recover and build a solid career, he admits to having had some concerns for McGrath's future.

'I remember thinking that injury was going to be Glenn's biggest problem,' says Gilchrist. 'He was such a wiry, thin fellow that I actually figured it might not be his destiny to be a fast bowler, given his shape and build.'

Gilchrist was not the first to wonder about McGrath's physical capability to survive the slog of top-class cricket, but McGrath was set for a different challenge that would test both his spirit and his spark – an on-field confrontation with the Australian Test captain that would make headlines.

13

The Bolter

I know you can grunt but can you speak?

Allan Border to Glenn McGrath,
4 November 1993

When Allan Border went out to bat for Queensland at the Gabba (the Brisbane Cricket Ground) in November 1993 and noticed the rookie NSW fast bowler's trousers only came up to his shins, he didn't even attempt to hide his smirk.

'Hey mate,' he sneered. 'Why are your pants so high? Are you expecting a flood or something?'

It was Test skipper Border's welcome to the big time for McGrath and he waited for an expletive-ridden comeback, but it never came. The veteran of 147 Tests was staggered by the rookie bowler's reaction: he stormed back to his mark and steamed in to bowl. Not surprisingly, the kid fired down a bouncer that hummed dangerously past the veteran's chin. Border decided to have another crack at the young bloke, telling him he looked like a television star – the yokel Jethro Bodine of *The Beverly Hillbillies* fame.

'He looked just like Jethro in those trousers,' says Border, chuckling at the memory. 'It looked as if he bought them when he was 14 and still only six foot, but he hadn't let the hems down as he grew. And I gave him heaps, saying things like: "Hey Jethro, you're not bowling too well today." But Glenn didn't say a word, and I thought that was interesting because most fast bowlers get stuck into you like school bullies, but not Glenn.'

Border continued his sledging for the four-and-a-half hours he was at the crease, during which he compiled a tidy 85 runs. After McGrath had replied to AB's best lines with nothing more than a stare, a snort and the predictable bouncer, the Test skipper cut loose with an insult that went straight from his mouth and into folklore.

'I know you can grunt,' fumed Border, 'but can you speak?'

While McGrath went a shade of red, he maintained his apparent vow of silence and refused to utter a single syllable.

'At the time I was still a quiet, shy kid from the bush,' he says. 'I was never a high-school bully – at least, I never viewed myself as one – and I never said much on the field back then. At the end of the day, Allan was captain of Australia and he was a player I grew up admiring. I didn't take any offence at what happened. I didn't think, "Bloody hell, Allan Border is opening up on me, it's the end of the world." I took it all in my stride. I was bowling well, and if I remember anything about that game, it wasn't getting angry or having my feelings hurt, it was only that I was out there and competing. I was playing for NSW and it was great – nothing could take the smile off my face. It wasn't as though I couldn't believe I was playing for my state – I was excited. Ego probably would have got the better of me later on in my career and I probably would have fired back at him; I would've had to say something.'

'Jethro' eventually had the last laugh at the Gabba when he dismissed Border for 11 in the second innings. New South Wales went on to win the game by eight wickets, despite a six-and-a-half-hour innings by Matthew Hayden, who scored 173. McGrath ended the match sharing the honours as best bowler with Phil Alley.

Says Border: 'It was a part of his initiation that he took it all in – he didn't feel as if he needed to say much, and most of us are the same. You sit in the corner, keep your mouth shut and it isn't until you get a bit more senior that you start offering more in team meetings or maybe geeing the boys up on the field. It's funny, I wonder how he might have reacted had I done that at the height of Glenn's career? Could you have imagined it? "Hey Jethro!" The thought makes me laugh!'

There were high expectations placed on the Narromine Express after his five-game rookie season with the Blues in 1992/93, which he finished with an impressive average of 21.56. McGrath and fellow fast bowler Wayne Holdsworth had won great acclaim for their effort against Queensland in the Shield final at the SCG. In the first innings McGrath bowled a marathon spell of 24.5 overs to finish with 4 for 64. In the second innings he underlined his love for hard yakka by bowling 18 overs straight for a very tidy return of 3 for 28. And Holdsworth bowled 19 overs from the other end.

'Holdsworth finished with his third seven-wicket haul for the season and it gave him a berth on the Ashes tour,' says McGrath. 'He went for more runs than me – he took 7 for 41 – but I was happy to keep it tight at my end. Wayne was on a roll that day. He bowled with plenty of energy and it was obvious he loved every minute of it.'

McGrath only enhanced his burgeoning reputation with his effort in the final of the domestic one-day competition, the Mercantile Mutual Cup, in February 1993, when he tormented the Victorians with his unforgiving line and length. While he went wicketless, the Victorians only managed to score 21 runs from his seven overs.

'We won the two domestic competitions – the Shield and the Mercantile Mutual Cup – and it was a great achievement. After we won the Shield final, our Aussie reps Steve and Mark Waugh and Mark Taylor joined our celebrations, and I remember thinking how good it was to be among the NSW blokes because they were such a good bunch. After we won the one-day competition, we all celebrated down at the Bourbon & Beefsteak at Kings Cross. It was all new to me, and I enjoyed the camaraderie and sense that no matter what happened I had been involved in a really special cricket moment.'

Against Border that day at the Gabba in late 1993, McGrath had continued to bowl short. But the batsman took it in his stride – after all, he'd stood up to the West Indies at the peak of their most terrifying pace attack, when the likes of Andy Roberts, Malcolm Marshall, Colin Croft, Joel Garner, Courtney Walsh, Michael Holding and Curtly Ambrose had targeted him in line with their philosophy: to kill the head (captain) was to kill the body (team). But Border had proved to be a *very* tough nut for them to crack. And at the Gabba he dug in while his team-mates fell cheaply: Matthew Hayden (9), Dirk Wellham (21), Stuart Law (3), Martin Love (11) and Ian Healy (6).

Border knew about the newcomer and thought he'd test him. 'I'd heard he'd bounced the crap out of the Waugh brothers in a grade game in Sydney and all of a sudden people took notice of him,' he says. 'They asked, "Who's this bloke?" And before he knew it, Glenn was playing state cricket. I came up against him towards the end of my career and I thought I'd stir him up a bit.'

The reporters covering the match didn't miss Border's verbal attack on McGrath and Wayne Holdsworth, who'd just toured

England as a member of AB's Ashes squad. BORDER CLASH, screamed *The Daily Telegraph-Mirror*'s back page.

'At one stage it appeared Border gave the NSW bowler a tongue lashing all the way down the pitch after one delivery – a verballing which continued halfway through McGrath's return to his mark,' wrote John Geddes in the same paper. 'Umpire [Tom] Parker was then seen to say something to Border who gestured he was within his rights to voice his opinion.'

'He was pretty worked up about the game,' Holdsworth had said of Border's tirade, adding that there was nothing sinister about a mid-wicket collision they'd had during the match. The Australian skipper had refused to comment about the on-field incidents.

The idea that his incessant bowling of bouncers at the national skipper might harm his claims to a baggy green didn't once cross McGrath's mind. 'I was loving every minute of the challenge, as it happened,' he says. 'I hadn't even thought of what might not happen later on in the day, let alone the following day or next week. I was just so happy to be where I was – taking on a great batsman.'

The old bull and the young fast bowler had crossed paths a few weeks earlier in a domestic one-dayer. Border wasn't around long enough to test McGrath with his wit and sharp tongue because he was dismissed for just 1 run. And he wasn't the only member of the star-studded Queensland team to fall to McGrath: Border's fellow internationals Dirk Wellham (49), Ian Healy (0) and Craig McDermott (13) were also among his 4 for 17 off 10 overs.

McGrath had picked the perfect time to impress the Australian selectors, who needed a replacement strike bowler after Ashes hero Merv Hughes was sidelined with a knee injury. Any hopes that Bruce Reid would slip straight in as a ready-made replacement bowler fell short because he hadn't recuperated in time from his own health problems. Wayne Holdsworth was mentioned as an option, but he hadn't lived up to expectations on the recent Ashes tour. A poor effort against NSW did nothing for Queensland's Carl Rackemann's chances.

The door was open for someone like McGrath – and his story as the bushie who lived in a caravan for his first 13 months in the big smoke had captured the public's attention. Journalist Phil Wilkins played on McGrath's outback origins when he wrote about him for *The Sydney Morning Herald*: 'In a rodeo sense it was young fast bowler Glenn McGrath from the NSW central-west who roped and tied the Queensland Bulls in NSW's overwhelming 127-run win in the Mercantile Mutual Cup game 4/278 to 151.'

Steve Rixon was cautious about the 'pick McGrath' push that started after NSW's limited-overs win against Queensland. He urged the selectors to show some restraint and not to make the mistake of exposing McGrath to Test cricket too soon. The NSW coach was worried by the possible fallout if McGrath was found wanting. He said at the time to the media: 'I just think at this point he needs to get some performances on the board for the Blues. Let's see how he goes in the next three or four games.'

McGrath was also very careful not to get too caught up in the hype. Although only 23, he was savvy enough to realise that the buzz about a bolter from the bush being considered for Test selection was an easy way to fill media space.

'Back then I'd like to read what the press had to say about the way I'd played – that changed midway through my career – but I'd always have a bit of a chuckle because I took none of it too seriously,' McGrath says. 'There were plenty of headlines and talk of Test cricket – and that pleased me – but I realised our win over Queensland was only the first game of the season. Steve Rixon was right – it really depended upon how I performed in the other games, especially the first-class matches. But I made it clear that if the selectors *wanted* to pick me, I'd grab the opportunity with both hands.'

McGrath was given his shot at the Kiwis a fortnight before the opening Test of the series, when he was picked for the Australian Institute of Sport XI to play New Zealand at North Sydney Oval. His frugal 1 for 21 from eight overs helped the AIS humble the New Zealanders by 110 runs – their third loss from as many games. McGrath's victim was the Kiwi opener Brian Young for 1. His effort against this international team inspired Rod Marsh to declare his prodigy had proved he was worthy of a call to arms.

'I'd have him in my side, obviously. But my opinion doesn't count; I'm not a selector,' Marsh told the media. 'I'm going to promote the kid because I think he's good enough and we have a lot to do with him. He's in pretty good rhythm. Still, he hasn't played a first-class game this season. We'll have to see how he goes [against New Zealand] in Newcastle.'

Martin Crowe was considered the steel spine of New Zealand's batting line-up and, following failures in the Kiwi's warm-up games, he was determined to get a few runs under his belt against NSW. But McGrath dashed that hope by having Crowe caught by Michael Slater at backward square leg for 15. Crowe's day in Newcastle ended in the nets, where he bunkered down for a few hours desperately trying to regain the touch New Zealand would need if they were to retain the Trans-Tasman Trophy.

McGrath, on the other hand, finished the Newcastle game with even more headlines after taking 2 for 30 from 15 overs. The media noted he had a unique control of the ball and that it appeared as if he'd be able to land it on a five-cent piece if required.

The selectors went into their meeting before the Trans-Tasman Trophy only to learn Jo Angel had suffered a numbing crack to his funny bone in Western Australia's match against Victoria.

By now McGrath shared a unit with Phil Alley at Cronulla. McGrath remembers the first challenge of his new living arrangement was helping to carry Alley's massive bed from the removalist truck and up the seemingly endless flight of stairs. The pair were the stereotypical odd couple: Alley cooked because McGrath could burn water, while McGrath found himself constantly picking up after his messy flatmate. Sharing house was Alley's idea, inspired by their mutual problem of surviving on scarce finances.

However, McGrath's circumstances were destined to change when the selectors leaked the Test team to the press. The quiet at the McGrath–Alley beachside apartment was broken just before 7 am by the first of a ceaseless stream of phone calls.

McGrath appeared on Channel Nine's news that evening celebrating his selection with a group of mates, each nursing a can of beer in his hand. After taking a sip, McGrath looked down the camera's lens and, with Queen's song 'Another One Bites the Dust' pumping from the stereo in the background, vowed he'd get 'stuck into' the Kiwis.

'I wasn't looking at anything in regards to Test selection,' McGrath says. 'I had only just made the NSW team and it was just great. Here I was, doing everything I wanted to do, and I thought it was exactly how it should've been and I was loving it. The fact I was reading about my name being associated with the Australian team was enough in itself. I didn't place any pressure on myself or put expectations about being picked in the Test team. I was out there and I thought, "Whatever happens, happens." About the extent of my thinking about getting picked was to say to myself, "Oh, playing for Australia, how good would that be?"

'I was half-asleep when the calls started to come through – the early mornings of the farm were long gone by then – but I was ecstatic. I was so happy. It was like a dream because I thought the selectors would give Jo Angel another go on top of the 10 wickets he took in the tour match against New Zealand. However, I felt as though I would – and could – do the job because I'd already played New Zealand twice that summer and I was happy with the way I performed. I was also happy because while all the talk of me playing in the Test excited me, I managed to put it to the back of my mind and perform – and that was what the selectors were looking for. Performance.'

The selectors picked 12 players to face New Zealand:

Allan Border (Queensland, captain, 147 Tests)
Mark Taylor (NSW, vice-captain, 46 Tests)
David Boon (Tasmania, 80 Tests)
Ian Healy (Queensland, 53 Tests)
Craig McDermott (Queensland, 49 Tests)
Glenn McGrath (NSW, 0 Tests)
Tim May (South Australia, 13 Tests)
Paul Reiffel (Victoria, 7 Tests)
Michael Slater (NSW, 6 Tests)
Shane Warne (Victoria, 17 Tests)
Mark Waugh (NSW, 27 Tests)
Steve Waugh (NSW, 58 Tests)

When McGrath checked his bag in at the airport to fly to Perth, a betting agency reported that he had been the focus of a

$100,000 betting plunge after odds of 80/1 were offered about his chances of taking the most wickets in the Trans-Tasman Test series. The odds were slashed quickly to 8/1 when others jumped on the bandwagon. While McGrath was confident of doing well in the three-Test series, none of his hard-earned dollars were riding on him because, despite having fulfilled a lifelong dream, he still struggled to get by.

Martin Crowe had no doubt Australia had unearthed a rare gem in the lanky shape of McGrath. He told *The Australian* that the selectors were right to place their trust in the young bowler, even though he'd played only eight first-class games.

'I think he deserved his selection. He looks to me like a very good fast bowler,' said Crowe. 'He has a fantastic line. He's fit, he's angry and his selection was fairly predictable from where we stood. He's got a little bit of Sir Richard Hadlee about him, because he's got that sort of build and he has a very good action which creates a very good line for him to operate on.'

14

Baptism of Fire

McGrath's Test career is only two days old yet a gut feeling tells me in about six years time Australia will be applauding McGrath's 200 wickets just as they did Craig McDermott's milestone yesterday.

Greg Chappell, *The Daily Telegraph-Mirror*,
15 November 1993

Craig McDermott, the backbone of the Australian pace attack, knew very little about the new bloke, McGrath, except that he'd played only a handful of games for the Blues and the NSW boys called him Pigeon because of his skinny legs. However, on the opening day of the First Test, he wanted to know if McGrath also felt like there were dozens of butterflies rioting in his belly.

He looked McGrath square in the eye and asked: 'Are you nervous?'

McGrath was a cocktail of pride and excitement, adrenaline and anticipation. He'd suffered writer's cramp signing 500 bats for Australian Cricket Board sponsors and friends. He'd given dozens of interviews, telling of the privilege he felt at being in the Australian squad. He found the attention from autograph-hunters and backslappers strange. He was determined to succeed – but nervous? That hadn't crossed his mind.

'Nope, not really,' was the rookie's quiet but respectful reply.

'Don't worry,' said the senior player with a cricket world-weary grin. 'It will get worse the more you play.'

McGrath nodded his head in the hope he at least looked as if he understood what the Queenslander with the shiny diamond stud in his earlobe was talking about. McDermott, however, chose not to elaborate. He knew that, in the Tests to come, McGrath would feel the pressure fast bowlers lived with: the sleepless nights when he'd wonder if the magic would still happen; the expectation to perform when his body was exhausted; and the constant demand to deliver, even when his feet and muscles howled in pain.

'I always believed pressure was something you put on yourself, and expectation for that matter,' says McGrath. 'You have a bit of success and you expect more, you set the bar higher. That's what it is all about; that was what Craig meant when he said it would only get worse. Playing a Test match is a lot more than just sitting somewhere and saying, "I'm off," and you leave to play. There's the mental build-up, the need to get yourself up for the game even though you wonder how on earth it is all going to turn out. Then there is the anticipation. It's not that it gets harder, but it becomes very draining. People develop higher expectations of you, but you demand even more of yourself. It never mattered to me what other people thought – it was how *I* felt and thought – but the build-up to a Test was incredibly intense.'

When McGrath arrived in Perth, his first job was to introduce himself to the half of the team who didn't have the slightest idea who he was. The last fast bowler to have enjoyed such a rapid rise to the Test arena had been Mike Whitney, whose seventh first-class match was the Manchester Test of the 1981 Ashes series, for which the selectors had plucked him from English league cricket.

In Perth, McGrath looked warily at his skipper, their last face-to-face meeting at the Gabba still fresh in his mind. 'I didn't hold a grudge or anything like that. I was a believer in what happened on the field stayed there,' he says. 'I certainly didn't take any of it personally. Anyway, when I played against AB at the Gabba I bowled well – I took a couple of wickets and we had a good win. That made it all so much easier. I went over to Perth and met most of the team for the first time and I was pleased to have him as my captain. I don't think he called me Jethro after that.'

However, McGrath still looked like Jethro when he was presented with his Australian blazer. The cricket authorities had sent through lanky bowler Bruce Reid's measurements to the tailor as a guide for McGrath's shape, but the resulting blazer was a poor fit and McGrath couldn't help feeling dismayed when the sleeves fell short on his longer arms. The only upside was that it matched perfectly his short long pants.

McGrath was roomed with wicketkeeper Ian Healy. It was a deliberate ploy to allow the hard-headed 'keeper to help the young blood negotiate his way through his biggest challenge – a Test debut. The Perth Test, however, was to be marred by sadness for Healy: while he scored an unbeaten 113 in the first innings, he learned his grandfather George Healy had passed away.

'It was a very distressing time for Ian, and it was awkward because I figured he obviously wanted some time on his own,' says McGrath. 'But what amazed me most was the way he kept it together – it was incredible. I won't forget his tribute to his pop either. After he hit his hundred he looked at the Channel Nine camera, patted his bat and said, "That's for you, Pa." '

Shane Warne, a leg spin bowler from Victoria and veteran of 17 Tests, went out of his way to make McGrath feel welcome. As they shook hands neither could possibly have imagined they would become what critics would describe as arguably the most lethal bowling combination in world cricket. Warne wanted to spare McGrath from any sense of awkwardness he might feel about being the new bloke on the block.

'Glenn was in a similar situation to the one I found myself in when I was named in the team a few seasons earlier,' Warne says. 'What struck me was he was green and a bit naive about what was going on around him. It was going so fast for him I thought he needed time to collect himself and say, "Okay, this is amazing." I was the first bit of new blood when I was first named in the squad. I walked in and there was Geoff Marsh, Bruce Reid, Allan Border, Greg Matthews, Merv Hughes . . . all those guys. From 1991 to 93 a lot of those guys disappeared – no Marsh, no Matthews, no Reid. It was a real changing of the guard, and in that time Michael Slater, Matthew Hayden and McGrath came in and out of the side. Suddenly we had a few young guys and it was quite good.

'So, because I'd been there I knew what it was like for a new guy to come into the side. It didn't matter to me if I'd played only five or ten games for Australia, my view was I would go out of my way to make any newcomer feel welcome and as if they were part of the furniture. I thought that was important.

'I remember Glenn as a stick-man: he had the big cricket boots; his trousers were way too short; he had one pair of whites and two tops which he wore over the whole five days. He was quiet, and there was nothing wrong with that. He seemed to me to be a quiet guy who just went about his business while on the field. He never seemed to let too many guys get to him. A lot of guys get white-line fever and lose the plot occasionally, but Glenn was always in control and always working away to a plan. But Pigeon settled in well. He is such a lovely bloke; such a humble man. He was always going to fit into the team. As he gained confidence he grew into the team's pest, one of the biggest pests I ever played alongside.'

McGrath welcomed the hand of friendship. Warne struck him as a confident, dynamic bloke and his warmth allowed McGrath to feel more settled among a team of strangers. While Border kept a close eye on his new bowler, he was happy to let him find his feet in his own time.

'Glenn probably didn't feel as if he needed to say a lot – and most of us are the same when we first start out, you sit in the corner and listen,' Border says. 'As you become more senior you start offering things in team meetings and maybe you start to say more things out on the field, as far as geeing your boys up. He has done the full gambit but I suppose he's just a nice, quiet country bloke.'

McGrath felt the adrenaline surge through his veins when Allan Border and his Kiwi counterpart, Martin Crowe, went out for the toss on the morning of the first day of his first Test match. McGrath noted how every player watched the coin as it spun through the air. When Crowe sent Australia in to bat, McGrath was surprised by McDermott's display of unbridled delight at the news he wouldn't need to strap on the bowling boots straight away.

'There was Craig, he'd taken 198 Test wickets and was expected to take his 200th in that Test, and he was so visibly happy to hear he didn't have to bowl first-up. I was like a sponge because I wanted to absorb as much as I could from him. My first observation was how organised Craig "Billy the

Kid" McDermott was. While guys like Steve Waugh turned their section of the dressing-room into a rat's nest by throwing their gear everywhere, Craig was meticulous. His socks were neatly laid out, his playing clothes were on a coathanger and he carefully placed his boots together. But when we lost the toss he jumped around like a big kid and looked very happy with himself. I was to learn it was totally the opposite when we were called on to bowl first, because that never pleased him; he'd moan and mention all his aches and pains. When he retired, Jason Gillespie and I continued to react like that in Craig's honour.'

But McGrath didn't dare say anything about how strange McDermott's reaction struck him that day in Perth. It was a return to his days at Narromine High when he didn't want to draw unnecessary attention to himself. He sat down among the players hoping he looked cool and calm, hoping against hope it didn't look as if he was in awe of McDermott, David Boon, Healy, Warne and Border.

While the persistent rain and dark clouds that draped Perth kept the spectators away, nothing could stop Beverley McGrath from being at the WACA to watch her son play his first match in the baggy green cap. She'd managed at the last minute to be on hand to witness one of the proudest moments of her life.

'I found out he was in the team on the Monday. The Test was to start on the Thursday,' says Bev. McGrath and Rod Marsh helped to get her a plane ticket to Perth – but when she arrived, there was no-one at the airport to meet her. 'I didn't have any phone numbers except for Rod Marsh's, so I phoned him and said I didn't know where Glenn was and I didn't know where I was going. He rang Glenn and told him to go and pick his mother up from the airport. He took a while to get there and when Glenn finally turned up in the team's car, he said it took so long because he was trying to find me a hotel to stay in. There was something like 20,000 American sailors in Perth that week and it was a struggle for him to find somewhere for me to stay. He was still making calls as I waited at the airport.'

It had also been expensive for Bev to wing her way to Perth. While McGrath was now a member of the Australian team, he was still battling to make ends meet financially. He paid for Bev's accommodation and she scraped the cash together to fly from Dubbo to Sydney to Perth. Her son gave her something that she would later use to help reimburse her fare – a bat autographed by each member of the Australian team.

Australia scored 398 in the first innings. McGrath's contribution was a first-ball duck after falling leg before wicket (LBW) to Murphy Su'a. He had better luck when he was given the ball, as Robert Craddock noted in *The Sunday Telegraph*: 'Debutant Glenn McGrath displayed an icy temperament in his first Test outing for a rock solid contribution which included Mark Greatbatch's wicket to an edge behind in the 10th over. As always he was accurate and had enough steam to thump a ducking Andrew Jones on the helmet.'

McGrath, who consistently launched the ball at 140 kilometres an hour throughout the game, took a second wicket – that of tail-ender Danny Morrison – to give him 2 for 92. In the second innings he again combined with Healy to remove opener Blair Pocock on his way to 1 for 50 from 16 overs.

While former Test captain Greg Chappell described McGrath as a future champion, Kerry O'Keeffe wasn't happy with the way McGrath was used in the opening Test and he held nothing back in his *St George Leader* column.

'Come on, Allan Border, young fast bowlers on debut must be allowed the freedom to express their talents – not forced to slave away at tactics quite foreign to their methods which gained them their national cap,' O'Keeffe thundered. 'Last summer it was the debutant Jo Angel against the West Indies who, to his cost, was directed to attack Richie Richardson with a succession of short-pitched deliveries and later, to adopt an unnatural defensive method over lengthy spells to stem the flow of runs. All of this without obvious assistance from a remote captain.

'Last week in Perth was Sutherland's Glenn McGrath's Test which was so decidedly affected by policy. The Australian game plan on the third morning was to create uneasiness in the minds of Andrew Jones and Martin Crowe by a full session of intimidatory bowling. There was McGrath pounding the ball in short, sometimes around the wicket – two methods he has rarely used on his quick progress to the top.

'The result . . . an unconvincing yet promising first game . . . more rational tactics by the Aussie power brokers may see McGrath's star rise in upcoming Tests.'

McGrath, however, had no complaint about the way he was used. The only pressure he felt was from being told ad nauseam that he had to swing the ball to be considered the real deal.

The First Test finished in a draw. McGrath was replaced by off-spin bowler Tim May in the Second Test (won by Australia) because it was played at Hobart's spin-friendly Bellerive Oval. He returned for the Third Test in Brisbane, where he snared three wickets in the second innings. The Australians' victory in Brisbane meant they won the Trans-Tasman Trophy, making it only the second time they'd won the Trophy out of the seven times it was contested since 1985.

Amid the celebrations and popping of champagne corks in the Australian team's dressing-room, McGrath drew extra attention in the press for his aggressive actions when he celebrated New Zealander Chris Cairns' dismissal.

'There is clear animosity between Cairns and the Australians, who lost respect for the Kiwi all-rounder when he was a late withdrawal from the Second Test because of a heel injury,' wrote Malcolm Conn in *The Australian*. 'But the level of visible displeasure directed at him in this Test was unnecessary. The most obvious yesterday was McGrath who clenched his teeth and ran past the dismissed Kiwi.

'It was McGrath's first wicket of the Test. The promising young fast bowler was 12th man in Hobart and claimed three wickets during the First Test in Perth, but he must learn to do more with the ball if he is to trouble batsmen at this level.'

15

Pirate of the Caribbean

Fast bowling is supposed to be an aggressive sort of job. When I bat I expect to get short balls, so I can't see why I shouldn't give it back to them in return.

McGrath's declaration of war before
the First Test of the 1995 series
against the West Indies

Standing at first slip during the opening Test of the 1995 series against the West Indies, it was obvious to Australia's captain, Mark Taylor, that the West Indies' fast bowler Courtney Walsh didn't fancy being on the receiving end of the style of bowling he loved to dish out: an attack of sustained short-pitched deliveries that made batsmen – especially tail-enders like Walsh – fear for their safety.

While facing Australia's new fast bowler, Walsh did all he could to appear 'chilled' by laughing and grinning as the latest McGrath bouncer whistled dangerously close to his chin, but the Jamaican's body language betrayed him. Taylor saw Walsh wasn't merely uncomfortable – he was very nervous. It was exactly what the captain had hoped for.

If Taylor's team was to become the first Australian side to

win a series in the Caribbean since Ian Chappell's men in 1973, and the first team from any nation to beat them in a series since the Kiwis in 1980, they needed to tame the Windies' fast bowlers first. While seemingly simple in theory, the plan to target the opposition's pacemen with 'chin music' whenever they batted would test the mettle of its implementers, because if the Windies' pace attack had proved anything in their domination of world cricket from the late 1970s, it was that they possessed short tempers, long memories and a disregard for mercy.

McGrath had no concern about the prospect of being bruised – or worse – when he bowled his grenades at Walsh and his brothers-in-harm Curtly Ambrose and the Benjamin boys, Kenny and Winston, that day in Barbados. He'd often dreamed of this moment as a kid at *Lagoona* when he'd waged imaginary battles against the West Indies during his marathon bowling sessions at the old 44-gallon drum – battles where Australia had relied on him to come through. He was now living the dream and – in a performance that had overtones of sadism – he dragged out Walsh's suffering by bombing him with bouncers rather than rushing to bowl the yorker that would have ended the number 11's torment.

'Glenn's bowling really shook Courtney up,' Taylor remembers. 'Courtney was trying to look cool about it, as the West Indies often do, but I think he was genuinely concerned because the Pigeon was ripping into him with plenty of short stuff. For a good half-dozen deliveries I don't think Glenn was all that worried about getting him out – he wanted to let him know we were there to play. When the rest of us out in the field saw that we thought, "You beauty!" – because we're now on equal terms here. His bowling made the West Indies appreciate we Australians weren't going to give them an inch, just as we knew they weren't going to give us an inch. It was game on, and that set a tone for us.

'Our plan was one any team who had been to the West Indies during the '80s and '90s would have hoped some of their bowlers would implement. We spoke about it in '95. We spoke about it in 1991 as well, and Craig McDermott did a pretty good job of unsettling them, but it was a bit of a one-man show in '91. In 1995, Glenn, in particular, ran with it – and it was a great effort because, to be fair, he was a pretty ordinary batsman and he was going to cop it, but it didn't faze him. He seemed to have the attitude of "I'm going to give it you blokes". And he did.'

The West Indies speed quartet was given fair warning of what to expect when, on the eve of the Test, McGrath made a public vow to take the fight to them. Reports suggest each of them chuckled at the skinny white man's threat, but that laughter was soon hushed when they stood before him with bat in hand. For the first time in their careers, Walsh, Ambrose and the Benjamins suffered the indignity of being forced to dance to another's tune, as McGrath peppered them in full view of the fans who'd long considered them supermen.

Thirteen years after the match that established McGrath as a spearhead bowler, Walsh won't reveal exactly how he felt about being targeted by a player determined to make his mark. He prefers instead to mention feeling a sense of solace that McGrath could humble more capable batsmen than himself.

'I thought he was a very good bowler the first time I saw him and realised he would give any batsman trouble on his day, much less me,' says Walsh.

McGrath wasn't naive, however. From the moment he unleashed the first bouncer of his campaign – one that almost kissed Winston Benjamin's nose – he knew his name had been entered into the West Indies' book of blood feuds.

'My bowling bouncers and intimidating their bowlers was the team plan; we thought it might unsettle them because it hadn't been done to them too often before,' McGrath says. 'We thought, "Well, we're going to cop it no matter how we bowl to them anyway." It didn't matter if we intimidated them, bowled at their stumps or short of a length, we were still going to cop it. I thought if the batsman did the business I'd be out of the firing line. But when I started, it didn't cross my mind I would have to go out and bat either. I think our team in '95 was luckier than other teams because we didn't have the psychological – and in some cases, physical – scars of other Australian teams, and that held us in good stead.'

McGrath, aged 25, had assumed the role of Australia's enforcer by default. Australia's most potent bowler, Craig McDermott, was forced to abandon the tour after injuring his ankle jumping off a sea wall before the First Test, and his new-ball partner Damien Fleming was sent home with an injured shoulder, the recurrence of an old problem. Their withdrawals were seen as serious body blows to Taylor's quest. McDermott's last act as a member of the team before he limped onto the aeroplane back to Queensland was to anoint McGrath as the man whose star was set to shine.

'If anyone is going to come through and make the big step forward, it will be Glenn McGrath,' said McDermott to the media contingent that saw him off. 'I have seen him make a lot of progress over the past 18 months – from someone brought in raw to the situation, to now where he is a genuine Test bowler.'

But nothing could camouflage the loss of McDermott and Fleming – their absence appeared to leave Australia's attack threadbare and exposed. With bowlers Brendon Julian, Paul Reiffel, the Waugh brothers, Shane Warne and McGrath left to carry the can, the Windies are said to have dismissed their bowling line-up as 'weak' in the privacy of their dressing-room.

After being rushed into the Australian Test team, McGrath was exposed during the Gabba Test of the 1994/95 Ashes series for lacking an important component in any top-class fast bowler's arsenal: the ability to bowl swing. He was yet to master the intricacies of that craft and made the mistake of listening to the critics who maintained that a bowler couldn't be considered to be of genuine international standard unless they understood the art. McGrath decided to become an instant expert, much to his own detriment.

'I hadn't cemented my place in the team and I listened to all the people who said you have to bowl consistent swing bowling to be considered successful at Test level,' recalls McGrath. 'It took me away from my game plan, which was being a seam bowler who hit the deck. I wanted to be successful, and while I did start swinging the ball, I couldn't control it.'

McGrath watched on in despair as the English batsmen plundered 40 runs off him in the first innings and 61 in the second. It would be one of the few times that McGrath finished a Test wicketless. It came at a high personal cost.

'I lost my bounce, I lost everything,' he says of that time. 'I was young and I didn't know my game that well, so it was a huge learning experience. I was dropped for the next three Tests, so I had a lot of time to sit down and think about things. Ultimately, I decided to go back to doing what got me picked in the first place – hitting good areas, getting a bit of bounce and seam movement, and going from there.

'Over the next three Tests I watched a lot of Damien Fleming. He bowled well, taking 10 wickets. However, he injured his shoulder and that allowed me to play in the last Test at Perth.'

McGrath made the most of his recall, reverting to his own game – 'what I did best' – and finishing the match with 3 for 88 and 3 for 40. The six-wicket haul ensured his selection in the squad to tour the West Indies, where he'd made enough noise to come under the scrutiny of a fearsome attack.

While McGrath ought to have been shaking in his boots at the retaliation awaiting him in Barbados when it came his turn to bat, he found inspiration from the battalions of Aussie supporters in the outer who chanted '*Ooh aah, Glenn McGrath*' as a tribute to his effort.

'It was the first time I'd ever been singled out like that and it was an incredible feeling,' he says. 'I looked at the people chanting it and they wore Aussie caps and T-shirts, waved the flag and had their faces painted green and gold. I looked at them and thought it'd be great to win the trophy for them.'

If the chanting wasn't enough, Steve Waugh also spurred McGrath on by offering words of encouragement loud enough for the likes of Walsh and Ambrose to hear whenever they were forced to duck for their personal safety.

'I just encouraged him to keep going – to continue bowling aggressively and not to back down in any situation,' says Waugh. 'I knew Glenn had great stamina and you could back him to keep bowling. I guess I may have encouraged him to bowl a bit aggressively, but I knew he'd find a happy medium and not go over the top. So, yeah, I encouraged him. I thought someone had to take a stance, and with him being a new guy, I thought it was a great opportunity for him to put his hand up and say, "I want to take the West Indies on." I bowled a few bouncers at them and I wanted a partner in crime. I think Glenn saw it as an opportunity to make his mark – I was simply throwing him a challenge. I was trying to push him in a direction where he was considered a spearhead. I think the West Indians respected those guys anyway.'

Courtney Walsh confirms that even though McGrath risked getting burnt by the fire he played with, there was a begrudging respect for the Australian.

'Once you decide to compete as McGrath did, you have to

be ready for *anything*,' he says of the Windies' plans to return serve at McGrath. 'But, that said, I think it was a brave move by Glenn [to bowl aggressively at the Windies' tail] and it was one that worked for him at the time.'

McGrath certainly deserved their respect by the end of the opening Test, which finished in a ten-wicket victory to Australia. He was named Man of the Match after he captured 3 for 46 in the first innings and in the second innings snared 5 for 68, his first five-wicket haul in Test cricket. His five-for included three wickets in ten balls.

Robert Craddock, writing for *The Daily Telegraph-Mirror*, documented the emergence of cricket's new star bowler when he wrote after the Test: 'The greatest dynasty world cricket has known is on the verge of collapse thanks to a bold young Australian who dared to put the wind up the Windies.'

Former Test batsman David Hookes covered the tour as a reporter and commentator. Hookes knew well the physical and psychological power the West Indies had over their opponents: his own career – and confidence – had never truly recovered from the time West Indies paceman Andy Roberts had broken his jaw during a World Series Cricket Super Test at the Sydney Showground in 1977.* But while he viewed McGrath's effort to bombard the West Indies with bouncers as a turning point for world cricket in the 1990s, he was convinced that Australia's great effort in winning the Frank Worrell Trophy was equally the result of deficiencies in the defeated West Indies team.

'I made the point at the time – and since – that Glenn McGrath's decision to bowl short at the West Indians in the First Test at Barbados was a defining moment in world cricket in the '90s. I believe that,' said Hookes. 'There is a bit of bluff and

* Andy Roberts was also coach of the 1995 West Indies team.

bullshit about the Windies in 1995; they were a pretty ordinary side in the two-and-a-half years before that series. Their record was pretty ordinary and they saved a few series, though they hadn't been beaten. They hadn't flogged sides; they were certainly on the wane, in a batting perspective particularly. Having said that, the end result – Australia winning – was fantastic.

'For as long as I can remember there was a lack of desire by any opposition fast bowlers to bowl at these blokes' throats and heads with the specific intention to hit them. To see McGrath, a bloke who couldn't bat, do that was what I call a defining moment. As a spectator who was there, I had no qualms about him being the leading bowler. Whether he was physically capable of doing it was what I thought remained to be seen – and he was. I don't know if he's been given worldwide recognition for getting rid of the old fast bowlers' unwritten rule of not bowling short or trying to hit tail-enders because, quite clearly from where I was sitting, he was trying to hit them – and that was fine. And they were shocked. It hadn't happened before. They'd treated everyone else like school bullies but some kid in the playground was prepared to pick up a slingshot and give it back to them. I didn't think either McDermott or Fleming was going to do it; they may have as a group, but they needed someone to do it first. The relentless way McGrath went about business proved he was prepared to give it to them.'

McGrath says Hookes did have a point that the West Indies side the Australians faced in 1995 weren't as formidable as the Windies of old, because the outstanding players of those years – Clive Lloyd, Viv Richards, Gordon Greenidge, Desmond Haynes, Andy Roberts, Michael Holding, Joel Garner, Colin Croft and Malcolm Marshall – had all retired.

But as he also observes: 'It has to be remembered we were considered by them the weakest team they faced. If you go through our attack there was me; Warnie was there but he hadn't played a lot; 'Pistol' Paul Reiffel was thrown in along with Brendon Julian – and yet we beat them. In one respect they weren't the same team as they were in the '80s, but they were still winning and when you know how to win it helps. And they still had guys like Ambrose, Lara, Richardson and Walsh, so they were still an awesome side. While I agree with Hookesy in that they weren't the same team when you compared eras, we could only play the team they picked and we beat them.'

While the likes of Hookes and Craddock highlighted McGrath's devotion to duty, the bowler credits Waugh for inspiring him to continue to dig deep and to stay true to the team's blueprint for success.

'The senior players, Mark Taylor and Steve ['Tugga'] Waugh, came up with the plan,' says McGrath. 'I knew Tugga always liked to get stuck into their bowlers and to give them a hard time. He might not have been as quick or got as much bounce, but I reckon he probably bowled more bouncers per over at the West Indies than anyone else in world cricket. He was always standing up to them and letting them have it.'

McGrath's success in unsettling Walsh and company also vindicated a view Steve Waugh had long held since the days when he'd taken on the West Indies with his medium-paced bouncers.

'I think there was the old fast bowlers' club, where if you didn't bounce the opposition's bowlers they didn't bounce you. However, that didn't work with the West Indies because they just bounced everyone. I always thought, "Why don't we get stuck into them?" I thought some of our bowlers may have worried too much about their safety, thinking if they didn't pitch 'em up they'd get nothing back. McGrath thought, "I'm not going to cop this any more; I'm really going to give it to them to see how they react." While I didn't have the same pace as Glenn, I had the same intent.'

The big difference between the pair, though, was that Waugh could bat; McGrath could not. And when Australia's number 11 eventually found himself out in the middle and facing the music, he vowed not to lose his nerve, even when the likes of Curtly Ambrose bored holes through him with murderous stares as his team-mates yelled, 'Let's kill him, mon!'

'I was not worried about being hurt by them. I was only scared of being embarrassed out there,' says McGrath. 'I got behind the ball and I watched it closely so I knew when to duck.'

Whilst Waugh admired McGrath's courage, he couldn't help but think there was an element of bravado in the way McGrath strode out to take strike, like the man who heads to the gallows without first offering a prayer. Waugh figured it wouldn't have been normal for McGrath – or anyone else in his situation – to feel anything but nervous as he watched his opponents charge in like deranged lions.

Waugh certainly believes McGrath must have been nervous in the Fourth and final Test, when Waugh was on 197 runs and McGrath walked out to join him at the crease. Waugh had upset the Windies early in the series: they'd accused him of cheating Brian Lara out of his wicket by wrongly claiming a catch in the First Test, and he had also been involved in a tense stand-off with Ambrose. On the way to his 197, Waugh had endured the closest thing possible to a mugging on the cricket field when he was hammered by the Windies attack. He boasted an ugly purple bruise that spread from his left wrist to his hand; the elbow of his right arm had been branded; he wished two of his fingers belonged to someone else because they screamed in agony where they'd been hit; and he'd been whacked in three other parts of his body. Yet Waugh had almost amassed a double-century when McGrath left the safety of the players' pavilion – and the Windies made it clear they wanted to give the new batsman a taste of the same medicine they'd been doling out to Waugh.

'I don't think Glenn *showed* fear,' says Waugh. 'You could sense there was some trepidation. I think it's to his credit he stuck to it, because you could see some West Indian bowlers didn't like what he'd done to them too much. They were laughing and trying to make a joke about what was happening, but they didn't like it. Glenn was always going to cop it. It was a test of his mental strength and his nerve. He didn't get hurt, which was amazing because you'd expect a guy who was averaging five or six runs to get cleaned right up.'

McGrath didn't get cleaned up in the Fourth Test. Instead he supported Waugh to his double-century, making Waugh only the fourth Australian, behind Neil Harvey, Bob Simpson and Bill Lawry, to score 200 or more in the Caribbean.

Ricky Ponting had been named in the 15-man squad for the 1995 West Indies tour – part of a long-term process to groom him for Test cricket – and he learned a lot from the impact his mate from the Cricket Academy had on the West Indies. Ponting later drew on this experience when he succeeded Steve Waugh as captain, to provide Australia with an 'X-factor' against teams good enough to challenge them.

'I remember thinking Glenn's decision to take on the West Indies bowlers sent out a positive message to the West Indies that the Australian side was really up for it,' Ponting says. 'Ambrose, Walsh, Kenny Benjamin had never been treated like that before. It made the West Indies sit back and think, "This Australian team is fair dinkum – they're really up for it."

'Even if you aren't the murder boys of cricket, you can show little things to let the opposition know you are serious. It might be the way you warm up, how you dress to go to the ground. Perception can be enormous. If you can give off the right signals to the opposition you're halfway to (a) bluffing them or (b) showing them what you're all about. McGrath, at that stage of his career, showed them what he was all about. His body language and the way he looked at their batsmen – the wry smile – it sent a signal to the batsmen and his own team-mates that he knew what he was doing. He gave us all the confidence in the world he could do the job.'

And McGrath did the job.

Although the Second Test finished in a draw and the West Indies bounced back to humiliate the Aussies in the third game at Port-of-Spain, Trinidad, by nine wickets on a dog of a pitch (a pitch for which Windies skipper Richie Richardson publicly apologised), McGrath maintained his rage.

While Reiffel was applauded for following the old dictum of bowling stump to stump, every McGrath bouncer – every delivery that made the West Indies fear for their safety – was cheered in lounge rooms across Australia by a generation of pacemen who'd been treated by the West Indies in previous years without a scrap of mercy. Geoff Lawson, whose jaw had been shattered by an Ambrose bouncer at the WACA during the 1988/89 season, was among their number.

'To the outsiders – and the outsiders being everyone but Glenn – the fear was he was going to get seriously hurt,' says Lawson. 'But he didn't care. It was as if he was saying, "My job is to bowl and to get people out. When they bowl at me I am going to back myself."

'In 1984 we didn't let loose on the West Indies until the end of the series, when we had the shits . . . we'd had the crap bounced out of us. I remember Rodney Hogg and I bowled 36 consecutive bouncers and Desmond Haynes got hit. They got upset that we bowled quick and short. We should have done it earlier. Pigeon didn't care. I'm trying to remember if he got hit. He was in the grand final as the game's worst batsman but he watched the ball and kept it simple. He kept his eye on the ball and, rather than complicate it, he went through the process of making sure his feet were here and there, he had his backlift, his grip was right – and by doing so he proved a simple plan is often the best.

'As someone who had dealt pretty closely with him, I was quietly confident Glenn could do the job even after McDermott and then Fleming returned home. You always keep your fingers crossed in those circumstances, but the great thing was he didn't wait for the West Indies pacemen to put pressure on him, he put it straight on them by getting in early. He didn't bowl anything too loose for them to hit. The West Indies didn't put *good* balls away, they put away *bad* ones. I had a quiet confidence that at worst Pigeon would be competent, and at best he'd be good, very good. You always think that of anyone until they become a veteran. In Glenn's case he always believed he could do it and that's half the battle.'

There was no tougher place in the world for a cricket team to tour than the West Indies. The illusion of virgin beaches, hibiscus flowers and fruit cocktails in exotically named places such as Barbados, Jamaica and Trinidad belied a harsh reality. Cricket – and more so the West Indies' ability to play the sport better than anyone else in the world – was the single thread that unified the island nations. And heaven help anyone who trespassed upon their turf, as Steve Rixon discovered in 1978. He was wicketkeeper for an Australian team sent there like lambs to the slaughter. Depleted of such trump cards as Lillee, Marsh, the Chappell brothers and Hookes because of their allegiance to Kerry Packer's World Series Cricket, the official Australian team was mentally bullied and physically belted in their 3–1 series loss. A photograph of Australian batsman Peter Toohey being cradled in the arms of Viv Richards after being floored by an Andy Roberts bouncer summed up the tour. 'Toohey copped it between the eyes,' says Rixon of the nightmare in paradise where Australia's batsmen literally batted to survive.

'I thought the danger at the time of the 1995 tour was the West Indies might retaliate by trying to break Glenn's hand,' says Rixon. 'But he said, "Enough is enough," and it was a courageous effort. However, I'd like to also give him credit for working out those blokes – he knew the West Indies would play their shots, so he bowled pretty good areas, which meant he was always a pretty good chance of knocking them over.'

The Australian's respected writer Mike Coward noted during the Third Test at Port-of-Spain that McGrath seemed comfortable at last with his place in the national team.

'McGrath's career was transformed in the First Test at Barbados when he had Lara caught at the wicket by Ian Healy,' wrote Coward. 'Not only was this the most highly prized of all wickets, it was a legitimate dismissal. From that moment it was apparent McGrath finally believed he was entitled to wear the baggy green cap. Gone was the self-doubt; the self-consciousness.

'He has since confessed he yearned to spearhead the Australian attack and despite the fact he was used behind Paul Reiffel and Brendon Julian – and, more often than not, Shane Warne – he seized his chance when Craig McDermott and Damien Fleming were lost to the cause because of serious injuries.'

Taylor, however, attributes McGrath's bowling success – he topped the wicket tally – to his superb control, and not just the short stuff. 'He showed magnificent control,' says Taylor. 'He knew where the ball was going. Glenn knew if he unsettled the batsmen he could fire in a yorker towards the stumps. There was no point in upsetting the batsmen if you can't get them out – and he could.'

McGrath proved it was possible to frighten the so-called Terrors of the Tropics. He finished the four-Test tour with 17 wickets at 21.71; his 6 for 47 at Queen's Park Oval in Port-of-Spain was his best haul. Among his victims were the men he was told to target: Ambrose (dismissed three times), Walsh (twice) and Winston Benjamin (once). In the aftermath of the West Indies' first series loss in 15 years, their skipper Richie Richardson dismissed the victors as the 'weakest' Australian team to have ever toured the Caribbean – and the Australians saw wrenching the Frank Worrell Trophy from the Windies as their best comeback to that remark. Coach Bob Simpson, however, took the time to pay tribute to the efforts of his bowlers.

'If we could bowl the right line and length, I believed we would always bowl them out for reasonable totals,' Simpson wrote in *The Sydney Morning Herald*. 'Our bowlers were able to do this and this was a great tribute to them.

'I have been privileged to watch from first slip some great bowlers, such as Miller, Lindwall, Davidson, McKenzie, Benaud, and thrilled to Lillee and Thomson's demolition of batsmen during the 1970s. But even they could not have given a better exhibition of controlled, tactical bowling than our team did on this tour.

'A testimony to the tenacity, concentration and skill of the Australian bowlers was that the West Indies' highest score was 265 and not once did they bat for a full day.

'While on the surface the Australian attack might not have had the colour or charisma of some of our past heroes, none of those greats of the past could have bowled with better control, nor stuck so faithfully to our game plan. A tribute to their skill was that approximately 70 per cent of the West Indies' batsmen got out in the way we had planned.

'Aiding and abetting this great control was a fiercely aggressive fielding team whose performances surely have never been bettered in Test cricket.'

McGrath returned home a hero. He also acquired a manager, Sydney accountant Warren Craig. A former wicketkeeper for the Sydney and Fairfield clubs, Craig had met up with McGrath through his cricket contacts to discuss the possibility of representing him.

'I knew a few people at Cricket NSW and had told them I wanted to break into sports management,' he says. 'I told them if ever there was an opportunity to assist a player to let me know. As it turned out, Glenn had a part-time person looking after his dealings and after the West Indies it was thought he needed a full-time manager and they called me.

'What I noticed in our first meeting was Glenn had the same outlook as a lot of athletes, in that he'd just come onto the scene and didn't know what he wanted from a commercial aspect: he didn't know what to expect, he didn't know what was out there. From a cricket perspective he definitely knew what he wanted, and that was to play for Australia. He'd had an outstanding tour of the West Indies but he didn't have much of a profile, so we formed a strategy to work out what we call "industry contracts" – the bat, the sunglasses, footwear and clothing contracts. I focused on getting stories written on him in the media. Initially they homed in on his batting, and I said to Glenn the day he improved his batting would be the day he'd make my job harder.'

Although Craig received requests for interviews and personal appearances, McGrath refused to rest on his laurels. He worked hard in the gym for three months and piled seven kilograms of muscle onto his upper body. It was a smart move. After his triumph in the Windies, he'd need extra strength to help carry the Australian pace attack in the years to come, something Mike Coward predicted in his report from the Third Test at Trinidad:

'In recent years there has been much angst throughout the Australian community because of an apparent dearth of quality fast bowlers,' wrote Coward. 'If the question has been asked once it has been asked a thousand times. Just who will take over from McDermott? On the evidence tendered in the Caribbean in recent weeks this is no longer an issue. McGrath has come of age.'

16

Soul Mate

Love is, above all, the gift of oneself.

Jean Anouilh, French dramatist

On tour in Hong Kong in September 1995, Australia's ICC Sixes team – Glenn McGrath, Michael Slater, Greg Blewett, Brendon Julian, Matt Elliott and Matthew Hayden – passed the South African players as they headed out for a night on the town at the famous Nathan Road, once known as the Golden Mile. The ICC Sixes tournament began the following day and the South Africans were on a strict curfew and alcohol ban. McGrath couldn't help thinking they looked envious as he and his mates clowned around as they waited for the lift and laughed about the possible nocturnal adventures that awaited them. Little could McGrath have imagined he would meet his soul mate that night.

Joe Bananas was reputed to be a good place to unwind, but when the Australians arrived it was loud and noisy, nothing like the oasis McGrath had hoped for. What made it different from any other pub he'd ever visited, however, was the attractive blonde English woman who was there with a group of her friends. McGrath left it to Julian – known as a charmer – to do the groundwork. The 'hosties' (for it turned out they were air stewards) were not only happy to chat, but they were celebrating the recent divorce of Jane Steele's friend Karen.

McGrath's first impression of Jane was one of joy and radiant beauty: 'She was tall, blonde, bright-eyed, bubbly and always smiling. She was brighter than any of the millions of lights that turn Kowloon's night into day. I was attracted to her and it was terrific that she didn't have the slightest idea of cricket. We went to another nightclub that was meant to be good, but it was dingy with expensive drinks, seedy types propped up against the bar and trashy music. However, that didn't seem to matter as Jane and I spoke. We could've been sitting in a Chinese laundry that night and it would've still been fun.'

Jane's friends had chosen to go to Hong Kong to let their hair down at the island's renowned nightspots. Virgin Airline's Hong Kong legs were 'two-nighters' and the time difference between London and Kowloon is eight hours, so it made it perfect sense for Jane and her Virgin crew-mates to party out all night and sleep all day.

'Sometimes we'd return to our hotel after a night out and we'd pass local children going to school,' she laughs. 'Our return flight was of an evening, so we'd be refreshed after sleeping all day and were able to deal with the demands of a 12-hour flight home.'

Jane almost didn't go to Joe Bananas that fateful night; she was tired. In the end she capitulated to Karen's persuasive charms, but she didn't worry about washing her hair, doing her nails or dressing up. Little could she have known that fate had arranged for her to meet the man of her dreams at Joe Bananas that night.

One of the flight team, a practical joker named Graham, told Karen and Jane there were members of the Australian cricket team at the pub who were asking if they could meet them. Karen and Jane thought it was another of Graham's jokes and nonchalantly told him to send the cricketers straight over. Jane couldn't believe it when Graham gave the nod and over walked a group of six not-too-bad-looking blokes. Glenn, the tallest Aussie, was the last to introduce himself.

'We started chatting away and I liked him,' says Jane. 'I told him I'd spent six weeks backpacking around the east coast of Australia, and he told me he came from a country town. In the back of my mind I thought it was a shame he lived so far away because, while he seemed nice, I thought we'd probably never see each other again. Before our evening ended we exchanged phone numbers and addresses and that was that.'

However, Jane left one impression before they said goodbye. She told McGrath and Brendon Julian her infamous water-melon joke, one that needs hand movements to be told properly. 'The fact it wasn't funny made it funny,' says McGrath. 'I also remember Jane turned bright-red after she said it. It is a bit risqué and I think she wondered why she'd told it.'

The next day the Australians lost their opening Sixes game to England – which came as no surprise because they'd been at a dance party until 4 am. Almost as punishment, McGrath and his team-mates then had to give a coaching clinic. While McGrath did his best to explain the benefits of bowling a good line and length, his thoughts were with Jane, the wonderful woman he'd met the night before.

'I was sincere when I told Jane I'd keep in touch, but she went her way and I mine,' he says. 'I didn't know if our paths would ever cross again.'

Jane returned to England just over a month after her 'Honkers' trip, feeling exhausted after an arduous flight from Miami. It had been a demanding shift and she was happy to be home in her cottage in a sleepy village in the Cotswolds, with

143

the kettle boiling. Jane had sent a letter to Glenn three weeks earlier but had received no reply.

'Pity,' she thought. She poured a cup of Earl Grey tea, played her answering machine – and was ecstatic to hear an Australian accent. Jane replayed the message so often the tape threatened to wear out. She decided to wait a week to call McGrath back, not wanting to appear *too* keen.

Jane phoned McGrath from Tokyo. After a game of phone tag they spoke and made arrangements to meet in Perth, where he'd be playing a Test against Sri Lanka in December. Jane had no idea what that meant, but it sounded like an adventure. She bought the book *The Rules and Regulations of Cricket*, but never read a full page.

'My dad wasn't too impressed about me going across the other side of the world to meet with an Australian cricketer he'd never heard of,' she says. 'And I have to admit, I began to feel apprehensive about going all that way to catch up with someone I'd met for a few hours in Hong Kong. I wondered if I'd lost my marbles, but common sense had gone out the window . . . I had no choice but to go.'

But there was no cricketer waiting for Jane at Perth international airport with a bunch of flowers. McGrath had been obliged to attend an afternoon team meeting to talk tactics. And when she arrived at the hotel and phoned his room, Jane was told to 'c'mon up'. There was no offer to meet her in the foyer and help with her luggage. Miffed, Jane dragged her suitcase behind her and didn't know what to expect when she knocked on McGrath's door.

'He was more handsome than I remembered – and I was glad to have made the journey,' she confesses.

And McGrath was happy to see Jane. The reason he'd taken so long to get back to her after receiving her letter was simple:

Glenn McGrath at the age of two.

With his mates from Narromine High School. Glenn is second from the left.

Dale, Donna and Glenn McGrath, on their family's farm in the late 1980s.

Jane Steele, while working for Virgin Airlines out of the United Kingdom.

Glenn and Jane on Kevin McGrath's farm in 1996.

Together on Australia's successful 1997 Ashes tour of England, shortly before the discovery of Jane's cancer.

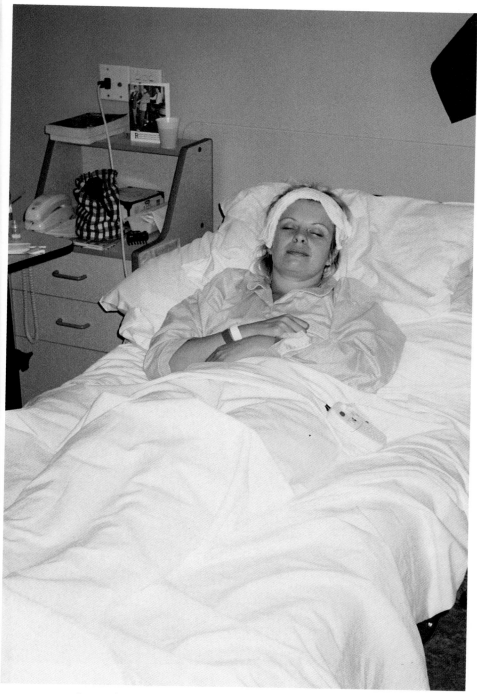

Jane in hospital in September 1997, after her first major surgery.

Engaged in 1998.
Photo by *The Sunday Times*, Perth

Jane, with bridesmaid Tracy Bevan, on the day of her marriage to Glenn, 17 July 1999.

The happy couple, married at last . . . 17 July 1999.

Photo by Brad Newman/Newspix

Jane and Glenn celebrated the birth of their first child, James, in 2000.

With James on the Ashes tour, 2001.
Photo by Hamish Blair/Getty Images

A proud father with his son at Lord's, the home of cricket, 2001.
Photo by Brett Costello/Newspix

Holly McGrath – 'Daddy's little girl' – was born in 2001.

McGrath with his father, Kevin, in the dressing-room at Lord's after taking his
500th Test wicket.

Photo by Hamish Blair/Getty Images

The entrance to Wancobra, McGrath's wool station in outback New South Wales, which is managed by his brother, Dale.

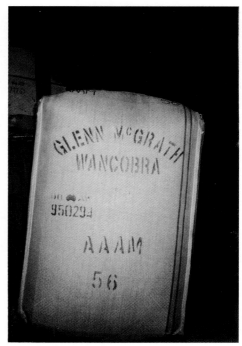

A bale of Wancobra wool.

After setting up the McGrath Foundation in 2002, Glenn and Jane continue to work with their many sponsors to raise funds for breast-care nurses.

Photo by Greg Wood/Getty Images

Glenn and Jane McGrath, arriving at the Allan Border Medal Awards in 2007.
Photo by Kristian Dowling/Getty Images

Glenn McGrath with Jane, James and Holly – 'my life's greatest reward'.
Photo by Chris Colls/acpsyndication.com

he'd been in the middle of what he called his 'summer ritual' – living out of a suitcase while he played cricket.

'I was a single guy enjoying life, and as far as I was concerned, that was not going to change in a hurry. Cricket was my main focus. However, when I think back on Jane's arrival to Perth – the airport, the suitcase – I can't help but cringe. Rudeness wasn't the reason I didn't pick her up, we had a team meeting and no-one is excused from them. When I opened the door and saw Jane smiling nervously, I felt bad for not going down to the foyer to greet her. The good thing, though, was we didn't miss a beat and picked up from when we met at Hong Kong. When Jane told me she had second thoughts about coming to Australia, I suggested she not worry about that and to see what happened. There was no need for pressure.'

Jane turned up at the WACA the following day at 2.30 pm. (She had no idea what time the match started and promised she'd get there earlier on the second day.) The Perth Test was the first game of cricket she had seen live – and while she thought McGrath looked athletic as he ran in to 'throw' the ball towards the batsman, she was struck more by a sudden understanding of why people felt the urge to streak at the cricket, seduced by the sun, blue sky and lush green grass. 'When Jane told me that at dinner, I couldn't stop smiling,' says McGrath.

Australia won the Test – McGrath took seven wickets – and they flew to Sydney to stay at his bachelor pad by the ocean at Cronulla. Jane fell in love with the area the locals called the Shire.

Their week together ended all too quickly and Jane left the Aussie summer for the cold bite of the northern hemisphere winter. McGrath was happy to have found Jane Steele was everything he'd believed her to be that first night in Hong Kong: happy-go-lucky, uncomplicated and very caring. They promised to keep in touch, but as Jane cleared customs she had her doubts: 'I got the distinct impression I wasn't the only woman in his life. I also thought he liked being single.'

Regardless, the pair kept in touch, racking up expensive phone calls so they could share each other's daily existence and writing letters. Glenn quickly learned to recognise Jane's distinctive handwriting.

McGrath then asked Jane to come to Australia for a month or two in April 1996. When she arrived in Sydney he was at the airport, although he was much the worse for wear, having been part of Sutherland's first grand final victory. He had been named Man of the Match after tearing through Bankstown, which boasted the Waugh brothers.

While Jane was in Australia they visited a remote resort at Bloomfield, on the fringe of the ancient rainforests near Cairns in far north Queensland. According to McGrath, Bloomfield was like the Garden of Eden, and amid the sweet scent of the tropical flowers they enjoyed long, romantic strolls; spent time alone on the beach; watched the sun set; enjoyed a champagne picnic on the rocks; sat on the Coral Sea floor during a scuba diving lesson; and even danced beneath the moonlight. It was perfect – until an elderly couple asked if Glenn and Jane were an item.

'Without thinking, I said we were just friends,' McGrath recalls with a grimace. 'Good friends, but just friends. It didn't go down very well – trouble in paradise . . .'

'An older couple asked if we were boyfriend and girlfriend,' says Jane. 'And when Glenn replied – quick as a flash, mind you – that I was *just* a friend from England and we were having a quick break, I felt gutted. It felt as if I was being passed off as his latest tart to two strangers. I didn't know whether to crawl into a hole or smack him across the face. I had begun to fall for him but if I could have flown home straight away, I would have.'

Luckily the tropical heat quickly thawed the ice that McGrath's remark had caused and the couple were able to enjoy the rest of their time together. Although Jane does still tease him about his insensitivity at Bloomfield.

'I was stupid. I never introduced her as just a friend ever again,' says McGrath solemnly.

Jane was soon to receive another lesson about McGrath. While she realised he played top-level cricket, she had no inkling of how famous her beau was in Australia until the night they went to friends Bev and Darren Mitchell's place for a barbecue. It was a pleasant night and Jane enjoyed mingling with the other guests.

But then Bev asked Jane a question that caught her off-guard: 'So, what's it like going out with Glenn McGrath?' When Jane asked her what she meant, Bev replied: 'You know, with him being a superstar and all.'

'What, like Ryan Giggs from Manchester United?' Jane retorted.

'Who's he?' Bev asked.

'Exactly,' said Jane. 'He's a great footballer but you haven't heard of him.'

'But Jane, Glenn's as famous as Robert De Niro!'

Her new friend's revelation made Jane's jaw drop in shock. But it did help to explain why every second person greeted McGrath with 'Glenn, mate', 'G'day Glenn' and even 'Ooh aah' whenever they went out. Until that moment, Jane had just assumed McGrath was a very popular bloke who knew a lot of people.

'I felt like a bit of a fool and took him aside to ask what it was all about,' says Jane. 'What I discovered from that was Glenn was just a down-to-earth, modest person who didn't brag about his achievements to impress people. I liked the fact he didn't tell people he was one of the world's best fast bowlers, if not the best. I loved that.'

As for McGrath, the fact Jane didn't know him as Glenn McGrath the cricketer but as Glenn McGrath the person – and she *still* liked him – was special. He began to dread the day she would return to England. Their two months together had gone too quickly.

When the time came for Jane to leave, both were misty-eyed at Mascot airport. Jane refrained from telling McGrath she loved him because it seemed too early to say that. Before she left, McGrath looked her in the eye and her heart melted when he said, 'Jane, this isn't the end, you know, it's just the beginning . . .'

For Jane, being back in England – separated by 20,000 kilometres from the man she'd fallen for – was painful. He was always on her mind and, as she says, 'it was doing my head in'. She put herself under enormous pressure trying to rearrange her schedule so she'd be assigned to flights bound for Down Under.

When Glenn finally told Jane during one of their marathon telephone conversations that he loved her, she dropped her guard and spoke from the heart. While his declaration made her happy, it didn't change the fact they were still separated by vast distances, and that broke her heart. So when they next met up in Sydney, Jane told McGrath their relationship had to end – because trying to find ways to be with him was tearing her apart.

McGrath was shocked, but he had a plan.

'It was the night before Jane returned to England – maybe for good, this time – and it was far from the happy time we were used to,' he recalls. 'It was pretty sombre and whenever we tried to be cheerful, it hit us she'd be leaving tomorrow. I was cut up. The image I'd built up of myself as a free-spirited bloke had crumbled quickly. I think it is fair to say up until that point I'd had the upper hand in our relationship, but I gave that up freely and willingly when everything was placed under a threat. I'd never been as serious about anything before when I asked Jane to move to Australia and be with me. She didn't answer straight away. Jane needed all of ten seconds to make her mind up.'

But life as the much-loved partner of an international cricketer wasn't quite what Jane had imagined. When she returned to Sydney, Glenn was in Sri Lanka and still three days away from returning. After being together for three weeks he was off again, this time to India, and there were other trips on the horizon.

'I realised I'd made a mistake having Jane come to Australia for two months during our off-season, because she may have gained the impression I just played a few games of cricket in summer and had plenty of time on my hands in between,' he says.

The reality of the life of a cricket widow was a shock for Jane. Watching the other players and their partners embrace as they said teary farewells only added to her distress – and it didn't help to hear that the farewells only got harder.

One day after the players had departed, Jane sat with Sue Porter (Mark Waugh's then fiancée) and her daughter Lauren, Tracy Bevan and Lynette Waugh, and made some firm and empathetic friendships over a cappuccino.

Glenn and Jane were in love. Nothing – so they thought – could ever hamper that, but the Department of Immigration's red tape provided an immediate reality check. Jane needed permanent residency. After failing to secure it for her, McGrath sought out anyone he thought might be able to help. He was offended that the Department considered Jane as just one more 'candidate for immigration'. She was the love of his life! But try as he might, he couldn't explain to the public servants the significance of that. They didn't seem to comprehend.

'It was frustrating,' he says, shaking his head at the memory of filling out form after form. 'I have to admit I was worried she might not get the residency because of how tough it was. We showed the correspondence we shared (and it was personal) – Christmas cards, newspaper articles on our relationship and how much we love one another – to prove we were being honest, but there was no certainty her passport would get the rubber stamp. So, there was lots of trepidation, though there was one bright spot. They gave Jane permission to travel to England when we headed over for the 1997 Ashes tour.'

But as it turned out, England became the place where the happy couple would begin a battle beyond their imagining, one that would make their dealings with Australia's Department of Immigration seem easy.

Part Two

17

Lord of Lord's

He maintains a good line and bowls little rubbish, rarely wasting the new ball.

Bob Massie after watching McGrath
take 8 for 38 at Lord's

Graham Thorpe, one of English cricket's shining lights, was up the night before the Lord's Test, the second of the 1997 Ashes series, doing his last-minute homework and studying the Australian attack. Thorpe had thrashed the Australians around Edgbaston, Birmingham, a fortnight before to score a brilliant 138, which, along with Nasser Hussain's double-century, put England on course for a nine-wicket victory. The Australians, the world's best attack, had struggled to find their rhythm – and answers – at Birmingham. When McGrath finished his first Test innings in England with 2 for 107, questions were asked about his ability to handle English conditions. Thorpe, however, thought it ridiculous to write the Aussie bowler off after one bad performance, and he put his head down to work out how he'd play him.

'I was up the night before thinking,' says Thorpe. 'I never over-complicated it but I had a game plan – I was going to be aggressive. Obviously I'd thought about McGrath. We batsmen knew if you tried to take liberties against him you'd come a cropper pretty quickly. But I realised that playing against any Australian attack with the likes of McGrath, Warne, Gillespie and later on down the track Brett Lee, you had to form an aggressive game plan. In the lead-up to a game I could picture McGrath's action very well. I'd wonder how far the ball would pitch; what shots I'd play. At times, getting in the right frame of mind to play was like getting into a game of chess – you just couldn't afford to slip up. I found throughout my career the days leading up to a Test were quite a nerve-racking time. It was actually a relief to get out there and to get on with it.'

While Thorpe had basked in the glow of victory at Birmingham, McGrath and the Aussie attack had been summoned by team coach Geoff Marsh to a special practice session the day after the defeat to study the nuances of English conditions. There was a sense of shock in the Australian camp as they tried to come to grips with the crushing loss.

'We all had an extra session the next day,' captain Mark Taylor says. 'We put some witches' hats down on the pitch. We thought, while we didn't bat too well (I made over 100 which was good because it made some people stop questioning my form and Warnie scored 50), they made 478. We wondered, why the disparity? They made 478 to our first innings 118. So we looked at the batting and we also looked at the bowling. The bowlers were keen to get out there and to bowl the right length. McGrath then showed everyone what was the right length and away he went.'

McGrath remembers the bowlers being summoned to the ground the following morning, to the centre wicket, where they were told to charge in off their long run.

'The idea was to find some rhythm and to hit the right mark,' he says. 'It is easier to work on things like that than in a Test match and, if I remember correctly, my biggest concern was that I was running in too fast. I slowed it down a little bit and that helped in the next Test at Lord's, because I ran in with a bit of rhythm on a wicket made for my sort of bowling.'

To win at Lord's, however, England needed to defy history, because the record books showed that they hadn't beaten Australia at the home of cricket since 1934. Lord's is viewed by many Australian players as their home away from home, and Taylor says playing there gave his team a big lift.

'We knew the next game was at Lord's and we Australians love playing at Lord's,' he says. 'People like Glenn McGrath love playing at Lord's because of the tradition and its significance. A kid who comes through club cricket at outback Narromine never thinks about playing at Lord's, so it is quite special for them to get there and they lift.'

One of McGrath's concerns about bowling at Lord's for the first time was that he would be overawed by the tradition and history of the ground. While Thorpe mentally prepared strategies he'd employ against the Australians, McGrath spent his afternoon before the Lord's Test soaking up the tradition and history of cricket's most famous ground.

'I didn't want to get overawed by the occasion, so I went there the day before and I took the time to really look around and soak up the atmosphere. I did that because once the game started I didn't want to be distracted by the things that make Lord's so special.'

When Taylor won the toss and elected to bowl, Thorpe's hair should have turned white with shock after he'd seen the pitch. The curator had dished up a wicket Thorpe realised was tailor-made for the old enemy's attack. It was on these occasions that Thorpe, who'd represented England in the national youth soccer team, could have been forgiven for wishing he'd pursued a professional football career.

'Over the past five years Lord's was as flat as a board,' he says. 'But we turn up to play Australia and the wicket was *good*. We didn't need a pitch that offered sideways movement or bounce, but that's what we got. It was a case of us looking at each other and thinking, "Bloody hell!" We'd tried to produce a pitch with a tinge of green in it! McGrath was one of the last bowlers you'd want to give a tinge of green when he had a Duke ball in his hand. We lost the toss and we eventually started to bat at midday the following day [because of the rain]. By 4 pm we were in serious trouble and struggling.'

While Thorpe and the English team tried to come to grips with the wicket that – thanks to the toss of a coin – they'd been condemned to play on, Steve Waugh sat next to McGrath in a section of the dressing-room Waugh had decreed his 'lucky' corner. In the 1989 Ashes campaign, the 24-year-old Waugh had belted an unconquered 152 at Lord's and returned to Australia hailed as the 'new Bradman' after averaging 126 in the six-Test series.

From their lucky window McGrath and Waugh enjoyed an uninterrupted view of cricket's most revered 22 yards of turf. The former Labor leader Doc Evatt once said that Australians would go to war to defend the hallowed pitch, but on this particular morning the ace bowler and star batsman spoke of how best to turn it into a minefield for England. While Waugh's name was already on the dressing-room's famous honour board, thanks to his ton in 1989, the pair joked that it would be great to have both their names painted in gold for their respective efforts in the Test. McGrath noted George Eugene Palmer, a right-arm medium-pace spinner, was the first Australian to make the board, taking 6 for 111 in the inaugural Test played at Lord's in 1884.

But if there was any obvious magic in Waugh's lucky corner, initially it was hard for McGrath to find – probably because it was buried deep beneath Waugh's debris.

'While I know tradition – and Lord's is steeped in it – meant a lot to Steve, I have to say his lucky corner at Lord's was treated no differently to the way he treated his spot in every other dressing-room in the world . . . it was a mess,' McGrath says. 'Pads, bats, gloves, his helmet, were strewn everywhere. But I felt good. There were only two times during my career when I had a feeling I was going to do something special. One time was Lord's – something made me believe I was destined to do well at Lord's that day.

'I don't know if you describe it as a feeling or a knowing. I just knew something special was going to happen that day, I had no doubts whatsoever that something really good was set and I didn't question it at all. I prepared as I always did but in the back of my mind was a feeling I was going to do very well. The only other time I felt it was when I took 8 for 24 against Pakistan in 2004 . . . maybe I should have felt it more!'

As Waugh sat next to McGrath, he shook his head in disbelief as the fast bowler annoyed yet another unsuspecting team-mate by smacking a grape into the back of his head or by tapping another on the shoulder and looking away as they turned around.

'He was a classic pain in the butt,' says Waugh of the team pest. 'He could hit someone with a bit of ice or a grape from 20 metres away – it was always an adventure as he found ways to entertain himself. If there was a gold medal for silly things he'd be the Olympic champion, but if he was a kid you'd have told him to go find something else to do.'

And yet, for all of McGrath's childish antics, Waugh figured his mate was destined to shine at the most revered of all cricket grounds – and it had nothing to do with cosmic forces or the alignment of the planets or the stars. He instead credited Lord's unusual sloping pitch, which favoured such things as McGrath's off-cutter.

'If anyone was made to bowl at Lord's, it was Glenn McGrath. His length when he got bounce made him awkward to play. England never felt comfortable leaving the ball outside their off stump – they had to play at him and that encouraged edging or, if it darted back, he'd either dismiss them LBW or he'd bowl them out. We were playing at the home of cricket; everyone was on edge and ready to play. If you were going to back a bowler to get a five-for that day at Lord's, it was McGrath.'

Shane Warne – who'd left psychological scars of his own on English batsmen since his first delivery against the old enemy, hailed as the 'ball of the century', dismissed Mike Gatting at Manchester in 1993 – also realised Australia's pace spearhead was ready to rise to the challenge.

'When you play at Lord's you look at guys like Glenn McGrath and see their eyes light up,' he says. 'But it's not easy, because I found when conditions were perfect for you – as they were for Glenn that day – your own expectations, and everyone else's for that matter, are very high. It's not easy. While it was a bit overcast, the ball was moving and it was a bit seamy, Glenn still had to get the ball in the right area, he still had to find the edges and people still had to catch the ball. It's hard.'

When play finally started, McGrath savoured the moment. He was opening the bowling for Australia at Lord's, one of sport's sacred venues, like Wimbledon for tennis and St Andrews for golf. As he ran in to deliver the opening ball of the match, he was struck by the silence. He later described it as an 'eerie calm', because there were no catcalls, no cheers or chants. Instead there was the type of respectful silence people normally reserve for graveyards or churches.

'It was so quiet,' says McGrath. 'I ran in to a mute tension so different to anywhere else I'd played, because in places like

Sydney or Melbourne every step of the opening bowler's run in for the first delivery is the signal for the crowd to go crazy. Lord's shocked me because it was so reserved.'

Steve Waugh concurs: 'The English are respectful of the traditions of places like Lord's and St Andrews. While St Andrews is not the prettiest course – it isn't how you'd expect a golf course to look – Lord's is the same for cricket. It's meant to be flat, but it has an incredible, outrageous slope. If you were playing park cricket at a place like that you'd ask, "What are we doing here?" It's ridiculous. But there is something there that makes you gravitate towards it, there's magnetism, because it has a special feel. You think, "This is the place where cricket started; this is where W. G. Grace played; this is the hallowed turf." As a cricketer, playing there is almost the Holy Grail. You know where you are playing and it is so very special.'

McGrath's first game on the hallowed ground unfolded rapidly. He made a quick breakthrough after England had hobbled to 11. Greg Blewett, fielding at short leg, caught opening batsman Mark Butcher after he played a limp shot. Mike Atherton followed one run later after edging a McGrath delivery low to Mark Taylor at first slip. And Alec Stewart rued what he called an 'error of judgement' every step of the way back to the dressing-room after he was clean-bowled – he'd let the ball go, only to hear the death rattle of his stumps when the ball came back down Lord's famous slope.

England was 3 for 13. McGrath had taken 3 wickets for 2 runs in just 13 balls – and the English jubilation that had followed the home team's triumph at Edgbaston was long forgotten by the time Thorpe walked out to the middle under a blanket of grey rain clouds. Thorpe planned to remain faithful to his aggressive strategy, but he needed to be smart. And this was reinforced when he edged the ball to wicketkeeper Ian Healy. Most of the

Australians thought the 'keeper had taken the catch clean, but Thorpe lived to fight on after Healy told umpire David Shepherd the ball had reached him on the half-volley.

Thorpe took time out to compose himself.

'I remember looking at the pitch and thinking, "I have to sit on this wicket. I'll get a good ball soon and when I do I'll have to be aggressive straight away,"' says Thorpe. 'I remember we were 3 for 20 and I was looking for anything short of a length so I could pull it. I decided if McGrath bowled anything short I would take him on; anything on the stumps and I'd leave it. That was it. I had one shot in my head.

'That's why I think you needed to have a very positive approach against him. Not reckless, positive. Drop and run – to take your singles – would always get a fast bowler angry, it'd really piss him off. You had to capitalise on anything. You also needed a lot of patience. You had to sit in there and go through it. You knew McGrath would be the bloke who'd get the ball thrown to him after lunch or tea. He'd get it at any crucial session because he could build pressure and take wickets. That is the hallmark of a great bowler: they don't get too cranky, they know they have to sit in and bowl maidens. And he could do that, and do it quite happily.

'But as a batsman, you always had to have the belief you could get to him to do something different. If you could take him on, have a go at his shorter ball, that was the one thing that would throw up a challenge to him. If he came back with a few more bouncers, you'd think you'd got under his skin.'

But McGrath had no reason to feel irritated by any of the Englishmen he bowled at that day. He was in control – and like any hunter from the Australian outback worth his salt, he realised patience was a virtue.

'I didn't lose my head or get carried away when the wickets

started to fall. I just kept chipping away and the wickets came. My ball that dismissed Alec Stewart summed up my match. He let it go, but the ball came back at him from up the slope. Alec said he had seen that happen to other batsmen before, but I felt like I'd won the lottery.'

England finished the first day at 3 for 38, with Hussain on 10 and Thorpe 13. While the batsmen may have tossed and turned that night, McGrath slept soundly – but even he couldn't have dreamed of what destiny had planned for the following day.

'We just picked up from where we left off,' he says. 'Paul Reiffel made a good breakthrough, dismissing Thorpe for 21 when the total was 47, then I grabbed Crawley and Hussain in succession. Dismissing Hussain was a personal triumph. He was my fifth wicket and it felt incredible – a five-wicket haul at Lord's, life as a fast bowler couldn't get any better. It came after another rain break and I was pumped.'

Being dismissed by Reiffel was a cruel blow for Thorpe, because he felt he'd been blind-sided after spending so much time digging in to counter McGrath. 'I was doing all right against Glenn and then Pistol got me – caught by Blewett at short leg,' says Thorpe. The first of Reiffel's two victims, he returned to what he called a 'shell-shocked' dressing-room. Thorpe and Hussain had shared a 288-run stand at Edgbaston; at Lord's, their 34 would be the highest of the England innings. Among the English players there was a hope that someone – anyone – could stop the rot, but in his heart of hearts Thorpe realised this was highly unlikely.

'It was an odd feeling back in the dressing-room, because there really wasn't much we could do,' he says. 'We were 50 for 5, the top order was gone – we were dealing with the rats and mice in terms of batting talent. But you get a bloke in that kind of form and it's very difficult. McGrath had the ball on a string that day, he was running up the hill, hitting the ball on the seam – he was pretty much unplayable.'

The only Englander enjoying the sight of McGrath tormenting the home team was Jane Steele. Even though she was sitting among the Lord's members, well aware that open cheering – or screaming, in her case – would be looked down upon by the battalions of old men in blazers, Jane couldn't help but let them know it was *her* man who was tearing the heart out of England's batting line-up.

'An attendant told me to keep quiet,' says Jane, recalling the numerous frowns of disapproval and symphony of 'tsks' that condemned her enthusiasm. 'But I replied, "I don't care because *he's* my boyfriend!" Well, I can tell you I got a few looks because the people sitting around me could tell I was English.'

Jane's unbridled happiness achieved something not too many other people can lay claim to – she made a Lord's attendant smile.

Perth's Bob Massie, who in 1972 had taken 16 wickets at Lord's against England, didn't enjoy such luck that day. He turned up to the game with the wrong tickets and, despite his place in the ground's history, the gatekeepers refused to grant him entry. By the time Massie returned to his hotel and found the right pass, McGrath had finished England off.

The non-playing members of the Australian squad who watched from the balcony of their dressing-room didn't need to worry about attendants or local sensitivities each time McGrath struck, as Adam Gilchrist recalls: 'It was my first Lord's experience and even though I wasn't playing, what stuck in my mind was the crowd appreciated what it was watching. It was the work of a true master craftsman; a guy who was in total control. I couldn't believe I was watching a guy rip a total batting line-up quite like the way Glenn was. It was very special.'

Andy Caddick's dismissal by McGrath resulted in England being rolled – all out – for a humiliating 77. The English tabloids went to town, ridiculing their team's perceived lack of fight. But not even the sharpest wit could match the cold hard facts of history, because England's total was:

- the lowest recorded by an English team at Lord's in the twentieth century;
- England's second-lowest score since the end of World War Two;
- the fourth-lowest score of the twentieth century;
- the thirteenth-lowest Test total of all time; and
- the nineteenth score under 100 in Ashes history.

And Glenn McGrath's 8 for 38 was the best bowling by an Aussie since Massie had taken his 8 for 84 (on his way to match figures of 16 for 137) in 1972. It was the best innings haul by an Australian bowler since 1909, when Frank Laver from Victoria snared 8 for 31 at Old Trafford. And it was ranked the third-best effort by an Australian bowler after Laver's 1909 effort and Arthur Mailey's 9 for 121 against England at the MCG in 1920/21.

An ecstatic Geoff Marsh beat the ground's official sign-writer to the job of adding McGrath's name to the honour board seconds after Caddick was sent packing, by scribbling *G. D. McGrath 8/38* on a piece of paper and taping it to the wooden board.

At the end of the Test, which finished in a draw because of the rain, Steve Waugh couldn't help but smile wryly when he looked at the board.

'We both said we wanted our names on the board by the end of the Test. But as it turned out, I was dismissed for a first-ball duck and Pigeon took 8 for 38,' says Waugh. 'It was an outstanding effort.'

Among the many faxes of congratulations from the likes of Australia's Prime Minister John Howard and the Narromine Council, the one that brought the biggest smile to McGrath's face came from his old Backwater skipper, Shane Horsburgh. He'd become a police officer and was based in rural New South Wales. Despite McGrath's sensational effort, Horsburgh didn't doubt his reasons for not giving him the ball when he was in the under-16s: 'I still didn't think you could bowl back then!'

As McGrath offered his old skipper from Backwater a silent toast of 'Good on ya, mate', England's media raked over the coals of their team's first innings disaster.

'England should stop playing at Lord's!' wrote the *Sunday Mirror's* Steve Whiting. 'They haven't beaten Australia there since 1934 and they won't this time either.'

Although the game ended in a draw, England finished the psychological battle battered and bruised. After Lord's, Mark Taylor's men went on to retain the Ashes – and the skipper points to McGrath's magic day at the home of cricket as a major reason for the eventual series victory.

'With Glenn McGrath's bowling and Matt Elliott's hundred at Lord's straight after our loss at Edgbaston, we *believed* we were a good cricket side,' he says. 'We went on with it from there.'

18

Reality

> Being the partner of a woman with breast cancer is like being a corner-man for a prize-fighter; no matter how badly your fighter is being mauled, you can't jump in the ring and mix it with the opponent. There were numerous times when I wished it was me suffering and not Jane, because it would've been so much easier to take. As her corner-man, all I could be was alert and tell my 'scrapper' to pick herself up after each body blow.
>
> Glenn McGrath

> I sometimes felt that maybe I had been chosen to get breast cancer because I was strong enough to fight it, to take it on and beat it. That maybe other women in a similar position would then see having breast cancer isn't necessarily a death sentence – that they might win their battle too.
>
> Jane McGrath

McGrath sat in the surgeon's office not knowing what shocked him more: confirmation that Jane had breast cancer or her reaction that she'd prefer to be buried than disfigured by a mastectomy. The desperation in her eyes and voice was unmistakeable, and it made his heart break. Worse still, there was nothing he could do except sit there and try to take it all in. It was the realisation of Jane's worst fears, a nightmare that had started a few weeks earlier, during the final stages of the 1997 Ashes series.

Jane had showered, her towel was wrapped around her waist and she combed her wet hair. She was in the team hotel, in the shadows of the grand Canterbury Cathedral, and she'd had a wonderful time with the girls exploring the old Tudor buildings for treasures and trinkets while the boys played cricket against Kent.

It had been a memorable trip. Apart from the cricket, McGrath and the boys had played golf at St Andrews and the Belfry, and had raced around the Formula One circuit at Silverstone. They'd been invited to the lawn tennis at Wimbledon, seen *Les Misérables* at the West End, and enjoyed a beautiful night cruise down the River Thames past London's famous landmarks – Big Ben, the Houses of Parliament, St Paul's Cathedral and Tower Bridge.

More importantly for the couple, McGrath had met Jane's family and she'd been overjoyed that they too were taken by him. Jane had also discovered how much her new country had come to mean to her. After England had shocked the Aussies in the opening Test at Edgbaston, she realised she'd embraced more about Australia than her boyfriend.

'While we waited for the boys to come out of the dressing-room, a few of the English players were at the bar,' says Jane. 'Tracy Bevan knew Darren Gough through Michael Bevan, who played county cricket for Yorkshire, Darren's team. She introduced me and I couldn't help but to end my congratulations with, "Make the most of it – it won't last long." ' Jane's intuition proved correct. While the next game, at Lord's, ended in a draw, McGrath famously took 8 for 38 in the first innings to help roll 'the Poms' – as Jane was now encouraged to call them – for 77. And the Aussies went on to win the series.

On this particular morning, though, as she combed her hair, Jane's intuition told her there was a problem with her left breast. She felt a chill, because her mother had been diagnosed with breast cancer aged only 49 and had needed a mastectomy.

'There was a lump in my left breast,' says Jane. 'For some reason my gaze was drawn to a section of my breast and I was convinced somehow it didn't look quite right. Instead of being curved underneath, it appeared to flatten out on one side. No matter how many times I told myself not to be silly, I became even more concerned. While my mother suffered breast cancer, I never thought it would happen to me. Mum was under a lot of stress when she was diagnosed and I thought that was the reason behind her illness. Also, none of her doctors had suggested I should be concerned so I didn't worry about it.'

Jane felt her breast so often for a lump she made the area sore, and that made her happy because she'd heard cancerous lumps weren't painful. She also sought Glenn's opinion. While he could see nothing wrong, he suggested they could go to her doctor in the Cotswolds. Instead, Jane elected to see Tracy Bevan, who was in the room opposite.

'She knew,' says Tracy. 'I think she wanted reassurance, to hear me say nothing was wrong. I looked at Jane and didn't speak . . . I didn't have to. My face said it all. I couldn't lie to her. Jane then said in that way of hers: "Right, okay, don't say anything." It was very hard. A few days earlier we'd celebrated the news I was pregnant.'

In ten or so minutes Jane had talked herself out of believing there was anything to worry about and she did her best to forget about it.

'The trip had been terrific because I learned a lot about Jane, her family and where she came from,' McGrath says. 'I enjoyed time with her family, saw the backyard pavers she enjoyed scrubbing as a little girl, visited her grandmother's old sweet shop. I saw her old school.

'However, when we were at Canterbury she was worried about her breast not looking right. I thought that because Jane was only 31, she was far too young to worry about breast cancer – that was an older woman's disease, wasn't it? I told her she had nothing to worry about. I could see the worry in her eyes and suggested we go to her doctor, because I thought we'd be better off dealing with whatever it was than sitting around wondering and worrying. There were a few problems. She had to be back in Australia by the end of August to comply with the conditions of her bridging visa, and I found out Jane was worried that if she did have cancer she might not be allowed back to Australia, which she thought would harm our chances of being together.'

Jane and Glenn, along with most of the Australian team and their partners, left England on Thursday 28 August with the Ashes still in their keeping. Skipper Mark Taylor was aware of Jane's visa requirements and midway through the flight he whispered in her ear that the plane had a mechanical problem and needed to divert. That meant, he said solemn-faced, they'd arrive in Australia a day later. Jane was beside herself until his face broke into a broad smile. She'd been had.

A few days after returning to Cronulla, the couple had dinner with Darren and Bev Mitchell. It was supposed to be a celebration – after all, Glenn had been named player of the tour – but Jane's mind was fixated on her left breast. When Bev, a theatre nurse, learned of Jane's concern, she took her into the bedroom and told her to lie down. (Jane's self-examinations over the past fortnight had been done as she stood up.) Bev felt the area and nodded. There was a lump. Jane wanted to cry but somehow she remained composed. When McGrath attempted to comfort her, she put her hand up to stop him. She didn't want to crumble.

'I saw tears in her eyes, but she didn't want a hug,' McGrath recalls. 'I could see she was . . . well, petrified . . . but I hung to hope. I hoped it was nothing more than a cyst and all would be well. I loved Jane. I couldn't believe anything would happen. I still believed breast cancer was an older woman's disease.'

Bev arranged for Jane to see a doctor at 9.40 the next morning. Glenn offered to drive her there but she told him to go to training. Regardless of what happened, she wanted their lives to go on as normal. The doctor examined her breast and found not one lump but two. He was comforting and said that, based on her age, the chances of them being malignant were remote. However, he thought it would be wise to have a mammogram, just to be safe.

Jane was so happy that she'd perhaps turned a molehill into a mountain that she decided to walk home. The doctor's tone had lifted the dark cloud that had settled over her – and the sun had never seemed brighter, the sky never as blue and life never more appreciated. McGrath returned to a happy Jane, and they rearranged their travel plans for his brother Dale's wedding back 'home' that weekend so she could go to the imaging centre for her tests on the Friday morning.

The metal plate Jane needed to rest her left breast on was cold. Another cold metal plate was clamped down on top of it to squash it in, and then the mammogram was taken. Her breast felt tender as a series of images was taken from various angles.

When that was finished, Jane was sent for an ultrasound, where soundwaves detected the two lumps, one at seven o'clock, the other at nine o'clock. The operator made her feel even more confident by saying they were probably only fibroid adenomas – non-cancerous growths. But Jane's hopes were crash-tackled when the woman who'd taken the mammograms said the doctor needed some more taken because a few of them weren't clear. Jane knew there was a problem, and she was blinded by tears of fear.

'The alarm bells were ringing,' she says. 'When I saw Glenn in the waiting room I was so happy to see him that I wouldn't let go of him. When we returned an hour later to collect the envelope, there was a post-it note with "Doctor, 3 pm", and I knew something was wrong. As we drove to the doctor's surgery, I hoped it was a nightmare and I was going to wake . . . soon. But my name next to the mammogram was all too real. The doctor's face said everything. He said the results weren't good and I'd need to have a needle biopsy to confirm if I had cancer. He told me to stop taking the contraceptive pill immediately, and that I was booked in to get my needle biopsy the next working day, Monday September 8.'

The walk back to the car was tough. McGrath had tears in his eyes, and when Jane turned to him and whispered helplessly in a hoarse voice, 'I have cancer, don't I?' his mind went blank. All he could do was hold her for dear life. Jane phoned her parents and she could hear the helplessness in their voices, so she somehow kept it together to make them think she was coping. McGrath went to Dale's wedding alone; there was no way Jane could make the trip, and when his family learned of her worry they prayed that her fears would amount to nothing.

'My grandmother was fighting breast cancer at the time, so everyone understood why she couldn't attend,' McGrath says.

'My family had met Jane a few times and they loved her – there was plenty of sympathy and support for her.'

'Two days after the biopsy I saw the surgeon. He was half an hour late and the delay added to my anxiety,' says Jane. 'Not long after I took a seat in his office, he confirmed I had it. I had breast cancer. I felt as if I was going to be sick. And then it got worse. He said the only realistic course of action was a mastectomy. It was hard to digest because he continued, saying things like I'd need chemotherapy that might make me infertile, and it might even bring on an early menopause. There was also a course of radiotherapy. In a matter of weeks, I went from not having a care in the world, being in love with the loveliest man in the world, to being told I could die.'

McGrath somehow managed to control his emotions and asked the doctor for any good news. The good news, said the surgeon, was if Jane had the mastectomy she might survive. But that wouldn't happen – and her vow to 'be buried rather than disfigured' stunned McGrath. He then listened as Jane tried to negotiate her life for her breast with the surgeon. She asked if he could do a lumpectomy, where the tumour and surrounding breast tissue are removed but the skin, muscle and lymph nodes remain. No. Could she have a reconstruction operation? Impossible. She was hitting brick walls and she was desperate. Mastectomy? She'd rather die. The doctor, however, didn't let up. He told Jane that after the mastectomy she'd require months of chemo and radiotherapy treatment.

'What I found cruel was hearing the drugs she'd need to take would mean that she – we – might not have children,' says McGrath. 'It seemed to me that this cancer was going to rob Jane of more than just her left breast. We sought a second opinion arranged through Errol Alcott's father, Kevin, a doctor, and it was just as grim. The other surgeon said there was a danger the cancer could spread to her right breast if we didn't take immediate action.

'Jane was worried about her femininity. She was worried that if she lost a breast she'd become unattractive to me but I swear, as her lover, that was not a problem . . . I just wanted her to be alive – and with me.'

On their return home, Jane decided to be fair and offer Glenn a 'get-out clause'. She'd return to England for the treatment so he could focus on cricket. She added with tears in her eyes that it'd do neither of them any good if they were bound by pity. Anyway, she could return to Australia after the treatment.

'We weren't engaged,' says Jane of her decision. 'I saw it as my problem, not Glenn's.'

'When Jane said that, I was scared she wanted to go home,' recalls McGrath. 'The thought of that was a greater worry than tackling the cancer head-on. I was under no illusions, it was going to be a tough battle, but I just couldn't imagine my life without her. The thought of breaking up never crossed my mind. We were in life together. I told her not to be stupid; I was there for her.'

They were well-chosen words, because Jane had promised herself she'd buy a ticket on the first flight to England if McGrath hesitated when she asked him the question about leaving.

There was a cancer counselling service, but there wouldn't be anyone available to talk to Jane for a few days because they were so busy. She felt cornered. There appeared to be no escape – or room to breathe. Despite McGrath's best efforts to tell her to have the operation, she remained committed to death before disfigurement.

Jane needed to get away, so they packed their gear and headed to Glenn's remote property a few hundred kilometres beyond Bourke and a ten-hour drive from Cronulla. If McGrath was certain of one thing, it was that they'd find an answer to their problems in the outback. After they'd dumped their luggage in the old homestead, he wheeled his trusty trail bike out of the shed and doubled Jane around the property. She saw baby kangaroos, emus and lambs in the first few weeks of their lives. In those few hours on the bike, Jane realised life was a gift to value and to fight for, especially when the odds were against you. It was not something to throw away cheaply. She'd fight. Jane Steele would fight to live.

When they returned from the motorbike ride, there was a message on the answering machine from Mark Taylor asking McGrath to call him as soon as possible. Taylor had learned of Jane's problem from Alcott. His call would help to reinforce Jane's decision to have the operation.

'My best mate Jack's brother is the cancer surgeon Dr Chris Hughes, and he was one of the people who started my charity, Sporting Chances Foundation,' says Taylor. 'I know Chris well and when I heard what had happened to Jane, I figured he was a good person to introduce them to.'

When McGrath spoke to Dr Hughes, he was told that if a breast reconstruction was what it would take for Jane to have the operation, he'd find a way to ensure it happened. At last, Jane felt as though someone was on her side, and it gave her hope.

Later that night when she looked at the breast in the mirror, she saw the ugliness of the cancer that was making her insides decay. She hated it. It spelled death and she had to fight it quickly. Before Jane had the operation – the mastectomy, a word she still couldn't bring herself to say out loud – she promised there would be no asking, 'Why me?' She would need all her energy to fight a long and tough battle. Jane also wanted to fight hard and tough for Glenn's sake. He'd proved his love for her was unconditional – and that gave Jane not only a sense of strength, but a determination not to let him down.

19

Life is Beautiful

Love is patient, love is kind. It does not envy, it does not boast, it is not proud. It is not rude, it is not self-seeking, it is not easily angered, it keeps no records of wrongs. Love does not delight in evil but rejoices with the truth. It always protects, always trusts, always hopes, always perseveres . . .

And now these three remain: faith, hope and love. But the greatest of these is love.

From Saint Paul's First Letter
to the Corinthians

Before the operation, McGrath held Jane's hand for as long as he was allowed to while she was wheeled into the operating theatre. It was so hard for him to see Jane crying and to hear her sob, and to be able to do nothing but say he loved her and that he'd be with her every step of the journey. There was a sense of disbelief it was happening . . . McGrath couldn't believe they were dealing with what the doctors called 'a life and death operation'.

When he looked at the statistics McGrath was horrified to realise that 27 Australian women died each day as a result of breast cancer. He would soon tell his mates to learn from Jane and advise their partners to have a check-up. To look at Jane, no-one could have guessed she had cancer – she was healthy, fit and happy. The only certainty McGrath felt was that regardless of how her breast looked after the operation, it would not change the way he felt about her. Ever the pragmatic boy from the bush, he reasoned that she'd still walk the same way, talk the same way, smell the same way, laugh and cry the same way she always had. She'd still be Jane.

McGrath warded off the negative thoughts that threatened to flood his mind before the operation. He opened it to only positive thoughts. He'd need to be brave no matter what, because he realised it would be devastating for Jane to see him collapse. Although sitting in the waiting room, he was with her in spirit, and for the hours the operation took he felt her pain, every awful morsel of it.

Jane was wheeled back into a room bursting with colours from the flowers her friends had sent, while the cards she had received exuded love and warmth. As McGrath watched over Jane in her post-operative sleep, he felt a deep sadness. Although she wore a gown, he could see her chest was swathed in bandages. She looked weary despite being asleep, and it struck him the fight would only get tougher when she began her chemo and radiotherapy.

Jane woke to see McGrath sitting beside her – 'a wonderful sight' although she was in a daze, having been pumped with pethidine to kill the pain. There was a button beside Jane's bed and her friend Bev explained that if she needed relief, she only needed to press it for a pethidine shot. She had two drains in her chest to empty the fluid from her wound. When she saw the yellow liquid flowing through the plastic tubes it made her want to be physically ill.

'The morning after the operation a nurse helped me into the shower so I could freshen up,' says Jane. 'It was awkward but I wanted to put my make-up on to look good for Glenn.'

On the rare occasions she was alone, Jane ran her fingers over the place where her breast used to be. Her worst nightmare was that there'd be a deep hole on the left-hand side of her chest. On the fifth day, she had to face her moment of truth – the way she now looked – when the surgeon examined the scar. She had already said Glenn would never see the scar and she would only look at it herself when she had to. The doctor thought that day had come. And he added that it should be up to McGrath to look at the scar to decide what he thought of it. Jane knew the surgeon was right, but she was terrified Glenn might take one look and run.

'I don't know which of us was the more nervous when the bandages started to come off,' says Jane. 'Glenn looked at it before me, and because he hadn't collapsed I thought maybe it isn't too bad. I took a deep breath and looked down. Thankfully there was no concave, it looked flat with a line of staples across a 15-centimetre scar. When I asked Glenn if he was fazed at all by the sight a few years later, he said it didn't bother him at all.'

'All I could do,' says McGrath, 'was to feel so impressed by what the doctor had done. In time I started to think of that scar as her badge of courage and honour. I saw that scar as her decision to live, rather than die. It wasn't ugly, it was a reminder to take nothing in life for granted. Jane wanted a breast reconstruction job, but I told her to do it for her, not me, because I had heard it was a painful procedure and that was the last thing I wanted her to endure – more pain.'

Jane's first mission the day after she returned home was to collect the mail from the post office box at Cronulla. Bev

Mitchell accompanied her for moral support. It was the first time Jane had to address what she'd call 'lopsided breasts'. It was frustrating and it was intimidating. Despite her concealing leather jacket, she still felt as if everybody was looking at her as she walked – exhausted – through the mall. At Jane's insistence, McGrath had gone to a sponsor's meeting in Brisbane, and Bev and Darren were staying in their unit overnight.

Jane was determined life would run as normal – but Glenn's phone call from Brisbane worried her. He'd been on the drink all night and she was concerned he was seeking solace in alcohol. McGrath insisted that wasn't the case at all – it was simply a case of one drink leading to another, and another, and another.

One of the biggest problems Jane contended with after her operation was the lack of guidance or information on her 'new' post-mastectomy life. Bev – a pillar of strength and loyalty – rang the Cancer Council and explained Jane's situation. They sent her a bra padding – a 'softie' made out of cushion stuffing enclosed in a silky pouch – which allowed Jane to wear the tight lycra tops she'd worn before the operation. Nevertheless, every day presented new challenges, as Jane discovered when she went to the ABC studios for the shooting of *Club Buggery*, Roy and HG's television show. She sat alongside Warren Craig in the front row and was mortified to notice her 'softie' sticking out of her jacket.

'I could've died,' she laughs. 'Fortunately no-one noticed and I nonchalantly pushed it back into my bra. After that little experience I used safety pins to secure it.'

Jane also decided it was time to get a prosthetic breast and some mastectomy bras, which are specially designed with concealed pockets to support a prosthesis. And she worked with McGrath-like determination on her exercises to help her arm heal after an operation to remove her lymph nodes. The fact that it took only ten days for Jane to be cleared to drive her car is testimony to the thoroughness of her exercise program.

But the hard work had only just begun. She was warned about the risk of lymphoedema, which results when lymph (a fluid) is retained in body tissue and causes swelling. With breast cancer treatment, doctors remove the lymph nodes to determine how far the cancer has spread; it is essential that after such an operation the arm is kept free of burns, cuts and scratches, which can cause an onset of the problem.

'You have to stay out of hot baths and showers, the sun, that kind of thing,' says Jane. 'Mum wasn't warned about it and after her mastectomy she did a vigorous cleaning and scrubbing at her home and her arm swelled up and never returned to its pre-operation size. The threat of it is with you for the rest of your life, but it can be controlled by such things as specialised massage, wearing a compression sleeve and elevating the affected limb – each aids lymphatic drainage. I have been fortunate to be able to control the slight swelling but it is something I'm mindful of.'

Jane also overhauled her diet. She found one of the best ways to counteract her loss of appetite was to drink fresh juices, especially pineapple and orange. She also learned more about the properties of various foods and juices – for example, that carrot juice is a wonderful source of vitamins A, B1, B2 and C, that it has strong antiseptic qualities, and that it is a tremendous blood cleanser. Jane also used the power of her mind to help her body to heal, imagining the power and strength being circulated through her by the pure juices. And her resolve was steeled by people like her best friend Tracy Bevan, who sent wonderful cards of love and inspiration. The messages would help Jane push through the dark days when she needed help most. 'I have never really been a religious person, but I found myself saying a prayer every night, asking for an angel to look after my very special friend,' says Tracy.

'I don't think I'll ever understand how brutal the chemotherapy and radiotherapy was on Jane,' says McGrath. 'Jane's an incredibly strong person who hides a lot with her beautiful smile, but I know there were times when she felt as if the treatment was tearing her apart. Yet on the days she couldn't get out of bed there were no hysterics or complaints, she'd just say dreamily that she needed rest. Jane used to call me her rock – but I gained so much more from her, though. Her inner courage was – is – incredible; her ability to smile when she should cry is amazing. She is the hero of our family. As a result of radiotherapy, she's battled fatigue, a loss of appetite, bleeding and sore gums, bloating, bone marrow suppression, and a terrible itch that left her clawing at her skin, which was red like the most severe sunburn. I had to stop her from doing it because I knew it would only make it worse. She loathed going to Sutherland Hospital, her veins had started to close up and the chemo treatment must have scared her too. But she'd confront all her fears and pain to go through it.'

Jane achieved one goal when she made it to Brisbane in November 1997 to be in the crowd for the First Test between Australia and New Zealand at the beginning of the 1997/98 season. It was daunting to be out in the public glare after her operation and treatment, especially as the day before she flew to Queensland she'd had another injection of chemo. She wanted to look – and act – like she did before the operation, and she gained strength by knowing she wouldn't be alone, that the girls would be there.

Jane and Glenn spent Christmas Day in Melbourne, where they were staying for the Boxing Day Test. They enjoyed Christmas celebrations with the team and their loved ones, but

Jane suffered some ill effects from her treatment. As she sat at the table, her chest – where the radiotherapy had been focused – felt as if it was burning. There was a pharmacy nearby, but Jane was too embarrassed to ask the chemist for a cream to soothe it. She tried to suffer in silence but ended up telling Sue Porter she was doing it tough. Sue responded immediately, practically dragging Jane to the chemist, who gave her sorbolene cream, which provided instant relief for her burning skin. Also around this time, Jane suffered shooting sensations of pain across her chest wall, jolts which would take her breath away. She was told they were caused by the nerve endings in her chest, and that although they were painful, they were nothing to worry about.

After the Brisbane Test, Glenn was ruled out of the following two Tests so he could have treatment on an entrapped nerve in his groin. He was sent to hospital so doctors could 'kill' the nerve by frying it with high-frequency waves. But the procedure turned out to be medicine's version of 'pin the tail on the donkey', as the doctor needed three attempts to locate it.

When he returned to play at the SCG for the Second Test against South Africa in January 1998, McGrath suffered a seven-centimetre tear in his abdomen early on the first day. It hurt like hell but he vowed that if he started the match, he would finish it. He slogged on through the pain, motivated in large part by Jane's presence in the crowd; he wanted her to know that he too could dig deep.

McGrath's injury turned out to be a blessing, because during the time he remained at home to recuperate, Jane endured her toughest treatment and he was there to help her through it.

'What made me laugh was when the doctor suggested I should do a pain-management course,' McGrath says. 'It was ironic because I had seen Jane and other women being left to fend for themselves after the most brutal of operations, and I was being offered a pain-management course. I also had doctors all over me, people sympathising with me and the media sweating on updates. The woman I loved was desperate for help but could get none apart from our family and friends, but there I was having a top surgeon making an appointment for me to do a pain-management course! I was grateful for his concern, but it didn't add up. When I returned home, I let Jane know I was frustrated about missing the Tests. It was like the end of the world. But when she'd offer words of encouragement I'd snap back into reality and think, "What are you saying?" '

To celebrate her last chemo session, Jane arrived at the hospital with a batch of homemade chocolate cookies. It was a day of great optimism because she was one shot from the treatment's conclusion – for the time being. However, the medical staff couldn't find a vein that was strong enough to withstand the needle. Jane saw it as a bitter blow. She'd pinned everything on the nightmare ending that day, and she cried. A doctor who heard of Jane's situation helped her to complete her treatment that day by putting a cannula into the back of her right hand to administer the chemotherapy. It worked.

A few days later it was Jane's thirty-second birthday. She'd never appreciated life so much.

'I think having cancer, although it has been very frightening for me and one of the worst things ever, is also one of the best because it helps make you the person you are,' says Jane. 'When I wake up of a morning, it doesn't matter if it is raining or sunny because every day is a great day. It's the simple things in life that count, and many people don't realise that because they don't even think about those things as they rush about. They don't stop to appreciate the little things, but we do.'

*

In October 1998 McGrath was sitting in his hotel room in Karachi before the Third Test against Pakistan when he realised it was time for him to marry Jane. It made sense: they were soul mates who'd overcome enough hurdles to realise they were meant to be together. She was everything he'd imagined his future wife to be when he was younger and had plotted how he'd like to have his life play out: represent Australia in cricket; settle down; be successful; and . . . have kids. It was time to ask the question.

When he returned from Pakistan, McGrath proposed. Jane's reaction – she screamed – made McGrath extremely happy he'd chosen to do the honours at home and not at a busy restaurant.

On Saturday 17 July 1999, Jane and Glenn were married at the historic Garrison Church at the Rocks, three weeks after Australia had won the World Cup. Jane was sold on the church because it had the Australian flag and the Union Jack hanging side-by-side, which Jane considered symbolic of their relationship. The church was crammed with family and friends who had travelled from afar to share their special day, and all agreed that Jane looked radiant as she walked down the aisle with her father. He would later tell the guests at the reception that he was proud to have a son-in-law who'd proven his love for Jane knew no bounds.

Steve Waugh was Glenn's best man. He later joked that he thought Glenn and Jane's life partnership would be longer and stronger than any of Pigeon's batting partnerships. The sister Jane never had, Tracy Bevan, was her matron of honour. Tracy would later reveal that the secret to Australia's great cricketing success was the lucky knickers Jane wore to the games.

When McGrath was asked if he swore to honour and protect Jane, the two words of his response – 'I do' – were the easiest words he'd ever said. The couple's union was sealed with a kiss.

183

'Our wedding day had many special moments,' says Jane, smiling at the memory. 'To have those great wooden doors open and to see Glenn standing at the altar, our family and friends, to be accompanied down the aisle by my father and to hear Glenn say "I do", made it one of the happiest days of my life. It was so beautiful.'

And there was a miracle in that church. When Jane walked down the aisle, she – and Glenn – had defied the doctors and the odds because she was 12 weeks pregnant. On 20 January 2000 a healthy boy was born – their son, James McGrath. They were blessed again in 2001 with the birth of their beautiful daughter, Holly. People who know them describe the McGraths as a perfect family.

At their wedding, Jane and Glenn picked for a reading Elizabeth Barrett Browning's poem 'How Do I Love Thee?' It could have been their creed:

> How do I love thee? Let me count the ways.
> I love thee to the depth and breadth and height
> My soul can reach, when feeling out of sight
> For the ends of Being and ideal Grace.
> I love thee to the level of every day's
> Most quiet need, by sun and candlelight.
> I love thee freely, as men strive for Right;
> I love thee purely, as they turn from Praise.
> I love thee with the passion put to use
> In my old griefs, and with my childhood's faith.
> I love thee with a love I seemed to lose
> With my lost saints—I love thee with the breath,
> Smiles, tears, of all my life!—and, if God choose,
> I shall but love thee better after death.

20

Spirit of the Rhino

Obviously there is an element of mental confusion or mental awe within the performance. There is a combination of the technical side and the mental side involved in the way they played the two innings they played.

Pakistan coach Bob Woolmer after
McGrath took 8 for 24 against his team

In December 2004 McGrath arrived at the WACA in Perth for the opening Test of the series against Pakistan disappointed with his record at the ground. It was supposed to be a paceman's paradise, and generations of fast men – including the likes of Lillee, Thomson and English bowler John Snow – had long gushed about the pace and bounce of the pitch there, yet McGrath had no reason to share their enthusiasm.

Merv Hughes was the WACA's highest Test wicket-taker, with 39 scalps. And while it was true that McGrath needed only two more wickets to claim the record, the statisticians noted the moustached Victorian had achieved his feat in six Tests compared to McGrath's nine. Although McGrath's average of 25.71 might've been one most bowlers would kill for, it was his highest at any Australian Test venue. His WACA hat-trick against the West Indies in 2000 was a definite career highlight, but his best return there of 4 for 49 was moderate by McGrath's lofty standards.

On the third morning of the Test, McGrath was wrapping up a meeting at the hotel with his friends from the Save the Rhino Foundation when he was stopped dead in his tracks by their latest request for memorabilia to auction at their next fundraiser. He had no problem providing them with autographed gear to auction. Indeed, he was proud that his match-worn shirts and other items had raised thousands of dollars to help preserve the great rhinos, but when asked to souvenir the match ball from the Perth Test, McGrath was consumed by what he'd later describe as a rare but familiar sense of 'knowing'.

'I'm happy to help the Save the Rhino Foundation because they fight for what I consider a great cause,' says McGrath. 'The rhinos captivated me when I first saw them during the Cricket Academy tour to South Africa in 1992. They earn *every* cent the hard way, too. There's no government handouts for them. I totally support what they do; the rhinos are glorious animals and it angers me to think they're close to going the same way as the dinosaurs. When I was asked if I could get the ball, my immediate reaction was to say I'd do my best. However, when I started to walk away to get on the team bus, I thought about it and returned to the group to explain that the only thing that would stop me from getting it for them would be if somebody took five wickets in the innings. Guys like to keep the ball as a trophy when they do that, and I'd always thought that was fair.'

As McGrath walked away from the group, he *knew* the Foundation would not be auctioning the prized 'rock'. He'd experienced the same sense of knowing only once before – at Lord's in 1997 – and it was the prelude to his name being painted in gold lettering on the honour board after he'd taken 8 for 38. It was more than a simple gut feeling.

'After I told the guys about the problems I'd have getting the ball if someone did well, I knew – I just *knew* – they wouldn't be getting it. I don't know why, but I pictured myself taking the ball home and it was so vivid. Is it making your own destiny? I don't know, but it certainly gave me reason to feel confident.'

The following day McGrath bowled through the opening session of the fourth day of the Test to take what would be his career-best figures of 8 for 24 from 16 overs. His lionhearted effort steered Australia to a commanding 491-run win after he'd helped to blast the Pakistanis out for a paltry 72 runs.

Early on day one, Pakistan had the Aussie batsmen reeling at 5 for 78. The home side was rescued by gritty opener Justin Langer, who scored 191. That determined innings said plenty about the West Australian's courage and tenacity under fire.

McGrath's own performance proved that he'd fully recovered from the ankle injury that had sidelined him for the better part of the year. While he'd returned to Test cricket in July with match figures of 7 for 61 against Sri Lanka in the Top End Series at Darwin, the Perth Test represented his welcome back to the big time – a point Australian captain Ricky Ponting emphasised during the post-match press conference.

'He bowled fantastically,' enthused Ponting. 'The conditions are suited to fast bowlers, but [McGrath] was great . . . a match-winner.'

Fellow opening bowler Jason Gillespie recalled clearly the confidence McGrath had exuded in the dressing-room – although he had no idea his mate had been buoyed by a mystical and rare sense of 'knowing'.

'I remember Glenn being upbeat and in a positive frame of mind,' Gillespie says. 'I can't recall him telling the team, "I'm going to take a bag of wickets." But he was just so positive. He gave me the impression he was going to knock them over, because he was leaping out of his skin and wanting to get among them.

'He was in such a positive frame of mind in that game; he was totally switched on and, after watching him bowl the first few balls, I couldn't help but to think to myself he was going to do something special.

'We all bowled well but Glenn grabbed the spoils, which was absolutely fantastic. He landed the ball on a dime and – try as they might – the Pakistanis couldn't do a thing with it.'

It appeared as though McGrath might take all 10 wickets in the second innings, but any hope of a clean sweep was dashed when Michael Kasprowicz replaced Gillespie at the other end and dismissed the opposition's number eight batsman, Mohammad Sami, in his first over. He finished with 2 for 4 from three-and-a-half overs – and his reaction to his success surprised McGrath.

'Yeah, he apologised!' laughs McGrath. 'When I took my seventh wicket, the thought crossed my mind that innings might be my best chance at taking a ten-for, but then Kaspa ruined the party. He had a big grin on his face when he said sorry and I could tell he didn't mean it! We all had a good laugh.

'It was a dream day in the field. I was swinging the ball so it would just hold its line . . . if I went a little bit wider it would swing more. It was like I had total control over the ball and nothing could go wrong. There was a bit in the wicket, good bounce and the wickets felt good.'

It felt anything but good for Pakistan as their batsmen – including skipper Inzamam-ul-Haq, who was dismissed for a golden duck – fell like flies. While Ricky Ponting would hail the mammoth win as another great team victory, he also expressed his concern to the media about the state of international cricket, commenting on the fact that the fourth-ranked team, Pakistan, was so clearly unable to compete with the world's number one outfit.

'I think that is a bit of a worry,' Ponting said. 'The last time we played them [in Sharjah in 2002], we beat them quite convincingly as well. It's hard to take a lot out of this game because the conditions here are so different to what they're used to and what they've played on. But it is a bit of a concern that they're the fourth-ranked side and they've been bowled out very cheaply in these conditions.'

Justin Langer, named Man of the Match after scoring 191 and 97, remembers McGrath's effort with the ball as 'ruthless', because the one-time sheep farmer grabbed the so-called 'Lions of Pakistan' by the throat and refused to release his grip.

'The ruthlessness was incredible,' says Langer. 'I thought the line and length he bowled in that innings was similar to that of great West Indians Ambrose and Walsh. You could just feel the pressure building up on the Pakistanis; they were suffocating under the pressure he applied. When he got into that rhythm Glenn was awesome, and the Pakistani batsmen were fighting for run-scoring opportunities – and breath.'

Says McGrath: 'I was just running in and trying to hit the deck. I just wanted to get the ball in the right areas and it turned out to be my career best effort. Fortune, destiny perhaps, was on my side, because instead of playing and missing the Pakistani batsmen nicked the ball. With each wicket I grew even more confident. It was tremendous to do so well in Perth because I'd never had a five-for there. It was great because I could cross that from off the list of the little goals that help to keep you motivated. I was really happy.'

Gillespie, who finished the innings with 0 for 37 from 12

overs, finds it ironic that the Australian pitch McGrath most dreaded bowling on had provided him with the perfect platform to punish the touring side.

'One thing I realised during my career was that most Subcontinent sides don't like bounce,' he says. 'The WACA is a bouncy wicket and I hadn't seen too many Subcontinent nations dominate on that wicket – they like slower wickets. Glenn always got great bounce, and it is fair to say a lot of his catches carried through to the 'keeper because of his extra bounce. Pakistan didn't have a chance in Perth that day.'

BEST BOWLING BY AN AUSTRALIAN, 1876/77 to 2007/08

9 for 121 – Arthur Mailey v England at Melbourne, 1920/21

8 for 24 – Glenn McGrath v Pakistan at Perth, 2004/05

8 for 31 – Frank Laver v England at Manchester, 1909

8 for 38 – Glenn McGrath v England at Lord's, 1997

8 for 43 – Albert Trott v England at Adelaide, 1894/95

21

Milestones and Magic

A true servant of the game.

West Indies great Courtney Walsh after
Glenn McGrath broke his record for most
Test wickets by a fast bowler

Courtney Walsh lugged his bags through Jamaica's inter-national airport in October 2005 when a stranger – who struck the paceman as appearing wide-eyed and breathless – sidled up and announced Glenn McGrath had just ended Walsh's reign as the game's most successful fast bowler. There was a pregnant pause before the stranger added that the Australian bowler had trapped Brian Lara LBW on the second day of the International Cricket Council (ICC) Super Series Test against the World XI at the SCG. The game, which pitted the world's best players against the world's best team (Australia), was granted Test status and while it promised much it delivered little, because the Australians dominated the game from the outset.

The man continued to babble, saying McGrath was a great bowler and Walsh shouldn't feel disappointed because he'd always be remembered as a champion by his people and cricket-lovers all over the world. Walsh would hear similar sentiments over the next few weeks but he nevertheless felt a strange calm. There was no sense of loss or regret because he'd accepted long ago that the record of 519 Test wickets would fall – after all, they're set to be broken. Now the day had come, the Windies great was happy it at least went to someone he considered worthy of the honour.

'There was no disappointment,' says Walsh. 'In fact, I was very happy for Glenn, just as I was for Murali when he passed the record first [in 2004]. I think Glenn will be remembered as someone who gave his all for his team and country; a true servant of the game and a great fast bowler. I had no problem with him passing me.'

For McGrath, leapfrogging Walsh as cricket's most successful fast bowler was a momentous occasion. He had spoken about it five years earlier when he was asked by the media to name his hopes and aspirations. And McGrath paid homage to the former record-holder at the press conference held at the end of the day's play: 'It's a big honour because Courtney was a cricketer I looked up to and admired,' said McGrath. 'He was a freak of a player who competed for 21 years straight without hardly taking a break.'

When McGrath dismissed Lara for just 5, it was the fourteenth time in ten years he'd fallen to the Australian. The West Indies great looked angry at himself and his anguish was extended when umpire Rudi Koertzen sought clarification from the third umpire 'upstairs', Darrell Hair. As he waited, Lara replayed the shot as if to chastise himself for getting it wrong the first time. McGrath was certain Lara was out. Casting a playful smile towards his old foe, he said, 'I think it's bad news, Brian.'

It took two very long minutes – an eternity for McGrath and his team-mates – for Hair to reach his conclusion. McGrath was right: it spelled bad news for Lara. At the time, McGrath's record suggested he was cricket's big-game hunter, having taken the Test scalps of Mike Atherton on 19 occasions, Lara 14,

Stephen Fleming eight, and Tendulkar and Jacques Kallis six. Shane Warne says the challenge of bowling at the big names brought that extra something out of his lanky brother-in-arms.

'When a Brian Lara or Sachin Tendulkar came in, Glenn wanted to get them out,' says Warne. 'He wanted to be the man to get them out. You can see in most people's eyes they don't want to bowl at the big boys through fear of being whacked, but Pigeon's approach was, "Give me the ball, I want to get him." I always thought it was a wonderful sign that he wanted to test himself against the best, and that was what made him great rather than very good. Glenn wanted to be the man.'

For McGrath, dismissing Lara added to the occasion of entering the record books – and the image of Lara trudging back to the visitors' dressing-room revived a treasured memory.

'The last time I dismissed him before the World game was when I took a hat-trick and he became my 300th Test wicket. It was a long time between drinks. I remember before bowling to him in the World game that I noticed the new ball was dipping around. When Brian came out to bat I decided to throw him the bait immediately; I'd bowl the first two balls across him and then attempt to sneak one back for the "kill". I guess what surprised me most was it actually worked . . . Lara went across his wicket and the ball swung back and hit him in front. I knew straight away he was gone, but the longer we waited for the third umpire to make his decision, the more I thought he might be given not out.'

McGrath admits he became motivated by the fast bowler's currency – wickets and milestones – early in his career. He studied hours of footage at home, hoping to pinpoint weaknesses that could be exploited; and he also visualised bowling at his opponents, a mental exercise that helps to reinforce positively how an athlete hopes to perform under pressure. His team-mates, former skipper Mark Taylor included, smile nervously when they reveal that McGrath could name any batsman he'd dismissed, their number on his personal tally and how he'd dismissed them – like a party trick. Fighter aces in the Battle of Britain could not have had such recall for dogfights and "kills". Although McGrath did find it hard to rattle off randomly the names of, say, his 83rd, 109th and 278th wickets towards the end of his career. Perhaps it was a sign that cricket's big-game hunter really was at the end of his tether.

Stuart Clark, who followed McGrath first at Sutherland and then in the Australian Test team, has a theory that Pigeon didn't start off playing for milestones and goals. Clark bases his assumption on his own feelings as he homed in on his first significant Test milestone ahead of the First Test of 2007 against Sri Lanka – his 50th Test wicket.

'I set milestones when I was younger but I was bad at it,' he says. 'I focused too much on them. I started setting game-by-game goals: do well in this game, move on to the next. I don't think Glenn was milestone-orientated when he started playing. I doubt very much that he would've said, "I'm going to take 563 Test wickets," after his first Test. Maybe that became his driving force in time; you need driving factors and I imagine Glenn realised them.'

Brad Haddin stresses that McGrath's seemingly insatiable appetite for wickets was never done at the expense of the team, be it NSW or Australia. The wicketkeeper used McGrath's final World Cup campaign to illustrate how he was definitely team- and country-first.

'Glenn was a great competitor and a great guy,' says Haddin. 'But he was also for the team, and we saw that in the latter stages of his one-day career when he gave up the new ball to Brett Lee and Nathan Bracken to play a different role. With him, it was always about what was best for the team.'

Nevertheless, when McGrath retired he reflected on his greatest moments:

- 8 for 38 against England at Lord's, 1997
- 8 for 24 against Pakistan at Perth, 2004
- 7 for 15 against Namibia in South Africa, 2003
- First Test wicket – Mark Greatbatch – 1993
- First five-wicket haul in Tests – included getting Lara out – 1995
- Hat-trick against the West Indies at Perth, 2000
- 500th Test wicket at Lord's – a match his family attended – 2005

'Other things stand out, too,' says McGrath. 'I remember bowling to Aamer Sohail at the Gabba in 1995. He had batted really well, and I decided to come around the wicket. He was on 95. I bowled a reverse-swinging yorker and he smashed it through the covers for four. That took him to 99 and I used the first five balls of the next over to try to set him up. On my last ball, it swung well and went straight through him and hit middle stump. Throughout my career I kept the ball up and hit the right area to build up pressure on the batsman. However, when I worked to a plan and it paid off, it just brought me so much pleasure.'

McGrath's résumé boasts everything a fast bowler could ever hope to achieve, with an innings of 61 and a classic catch at Adelaide thrown in for good measure. The only jewel missing from the crown was ten wickets in an innings, though he came close with eight against England at Lord's and eight against Pakistan at the WACA.

'I was lucky to be able to cross a lot of things off. A lot of it was things you could only dream of and hope they happen.

There are special moments and, from a selfish point of view, I treasure them because they were out of the ordinary.

'The hat-trick against the West Indies at the WACA in 2000 was definitely one of those moments. I'd stirred the media before the Test and said Sherwin Campbell would be wicket number 299 and Lara 300. I didn't think about 301 . . .'

On that day, McGrath – operating from the Swan River end of the WACA made famous by his childhood hero Dennis Lillee in the 1970s and early '80s – became only the eighth Australian to take a hat-trick in the Test arena when he sent Campbell, Lara and Jimmy Adams packing. The exclusive club was established over 120 years before when Fred 'the Demon' Spofforth took a hat-trick against England in 1878/79. Hugh Trumble (1901/02 and 1903/04), Jimmy Matthews (twice in one match in 1912), Lindsay Kline (1957/58), Merv Hughes (1988/89), Damien Fleming (1994/95) and Shane Warne (1994/95) are the other members.

'When Brian came in to bat, I knew what I wanted to bowl,' McGrath recalls. 'I'd knocked him over a few times so I decided to bowl the ball straight at the stumps, hit the deck and commit him to play at it. I thought if the ball went away a little bit on the seam he could nick it – and he did – but my heart was in my mouth as I watched Stuey MacGill juggle the ball before finally taking it.

'I was on a hat-trick and, while I was really excited, I decided not to bowl the ball straight at the stumps when Jimmy Adams took strike, because that was just what a batsman would expect. I bowled the ball so it dug in around his ribs. I figured he'd play at it. I didn't think the ball was steep enough, but he fended the ball off the shoulder of his bat and it popped straight up to Justin Langer at short leg. "Lang" was someone you could rely on to do the job and I was bloody pleased he came through again.'

Langer, who prided himself on the loyalty he felt towards his band of brothers, would have willingly lost an arm before dropping what he considered to be a straightforward catch: 'It wasn't a hard catch at all. It was straightforward, very basic. But you don't take them for granted . . . and you don't celebrate until after you catch the ball. But even though there was a lot hanging on it for Glenn, that was one of the easier catches I took.'

While McGrath celebrated his hat-trick, he remembered thinking as he strolled back to field on the boundary how lucky he was that his career coincided with what many argued was perhaps cricket's greatest fielding team.

'The hat-trick was a tremendous achievement; one of those special moments you dream about,' he says. 'But I was so appreciative of the fieldsmen I played alongside. I was so spoiled because the calibre of fieldsmen who played for Australia during my time was brilliant. I had blokes such as Mark Taylor, Mark Waugh, Ricky Ponting, Shane Warne and Matt Hayden in slips. And then there was Ian Healy and Adam Gilchrist, two of the greatest ever wicketkeepers – they helped get me a great deal of my wickets.'

England's vice-captain Marcus Trescothick was the bookies' favourite to present McGrath with his 500th wicket when the bowler marked out his run-up at Lord's during the 2005 Ashes series. British bookmaking agency William Hill listed him at $3.30 as the man most likely to be McGrath's historic dismissal. McGrath's family were all at Lord's, waiting to celebrate him becoming only the fourth man in the game's history to take 500 wickets.

'I was on the verge of getting my 500th wicket at Eden Park against the Kiwis, and even though I was taking a few wickets, some of the blokes were adamant I was holding back to take it at Lord's,' says McGrath. 'One thing about my career is I never didn't try to take a wicket. To be honest, Lord's, the home of cricket, was the ideal place to reach that kind of milestone, but against New Zealand there were three wickets left, and I would have had to take each of them to get 500. I was committed to doing it, but I have to admit I felt relieved when Daniel Vettori hit a catch down towards me and I took it. It was then taken out of my hands and I'd have to try my luck at Lord's.'

Kevin McGrath was sitting among a sea of English supporters when his son lived up to the faith the bookies had placed in him – and McGrath and Langer combined to dismiss Trescothick for 4. Words couldn't describe the pride he felt.

'They're emotional moments,' says Kevin, picking his words carefully. 'I was at the Sydney Cricket Ground when he took his last Test wicket with his last ball. The prime minister, John Howard, was sitting next to me, and I'll never forget how he leapt to his feet and yelled, "What a fairytale finish!" – and he shook my hand. I felt, well, funny . . . as in emotional, because they are special moments. But Lord's for Glenn's 500th wicket was the highlight of my life, it was unreal.

'A friend of ours mentioned to the people around us I was Glenn's dad and the response was incredible. People shook my hand and made a fuss. When he took the 500th wicket, you would have thought I'd run out and taken the wicket for him. People were so happy for him to get the wicket even though he was Australian. The crowd was pleased to see some history at Lord's and their reaction was unbelievable. I'll never forget it. I was in the wrong place at the wrong time and, of course, was stuck in front of a television camera. I did the interview thinking because I was in England no-one back home would see it. But it was played on *Sunrise* the following morning and I copped heaps!

'But seeing Glenn take 500 wickets was amazing. As I tell

people, I'm a failure. I tried to make a farmer out of my son and he became a great cricketer.'

For Glenn's mum, Bev, it was also a highly charged, emotional thing to see her son establish himself as one of the sport's genuine all-time greats. That one dismissal made all the hardship and occasional heartache worth every second.

'He had a lot of knockers, but Glenn became the number one bowler in the world,' Bev says proudly. 'It's because of what Glenn achieved I tell people, "You'll never know how you can go unless you have a go." I was proud to be there to see him take his 500th wicket, it was special. Things like that can pass you by if you're not careful, but I'm happy I was there for the important times.'

McGrath celebrated his 500th wicket by taking 5 for 53 in the first innings of the Lord's Test and 4 for 29 in the second. It was a ruthless display that helped to set Australia up for victory by 239 runs. Shane Warne nominates that effort as one of McGrath's finest moments: 'He was outstanding. It was perfect and I put it up there with his 8 for 24 against Pakistan at the WACA. I can also tell you about the times he didn't get the wickets but bowled just as well. When conditions are in your favour, you should get good rewards. If you bowl consistently over a period of time, you'll have one of those days when things just click and things can go your way. But Lord's 2005, that was one of his best efforts.'

Now he's retired, McGrath expects the day will come when his record as Test cricket's most successful fast bowler will be bettered. But for someone who fought so hard for his initial recognition, then for his selection into bush representative teams and ultimately against the threat of being dropped from the national side, it is surprising to learn that the record is something he'll quite happily surrender.

'The good thing about cricket is the respect we have for each other,' he says. 'It pleased me to learn Courtney Walsh was happy for me when I passed him. I think there is a sense of brotherhood among all fast bowlers because we understand what we have to go through to bowl; it doesn't matter what their nationality or culture is. Courtney and I always got on well. He bowled 21 years straight, and that makes him a special athlete . . . I think I was like him, in the sense that the more I bowled the better I felt, while other blokes needed to rest.

'When you look at the fact Warnie, Murali and Kumble have all taken over 600 wickets, you have to be impressed; they are amazing figures, and when you think of the amount of time it has taken for them to achieve that, it is mind-boggling. When I thought of who might be the next fast bowler to take 500 wickets I pinpointed Shaun Pollock, but he's since retired. Brett Lee is bowling the best I have ever seen him bowl. You can tell he loves being the main bowler. Who knows? Maybe it'll be him. Though bowling at the pace and speed he does is tough, and there's more danger of an injury than someone who bowls at my pace. He might get there; the way he bowled during the 2007/08 season was sensational.

'What I have learned in retirement is that I am very happy with what I achieved. I don't feel as if I have anything to prove to anyone or myself. If seven people go past the record, well, that's fine by me because I'm not attached to it; I hold it but I don't own it. I can't feel jealous – or concerned – if someone breaks the record. If someone is good enough to beat the figure and tough enough to overcome all the hurdles fast bowlers need to contend with, I'll respect them. While it is nice to have these milestones, awards, accolades and even 500 wickets – what I realise is that at the end of the day, it isn't anyone's right to have them. It's a privilege.'

22

Crushing the Kiwis

I asked New Zealand's captain, Stephen Fleming,
and also Daniel Vettori how they felt about
McGrath hitting 61 against them. I really wanted
to know. Fleming said they felt exactly as I would
feel if Glenn McGrath had done that to me,
because 'it doesn't get any worse'. The Kiwis were
hurting . . . but it was absolutely brilliant.

Adam Gilchrist on Glenn McGrath's highest
Test score, against New Zealand in 2004

McGrath was steaming beneath his helmet when he
walked out to join Jason Gillespie against New Zealand
in the Brisbane Test of the 2004 series. Waiting to bat, he had
been ribbed by his team-mates for almost taking more Test
wickets than the runs he had scored – 454 to 477. Adding
to his annoyance as he left the dressing-room was the sight of
Adam Gilchrist bandaging his fingers – in preparation to start
keeping wicket sooner rather than later.

'I always started to get myself ready to 'keep when we were
eight down, just in case there was a quick collapse,' says Gilchrist. 'As soon as the ninth wicket fell that day, I raced down
to get dressed. Pigeon had often seen me as he was putting his

helmet on and he'd mutter, "Thanks for the confidence," when he saw me taping up my fingers. I did it that day at the Gabba and I ended up sitting in my whites for two hours while he batted. It was sheer fun, absolute sheer fun. I couldn't believe it. I put that innings among the two most entertaining hours I've ever enjoyed at the cricket because of the unexpectedness of it all. I don't think anyone could have expected that.'

Ricky Ponting certainly didn't. He had also changed into his whites in preparation to lead Australia out onto the field to bowl at the Kiwis.

'I remember looking up at the clock and it was 3.39 pm, and Darren Lehmann walked into the viewing room and said, "Skip, I think we should bring them in. I think we should declare,"' Ponting told the media after the tail-enders' grand stand. 'An hour and a half and 90-odd runs later, they were still out there . . .'

What the Australians didn't realise was that during his recuperation from an ankle operation in the lead-up to the series, McGrath had spent hours in the nets finetuning his batting skills.

'The boys were having a good old laugh about my runs versus wickets,' he says. 'But what a lot of them wouldn't have known was that when I couldn't bowl, I'd go to the SCG indoor nets twice a week with my trainer Kevin Chevell and he'd feed the ball machine. I'd face 250 a session – 500 a week. I wouldn't have faced that many in a year previously, and I improved. I had always put my time into bowling and focused on getting fit and strong, but because of the ankle I had time on my hands, and my innings was to prove I'd spent it wisely.'

The New Zealanders greeted McGrath to the wicket with some short, sharp bowling intended to rattle him. While the Kiwi attack was without its trump card, Shane Bond, McGrath treated Chris Martin, Kyle Mills, Scott Styris, Jacob Oram and Daniel Vettori with respect.

'I copped a bit of short stuff,' McGrath recalls. 'I was dropped when I was on 11. I pulled a ball right up in the air and Mark Richardson dropped me. I then nicked the ball and Brendon McCullum fumbled it – thank goodness.'

Jane McGrath, who had sat in grandstands all around the world as a loyal witness to her husband's many trials and tribulations as a number 11, could not believe her eyes when she turned on the television and saw her husband 'tonk' the Kiwi attack all over the ground. While her every instinct told her to rush to the ground and make hay while the sun shone, a cricketers' wives' tale wouldn't allow her to budge from her seat.

'The children were with us and because Australia batted – we were always there for when Glenn bowled – I thought it would be too long a day for James and Holly to be at the ground, so I took them to a park near the hotel to let them play,' she says. 'When we went back to the hotel, I turned on the television and Glenn was batting *and* he was getting a few. When they went in for tea I wondered, "What do I do?" I thought I couldn't move because I feared he might get out if I moved. I always remember Sue Porter, Mark Waugh's then partner, would sit there throughout his innings and all the girls did the same. So even though I was watching it at the hotel, I *couldn't* move.

'In the end a friend looked after the kids while a girlfriend and I went to the ground. As I made my way there I kept thinking, "Please don't let him get out!" I just couldn't believe it, and to see Ricky and Gilly's faces in the glass enclosure as Glenn batted was priceless. Their joy was great. For him to be out there with Jason Gillespie was one of my favourite moments . . . it was brilliant.'

Gillespie was laughing his head off the entire time he and McGrath made their stand. He'd advised his mate that if he played straight, stuck to his guns and batted properly, they wouldn't get him out.

'Glenn played every shot and it was bizarre! He was laughing, I was laughing . . . the Kiwis were spewing. We had a great partnership and I spent a lot of my time urging him to get his half-century – and once he reached it, he urged me to mine.

'Seeing him get those runs was really pleasing because I knew how much he wanted to bat. Statistically speaking, his 61 was one of the greatest knocks of all time because, if you think about it, he was averaging about four or five with the bat at the time and he bettered it by 12 times in that innings – 12 times! If you think about it, for someone like Ricky Ponting, who averages 60, he'd need to score 720 to improve it by 12. When you put it into that context, it was a bloody good effort by Glenn.'

'I was very pleased,' says McGrath. 'The hard work paid off. Jason was a good batsman. He was very patient and could get right behind a ball. He didn't need me to yell encouragement for him to get his 50, because I knew he'd have made it even if it took 500 balls. We were having a grand old time, though. We were laughing and cracking jokes – it was one of the most enjoyable times I ever had on the cricket field.'

Gillespie had an extra incentive to score his 50. He'd promised the boys a special treat if he scored a half-century: to 'ride' his cricket bat like a horse. He pinched the idea from the movie *Happy Gilmore*, in which Adam Sandler's character, a golf maverick, has little respect for the game's traditions and stuffiness. Gillespie's pledge, however, had nothing to do with disrespect – it was simply an excuse to give his team-mates a giggle.

'The general feeling was, "Surely he wouldn't do it?" Because it was a bit off the wall,' Gillespie says. 'Adam Gilchrist was left in no doubt I'd do it – I had a mullet, for God's sake – and when I brought up the 50 I thought, "Here goes, giddy up" – and I rode my bat like a horse!'

As McGrath and Gillespie whooped it up, former Kiwi fast bowler Richard Collinge took a very close interest in the knock. Apart from the trans-Tasman rivalry, Collinge had reasons of his own to want McGrath to be sent packing: the Australian threatened to erase his name from the Test record book. In 1973 the tall left-arm bowler had scored an unbeaten 68 when he and Brian Hastings scored Test cricket's highest tenth-wicket stand of 151. After watching McGrath spank the Kiwi attack around the Gabba, Collinge told *The Sydney Morning Herald* he was surprised by just who was challenging his benchmark.

'I always thought someone might get it,' he told journalist Alex Brown. 'But if I was to have picked who that person was, I'm not sure I would've said Glenn McGrath. I've been getting a bit of shit thrown at me today.'

McGrath revelled in the moment. He brought up his 500th Test run with a towering six – the first of his Test career – off Daniel Vettori's bowling.

'It was my first and only six in Test cricket, and from the instant the ball left my bat I knew I'd struck it well. It was so great to watch the ball soar into the air, and the fact that it was off Daniel Vettori made it even more special because he's a great bowler. There was no-one fielding down there and it was such a great feeling. I looked down towards Dizzy and he was smiling and laughing.

'That innings was a career highlight. I knew while I was out there it was going to be something I'd be very proud of, but what I enjoyed most was the reaction of the boys – they were loving it; they were enjoying the moment for me.'

Collinge's record enjoyed a brief reprieve when McGrath fell on 61; his benchmark would ultimately fall to Zaheer

Khan a few weeks later, when the Indian smacked 75 against Bangladesh.

Ponting later described the last-wicket partnership between McGrath and Gillespie (who scored 54 not out) as 'the straw that broke the camel's back', and it all but sealed an emphatic Australian victory. The Kiwis went on to be rolled for 76 in their second innings, of which McGrath took 3 for 19.

'You could just see their whole body language change as the partnership grew,' said Ponting. 'But more than what it did for them was what it did for us. It gave us a lot of momentum and a lot of energy to go out and play well for the rest of the game.'

McGrath lived it up in the dressing-room, telling Ponting he'd scored 10 runs more than Ponting had and that he expected to be elevated above Shane Warne in the order and bat number eight for Australia. He taunted Gillespie by asking him over and over what his highest Test score was until the mullet-haired paceman felt like his nickname – dizzy. While Gillespie's 54 was seven runs short of McGrath's 61, he was to have the last laugh – in 2006 he would score a double-century against Bangladesh.

23

Last Man Standing

Before we even started our mid-wicket chat, Pigeon said, 'Mate, if you want your half-century, start playing your shots . . . NOW!'

Bowler Nathan Bracken on the advice he received from McGrath during the First Test against the West Indies at Brisbane in 2005

West Australian batsman Michael Hussey, who'd scratched and scraped his way to 27 in the first innings of the 2005 Boxing Day Test against South Africa, felt a wave of calm wash over him as Glenn McGrath walked onto the Melbourne Cricket Ground. The World Champions were on the ropes at 9 for 248 against an aggressive South African attack and, while Hussey had only made his Test debut a few weeks earlier, he understood McGrath's arrival at the crease was generally viewed as the equivalent to last rites being read over an Australian innings. As McGrath imitated the warm-up style of the game's ace batters like Adam Gilchrist and Brian Lara by swinging his batting arm around like an old Tiger Moth propeller, Hussey committed himself to attack the Proteas' bowling.

'When Glenn walked out it was initially a case of the pressure being taken right off me,' says Hussey. 'I decided to enjoy it: to take as much of the strike as I possibly could and then tee off. From my point of view, it was very simple: I had to make as many runs as I possibly could.'

Ricky Ponting, who'd plundered 117 runs off the South African attack before being caught by Herschelle Gibbs off Andre Nel, also watched his number 11 saunter to the crease. Minutes earlier Ponting had looked on with impatience – and some mirth – as McGrath had 'stuffed around' to get kitted up.

According to Ponting, McGrath was always late onto the field. 'The second-last wicket would fall and Glenn would just sit there and have a drink, pick his helmet up and muck around with it for a while. Then he'd struggle to put his arm guard on properly – the strap would go here, it would go there – he'd wait to put his pads on, and finally he'd be ready to go.'

The television and radio commentators waxed lyrical about McGrath's batting record, pointing out that he vied for the record number of ducks in Test history, or perhaps noting that Steve Waugh had once said a pair of old stockings had more runs in them than McGrath. There was also the story of the time Waugh – who was within reach of becoming just the seventh Australian to score 200 against the West Indies – had consoled himself, at the sight of McGrath taking guard, that 197 not out in the Caribbean would be something to tell his grandkids. But Australia's so-called 'bunny' had passed the test on that occasion, helping to nurse his friend to a historic double-century. Indeed, McGrath was to criticise Waugh – who was caught in the slips on 200 – for leaving *him* stranded on 3 runs.

When McGrath joined Hussey in the middle, the more optimistic members of the Melbourne crowd pointed out that he'd scored 61 against New Zealand the previous summer – but that hopefulness was tempered by the view of his former team-mate Mark Waugh.

'When I heard he scored a half-century in English county cricket a few years earlier, I almost ran off the road,' laughs Waugh. 'But I was glad to have seen that innings against the Kiwis with my own eyes, because I would *never* have believed it.'

Jane McGrath, who sweated on the day Glenn would raise his bat in acknowledgement of a decent score, would not have appreciated hearing that.

'I never worried about Glenn getting hurt when he was batting, but I used to get really, really cross when people didn't take his wicket seriously,' she says. 'I knew how hard he worked on his batting, and it meant a lot to him – yet it became a standing joke: "Yeah, number 11, he can't bat for toffee." And he could, *he could*, and nine times out of ten he'd be given out when he wasn't. I'd think, "There's another 50 nipped in the bud." It was like, as long as the batsman at the other end got his 50 or ton, don't worry about Glenn, don't worry about the workhorse! And that, as you can see, used to get me really fired up.'

McGrath says he never allowed the criticism – or the jokes – about his batting to upset him. However, Steve Waugh, who coached him for a while, is adamant McGrath was driven to work harder because he didn't like being taunted by his team-mates. McGrath's sole demand was that his critics should at least credit the fact he showed ticker, even though common sense suggested early in his international career that he was in above his head.

While another Australian fast bowler – Rodney Hogg, who played in the late 1970s and early '80s – phoned his wife from the dressing-room to demand she erase from a video a soft dismissal to the West Indies because he didn't want his son to see it and grow up thinking his old man was a coward, McGrath never backed away from the bowler.

'Early on in my career, I didn't wear a chest-guard against the West Indies because it was an ego thing. I didn't want it to look as if I was scared of them. I came around, though, when I thought if I was hit and my ribs were broken I wouldn't be able to bowl. But I was never scared of the ball. The most surprising thing about being hit is it doesn't hurt straight away. I think the adrenaline helps to mask the pain, but you certainly feel it later on. They always left a deep-purple bruise. However, I was prepared to cop that – any time – rather than get out for another duck. My only fear when I batted was of embarrassing myself. People will never understand how bad I felt when I was dismissed for a duck, because I put a lot of effort into my batting.

'But I never worried about criticism, and I know a lot of people had a good laugh about it. While I would've liked some more runs, what I was most proud of as a batsman was that I didn't just go out there and throw my wicket away, and that I didn't look scared. I really tried to get behind the ball, and if need be I'd put my body on the line. I worked hard on my batting and I tried my best.

'I never had a problem picking the ball up. In the early days I just didn't have the defence to get myself set, and I also didn't allow myself time to get in there and play shots. I figured that as the number 11, if I went out and blocked five balls in a row it wouldn't be appreciated back in the rooms, because the feeling would be, "Get on with it, try to get some runs." A batsman has the luxury of being able to take four or five overs to settle in without scoring a run, but if a tail-ender does that it's considered a waste of time. If we look as if we aren't going to score runs then the captain will bring us back in. More often than not, my innings depended on where the team was and what was needed.'

On 26 December 2005, Australia needed McGrath – and Hussey – to hang on for grim life. In the two minutes it took for McGrath to reach the pitch, Hussey had devised a plan – to keep as much of the strike as possible.

'We'll wait until the last two balls of the over, and if they bring the field in I'll try to hit a four and then get a single off the last ball,' he told McGrath with the cool, calm and collected demeanour of a fighter pilot. 'If they leave the field out, you'll have to face the last ball.' McGrath nodded in agreement.

The West Australian batsman lifted to the challenge, responding brilliantly to the simplicity of his own plan. South African skipper Graeme Smith consistently took the pressure off Hussey by moving the field back when McGrath was at the non-striker's end. Hussey exploited the gaps in the field, and, by his own admission, what had been a scratchy knock was transformed into a confident, fluent innings, which frustrated the Proteas. Hussey reached 50 and when he made it to the nineties, the man they call 'Mr Cricket' – because of his renowned and all-consuming love for the game and its stats – tempted fate by sticking to the plan that had worked so well.

'When I reached 96, I thought for a second or two that maybe I should hold the strike until I got my century,' says Hussey. 'But I decided to keep to the plan that Glenn and I had followed – it had worked well until that point. I took a single off the second-last ball of the over, leaving Glenn one to face.'

South Africa's wicketkeeper, Mark Boucher, saw the moment as an opportunity to unsettle Hussey by asking, in an incredulous tone, 'What have you done?'

'Glenn had shown amazing courage and patience,' Hussey says. 'I heard Boucher's comment, but I didn't allow it to worry me. I thought to myself that it didn't matter what happened; we'd scored more runs than people probably thought we would, and we'd had a lot of fun frustrating the South Africans. I was happy we'd put up a fight.'

The tone of Boucher's words wasn't lost on McGrath either, but as a self-proclaimed master of mind games, he refused to allow any negativity to creep into his head.

'I'd helped get Steve Waugh to plenty of hundreds, so I treated this innings as my helping another batsman to three figures,' McGrath says with a grin. 'It's funny, but of anyone in the Australian team, no-one could justify going the tonk quite like me. But when I practised my batting, I'd work on getting behind the ball and playing it. I always felt that when Stuart MacGill was at the crease, he had a license to swing and hit. But over the years, my defence had improved to such an extent I could hang around, especially if there was an established batsman at the other end. As I faced up to the bowler that day in Melbourne, I didn't think about Huss being on 97. I didn't think about the scoreboard or even that we were trying to set South Africa a first innings target to chase. I only worried about getting behind the next delivery.'

And it proved to be an unbeatable approach. McGrath kept his wicket and supported Hussey to his century. Makhaya Ntini finally knocked Hussey's stumps over when he was on 122. The delivery ended a brave innings in which the West Aussie rescued his nation by batting bravely for over four hours, facing 203 deliveries and hitting 14 fours and four sixes. Hussey and McGrath entered Australia's record book for their 107-run tenth-wicket partnership. Australia triumphed in the Test by 184 runs and Hussey's knock secured him the Man of the Match award. Australia's last man standing, McGrath, finished his two hours at the crease on 11 not out, although he was later to lament his score should have been higher.

'We turned down about 10 possible runs, maybe more,' says McGrath. 'I told Mike, "You get your runs everywhere and I'm turning mine down!" Every run I scored during my career was like gold, so it was extremely hard to stand around that day and watch them go begging. On a serious note, though, that was exactly what we needed – and it worked.'

While McGrath was warmly congratulated by his team-mates and their support staff for his last-ditch stand, he finished his 56-ball dig feeling footsore and exhausted, although that wasn't uncommon for him after a 'longish' stint at the crease.

'I'd always feel more buggered after facing ten balls than bowling 20 overs,' says McGrath. 'I don't think people realise how hot it is under the helmet. I always found I started sweating badly after wearing it for just a few minutes – it was like someone had turned a tap on. But I think the reason I'd feel exhausted after batting was the mental side of it, not the physical. In Melbourne that day I had to really concentrate.'

Hussey was well aware of the level of discomfort the fast bowler fought through that day at the MCG, as he recalls: 'I remember during one mid-pitch talk Glenn told me he was feeling tired. He found the level of concentration exhausting and I was also hammering him. But in the next breath he'd settle himself by saying he knew the longer he batted, the less he would have to bowl. He was good value and it also made him happy to see how frustrated we were making the South Africans by hanging around.'

The euphoria McGrath felt having done his job as a batsman at Melbourne was a far cry from the sense of humiliation that weighed down on him 11 years earlier at the SCG, where he was dismissed for 1 in the Second Test of the Australia–South Africa series. McGrath remembers 6 January 1994 as the day of arguably his worst cricket experience. Australia needed an apparently easy 117 runs to win with a day in hand, but fast-medium bowler Fanie de Villiers single-handedly routed the

Aussies by taking six wickets. The Australian batsmen fell like flies: Mark Taylor for 27; Michael Slater for 1; David Boon for 24; nightwatchman Tim May for 0; Mark Waugh for 11; Allan Border for 7; Damien Martyn for 6; and both Ian Healy and Shane Warne for 1.

Craig McDermott, with 29 runs to his name, waited for McGrath to join him at the crease. McGrath walked out slowly, painfully aware that he – and six lousy runs – were all that stood between defeat and victory.

Facing the bowler and sweating profusely, McGrath managed to make contact with the ball and scramble through for a single. But the pressure ultimately swamped him and he fell, caught and bowled to a regulation de Villiers delivery. McGrath was de Villiers' tenth wicket of the match. A sense that he'd capitulated burned in McGrath that day.

'I just wanted the ground to open up and swallow me whole,' he says. 'It was humiliating. I could live with being dismissed by a decent delivery, but to be caught and bowled the way I was that day – a gentle defensive shot – really hurt. Nine times out of ten I would've hit straight through the ball. A lot of people tried to cheer me up by saying it wasn't my fault, that our batsmen should have scored the runs and it shouldn't have been left up to me – but the job was there to be done and it *was* up to me.

'I carried the hurt from that day for a long time because I really felt as if I'd let Australia down. I've always thought the only person I could have any control over is myself. The fact is, I was the last batsman out and, up until that point, we had a chance. Whenever we lost a game or performed poorly as a team, I'd think about what I could have done to help the side. That was one reason why I never had a go at anyone else for something they may have done out in the middle – I realised that no matter what I said or did, I couldn't change what had happened to them. But I could change things about my effort.'

Former Australian fast bowler Geoff Lawson was one of many who argued that Australia's top order – not McGrath – had to answer for the SCG capitulation to the South Africans.

'People who watch the game expect numbers one to 11 to bat, but it's not like that at all,' he says. 'Numbers eight to 11 get picked to bowl, not for their batting ability. Yet with Pigeon, one thing I noticed was that every time he was dismissed during his career, it was treated by him as a shock. It was as if he was saying, "How did I do that?" His head would drop. He'd then shake his head in disbelief and he'd still be standing on the wicket when everyone else was three-quarters of the way off the ground. Everyone had a bit of a giggle about it – but if your number 11 gets out, it isn't his fault you've lost the game. It's normally the first six who should be answering questions.'

Insiders swear McGrath's reaction to being dismissed bordered on psychotic at the best of times. While he didn't quite follow Michael Slater's symbolic act of jamming his bat and pads into a toilet bowl because he was dismissed playing a 'crap' shot, McGrath would put on a performance that Ponting likened to a comedy display rather than drama. The SCG loss to South Africa, however, was the exception.

'We all knew Glenn worked his backside off to improve his batting,' Ponting says. 'He took it seriously – probably a bit too seriously, because when he was dismissed he'd storm into the dressing-room, chuck his helmet, throw his gloves and hurl his bat. While he'd be seething, most of the other guys would hide their heads in the lockers, pissing themselves laughing.'

Jason Gillespie, however, welcomed McGrath being on the receiving end of an alleged poor decision because it normally meant an easier day in the office for the bowlers.

'Glenn was always funny when he got out,' says Gillespie. 'He'd be fuming, saying the umpire got it wrong – in his book he was never out. Most times he'd wear his bowling boots out to bat, and he'd be pacing as he waited to bowl when he got what he called a "dodgy decision" – and he'd go out there and bowl really well.'

While Ponting was one who enjoyed the locker-room banter concerning McGrath's batting, he admits to a genuine admiration for his old number 11's courage – and his willingness to take guard against pace bowlers who threw all they could at him.

'We always have a bit of a laugh and joke about how scared some of these tail-enders must be,' says Ponting. 'But when you sit back and think about it, it must be scary to go out to bat knowing there is no way you can really protect yourself against someone who is bowling at 150 to 160 kilometres an hour. It must be really scary knowing there is nothing you can do if they bowl a good bouncer at you. If you remember that over Brett Lee bowled to South Africa's Nante Hayward in Adelaide a few years ago, when he was running off the wicket to get away from the ball and Brett was following him; that must be terrifying.

'At the end of the day, a lot of the tail-enders don't have the skills to protect themselves. It would be a bit like me getting into the boxing ring with Mike Tyson and knowing he could kill me if he wanted. Cricket looks so easy on television. You can sit back and think, "This game can't be that hard to play." But I remember when some rugby league guys got in the nets – they were all talented athletes in a physical sport – they didn't look comfortable at all when the NSW boys bowled a few bouncers at them. It's brave for blokes like McGrath to show no fear out there even though they must be absolutely shitting themselves. Glenn never got hit badly. He ducked well, but he'd get behind the ball. He wore a few glancing ones off his helmet and he copped a lot on the gloves, but one thing about him is he never showed signs of fear.'

McGrath hadn't always been so wonderfully inept. When he played in the Far West competition for Backwater and then for the Rugby Union XI, he was a slogger who could score a rapid-fire 50 or 60. There was nothing brilliant about his technique, although he did lay claim to owning the best bat in the district – a Stuart Surridge Jumbo, bought via mail order from the Greg Chappell Cricket Store in Brisbane for about a hundred hard-earned dollars. McGrath was attracted to the bat because of its chunky appearance – it looked mean, as if it were crafted to score runs. And it did, though McGrath admits the English willow performed as many air swings as scoring shots.

'I looked at the scorebooks before I moved to Sydney and saw that I normally scored 60 to 70,' he says. 'I'd just go out and play my shots . . . back then defence wasn't my strong point. My first scoring shot might have been to charge down the wicket and slog the bowler over his head for six. You can do that on a synthetic wicket because the ball comes on to the bat better than it does off turf. I was never considered a gun batsman – it was just a bit of fun. Actually, while I have often said my bowling benefited because no-one took much interest in me as a young cricketer, I reckon my batting suffered because no-one ever showed me the fundamentals when I started out.'

Stuart Clark, who played alongside McGrath for Sutherland and NSW before breaking into the Australian Test and one-day teams, is a tail-ender who gained great heart from the way McGrath approached his batting.

'He tried very hard,' Clark says. 'He tried, he tried, he tried – and Glenn actually went from the stage where he couldn't bat to save himself to scoring 60-odd in a Test. He also helped a few batsmen get to their centuries – and if you look at it, he was probably cricket's most improved batsman by the end of his career. I know people look at tail-enders and say it's bad batting, however unless you experience it you can't appreciate how quickly the ball can come at you. It can be scary at times. There are nerves when you're sitting and waiting to bat, and once you get out there you have to overcome those.'

The public, however, was genuinely fascinated by McGrath's batting. Perhaps it was cricket's equivalent to motorists gawking at the aftermath of a car crash, but people just couldn't look away. McGrath's father felt a sense of pride during the 1996/97 series against the West Indies when his son was facing their bowlers at the SCG and the entire electronics department of the Grace Bros store in Dubbo came to a standstill. Staff and customers stood transfixed at the bank of television screens showing McGrath batting. As Kevin McGrath later told his son, the mob wildly cheered each of the 20 runs he scored before lunch as if Bradman himself were batting.

At the SCG that day, the members gave McGrath a standing ovation. On his arrival back in the dressing-room, his peers also celebrated as if he'd scored a century. One of them even chided him for not calling for a second pair of gloves like a 'real' batsman. The reason for that was simple – he didn't own a spare pair. McGrath scored 24 that day – and his 57 minutes at the crease filled inches of newspaper space and commanded prime-time television coverage. It was because of the public's fascination with McGrath's batting that he never lacked interest from bat sponsors. Despite a frustrated Steve Waugh advising McGrath after a not-so-good net session to extort cash from bat manufacturers by threatening to *use* their product, Warren Craig had no problems getting his foot into plenty of doors courtesy of McGrath's batting.

'It was never hard to negotiate bat deals for Glenn,' says Craig. 'They were never lucrative deals, never the ones we hung our hats on financially or commercially. There was always interest in Glenn's batting – you only had to go to a game and listen to the crowd cheer when he went out to the middle. I always thought the concentration of the television cameras, the photographers, the radio and TV commentators when he batted was something else. It meant, however, that there was always exposure when Glenn batted, and that meant sponsors saw value in getting on board. In the 12 years I represented him, there was only one time when he didn't have a bat sponsor.'

Test opener Phil Jaques, who, like Clark, played the occasional first-grade game alongside McGrath for the Sutherland Sharks, says his earliest memories of McGrath are from when he'd make a rare return to grade cricket and he'd badger the captain to name him at number six. He'd point out that batting at number 11 at international level should entitle him to bat in the middle order in grade.

'No matter how hard he pushed, Glenn would end up batting at nine, ten or jack,' says Jaques. 'But it always made me smile to hear him ask the captain to promote him. He was certainly passionate.'

McGrath did, however, convince John Dyson he was a talented batsman when he first played for Sutherland.

'I asked where he batted and he told me he was an opener,' says Dyson with a smile. 'I thought to myself that was a bonus: an opening bowler who could open the batting. I thought the standard at Narromine couldn't have been too great so we put him in at number seven. In his first innings for us, his off-peg disappeared. Unlucky – could've happened to anyone. In his second dig, he batted at seven again and was bowled middle stump. Suspicious. In the third game, I asked Evan Atkins what the chances were of Glenn getting some runs. He replied "none" and was right. His middle peg disappeared. He was dropped to bat at number 11 until he proved himself.'

Steve Waugh, who volunteered to act as McGrath's batting coach, remembers how hard McGrath worked in the nets to 'prove himself' with the blade. While he recalls being terribly underpaid, Waugh at least had a willing student.

'With Glenn it was a matter of getting the basics right, because he was playing a million shots without having a solid foundation,' says Waugh. 'I thought that if Glenn could get his defensive technique right, the attacking shots would follow. My main priority was to try to get his arms working together, and to help that I gave him a mental image. I'd say to rock the baby. The idea was to help him develop the action required to play a straight bat. Every time he dropped his front elbow, I wanted him to have the mental image of the baby falling out of his arms, and I'd reinforce it by saying he'd dropped the baby.

'When he started, he looked as if he was going to get massacred every time he trundled out to the crease, but towards the end of his career he could handle it. He was always up for a partnership; he could hit a couple of fours and he even nailed the slog sweep at the very end. And when he tells you he never backed away – even when the West Indies were hunting him in '95 – he's telling the truth. He may have lacked technique then, but he was never once short on heart; never found wanting for courage.'

Towards the end of the 2007 World Cup – McGrath's last appearance for Australia in international cricket – Ponting used McGrath's absence from the team's dressing-room to answer a question that had bugged him for years: what were the contents of McGrath's batting kit? He couldn't help but shake his head in disbelief when he opened it to find out.

'I knew he'd had the same two pairs of batting gloves for the last four years – I go through 40 pairs a year – but when I rummaged through his kit I found he only had *three* gloves. Pidge had lost one somewhere along the way and hadn't worried about replacing it,' Ponting revealed. 'He had two left-hand gloves, one right. I also noticed he'd broken his bat but didn't have a replacement. I think that summed up Glenn's batting.'

While McGrath defied his teenage tag of 'the boy who couldn't bowl', despite all his hard work in the nets and the courage he showed under fire as a batsman, he never changed the perception of his batting. Throughout his career McGrath's batting was analysed, criticised and ridiculed, yet not even his fiercest critic could ever accuse him of 'dogging' it. He was offered the chance to bat at number three in his farewell Test, when Ponting imagined the sight of McGrath striding out to bat would be greeted with thunderous applause from the crowd. However, Australia's frustrated batsman made his farewell to arms on his own terms.

'Punter,' McGrath said, looking his skipper square in the eye, 'I either bat first or I bat last.'

24

Dissecting the Pigeon

I know as a former fast bowler you have dream days where the ball hits the right spot and you feel as if you've found Nirvana. But you can come out the next day and bowl like a drunk and go for a hundred. Glenn bowled that in-between length that terrorised batsmen; the best in the world. I don't think I can ever remember a bowler doing that . . . you could count the number of deliveries he bowled down the leg side throughout his career on one hand.

Dave Gilbert, former Australian Test player
and CEO of Cricket NSW

'He's not a fast bowler. Glenn McGrath is *not* a fast bowler. Pigeon will get the shits with that, but he's not a fast bowler. Not that he gives you balls to pull, but if you were facing McGrath I reckon if you elected a ball to pull, you could do it; you couldn't do that against Brett Lee, you couldn't do that against Jeff Thomson, Michael Holding or Andy Roberts . . .'

David Hookes' forthright views and his willingness to express his thoughts, no matter how close they cut to the bone – be they about the form of the Australian team or how

McGrath's bowling should be defined – made him a top-line media commentator. He attacked issues without fear or favour, and his comments would invariably evoke public reaction. His antagonistic approach didn't always win him friends, and it could be argued, sadly, that this very trait led to his tragic death in 2004. Hookes was killed after an altercation with a bouncer outside a hotel in St Kilda when a night out with the Victorian players he coached turned ugly.

Hookes was at his 'media best' in 2003 when asked for his thoughts on McGrath. However, after a few minutes of describing how the likes of Lee and Thomson were his idea of 'fast' bowlers and McGrath wasn't, Hookes made sure it was understood he believed McGrath was a great player.

'It's probably unfair to say he's not a fast bowler; he's not an *express* bowler,' said Hookes thoughtfully. 'The quote Martin Crowe gave me one day was right: he's a similar bowler to Sir Richard Hadlee. As good as Hadlee. He's the same style of bowler – medium-fast, fast occasionally; on the spot, can seam it around a bit, a bit of movement . . . just relentless. Martin Crowe is a cricketing aficionado and loves the Australian way of cricket. He's a great friend and understands our style and our approach to life. For him to give McGrath that kind of praise, well, I think it should go on the cover of Pigeon's book.

'He's basically a boring bowler, but we use him as an example to our kids in Victoria and say if you land it on the upside-down saucer 85 times out of a hundred, you'll get 400 Test wickets. It's pretty simple. He's not a fast bowler – he's not bouncing blokes out, he's not slinging them out – he's just getting blokes out. I can't compare him to Lillee or Thomson or Holding and Roberts. John Snow was a bit before my time but he might have been faster. He would've been second change for the West Indies at their best . . . that puts him in the top four bowlers over the last 20 years, and that's probably unfair on Wasim Akram.'

Hookes aimed to entertain whenever he batted – and whenever he spoke about cricket. While McGrath worked hard to perfect his bowling technique from a young age, Hookes lamented that he should've probably spent more time in the nets finetuning his footwork. While McGrath was hailed as the consummate pro and nightmare of the game's best batsmen, Hookes insisted the New South Welshman didn't play 'his' kind of game.

'He is boring,' said Hookes. 'For the majority of Steve Waugh's career, you would not have rushed to watch him bat. At the start you wouldn't have, now you would – if you're talking about entertainment value. If you knew Australia was trying to save the game and Steve was 4 not out overnight, of course you would go and watch him. The same with Pigeon. You wouldn't rush to watch Glenn McGrath bowl. I would rush to take a young fast bowler to watch Glenn bowl – that's different. I'd put my sunglasses on and go to sleep. It [Hookes' view] might look shithouse when it appears in black and white, but that is a huge compliment to Glenn . . . it's not a derogative comment at all. But why would you go to watch Glenn McGrath bowl? He's just going to concede 2.8 runs per over or whatever it is, take his four wickets – two in the first session and two in the last – and then get in his car and go home.'

And yet Allan Border – McGrath's first Test captain and later a national selector – sees a beauty in McGrath's consistency and a genius in the way he compensated for not having the express pace Hookes thought necessary for a bowler to be considered 'exciting'.

'Different people talk about him being a boring bowler,' says Border. 'Okay, Brett Lee is an exciting bowler and Shane

Warne is an exciting bowler because one bowls a million miles an hour and the other bowls ripping leg spinners. However, if you don't have those skilled traits, what do you do? Let everyone belt the crap out of you? Glenn's attributes are that he's six foot five, he has incredible willpower, the ticker to back it all up. But he knows he is not an express bowler so he uses other attributes. He uses his height well and has an unerring accuracy – and that's what playing sport at the highest level is all about. He has enough pace to stick it up a bloke. Unless you are freakishly talented, most people get there by understanding their games well. He does a little bit with the ball, so even on good wickets he can maintain a good attacking field, and that means any half-chance is more than likely to go to hand, so it is like a self-fulfilling prophecy. He keeps the bowling tight, keeps an attacking field and that can lead to wickets.

'If a batsman is doing well and the captain of the fielding team has to spread his men out, there aren't going to be as many catching opportunities and all of a sudden you start to wonder, "How are we going to get them out?" A lot of blokes also looked at what he was doing and at the fields Steve Waugh sets for him, and that expectation gets placed on everyone else. If you get a Brett Lee – and you do like those strike weapons – you sit back and think, "Oh, no! He's going for five an over, bloody hell!" And then McGrath comes on and he steadies the ship. He's a captain's dream.'

Dennis Lillee, who captured the imagination of Border's generation as the consummate fast bowler and is remembered as the greatest, appreciated McGrath's ability not only to bowl with pinpoint accuracy, but also to dig deep and give everything even when he might not have had much left in the tank. Lillee points out a key to McGrath's success was that he exploited his greatest natural resource – his height.

'Glenn was never express,' says Lillee. 'If you're not express you have to have something else, and I'm sure that's the reason he homed in on that pinpoint accuracy. If you're bowling from 130–137 kilometres an hour, you need to be accurate, otherwise the batsmen will get hold of you. The other thing that was helpful was his height, six feet five. When you talk to batsmen about what troubles them most, it's not pace but bounce – awkward bounce and not being able to pick it. Guys like Glenn, Courtney Walsh and Joel Garner all had a big advantage because, apart from being skilful, they came from a different trajectory at the batsman.

'For most of his career Glenn was very machine-like. He could put the ball where he wanted it and he'd play at the batsman, so just when they thought they were on top of him, he had the ability to be able to call upon that terrific bounce that hit the right spot . . . and he developed this amazing reverse swing or the searing yorker that was bowled on the right spot. It didn't have to be super-quick, but in the right spot it was quite dangerous. Glenn also had the ability – and conditioning – to bowl all day, but he could also be very effective whether the ball was new or old.'

Brad Haddin was a fresh-faced 23-year-old from near Canberra when he shaped up to McGrath in the nets for the first time in the summer of 2001. It wasn't so much nerves he had to overcome, but rather the sheer thrill of facing a player he already rated a legend. Haddin was pleased to have survived the first four balls he faced from the man who'd annihilated the likes of Michael Atherton, Brian Lara and Sachin Tendulkar.

'It was one of the first times I was at state training and I remember thinking to myself that I wouldn't get out to him: *I won't get out to McGrath,*' says Haddin. 'The first four balls all landed in the same spot and I let them go. As I congratulated myself for doing so well against McGrath I noticed he smiled at me. He just smiled. The next ball landed in exactly the same spot and I played it exactly the same way. However, instead of going away off the seam, it crashed into my off stump. He'd used those first four balls to set me up and then made me look like a goose. He was world-class – he just asked so many questions of the batsman. His consistent line and length got you in the end.'

Jason Gillespie has a story he already knows he'll share with his grandchildren in the years to come; it's that, statistically speaking, he and McGrath took the most wickets of any opening partnership – and that includes the combinations of Lillee and Thomson, and Lindwall and Miller.

'I will tell them that,' says Gillespie proudly. 'I'll say, "You know that bloke McGrath? I was the joker at the other end." I felt very lucky to have him bowl from the other end because Glenn never went for many runs. I just kept it nice and tight. I always thought I was in with a real chance because, given the choice, I was the one who seemed to be targeted a little bit. The opposition thought they could go me, play more extravagant shots, and I'd get some wickets. He kept it tight and I was lucky to get the spoils.'

Steve Rixon pulls on a pair of imaginary wicketkeeper's gloves when he reflects on what made McGrath a standout in a field where demi-gods such as Thomson and Frank 'Typhoon' Tyson scared batsmen and thrilled spectators by hurling fire and brimstone from long and frightening run-ups.

'Thommo is a good example, because *he* didn't know where they were going, so how could anyone else pick them?' Rixon muses. 'When Glenn bowled, a wicketkeeper could wear a blindfold and he'd know where the ball was going to land. You knew Glenn wouldn't go past what he knew; he was too disciplined for that. And it was effective.

'I remember an instance in Kiwi-land where the New Zealanders looked as if they were a chance to win with Craig McMillan and Chris Cairns in. Glenn bowled seven or eight overs for only two or three runs. He didn't get a wicket – Colin Miller and Shane Warne got them – but Glenn . . . he squeezed them like a sponge. I could see the pressure build up. When I heard the radio commentators describe how well he was bowling, I pulled my car over and watched it on a television on display in an electronic store's window. I had to watch it because they were the Kiwis and I had coached them the year before, and secondly Pigeon was on song – I *had* to see that. I heard the accolades go to the other two bowlers but I stood outside that shop window and clapped Glenn because it was such a great display of bowling. And he put the Kiwis under pressure. At some stage it seemed as if they said, "We need 50 more runs." But before they knew it the game was over. As I said, Glenn just squeezed them like a sponge.'

When Rixon coached New Zealand from 1996 to 1999, he tried to 'humanise' McGrath for the New Zealanders and strip away the veneer of 'legend' that had the Kiwis psyched out before they even stepped onto the playing field.

'He was like a god,' says Rixon. 'The one thing I had to get through their heads was they were not out before they even got there. They just knew he would bowl *there* regularly and it was a case of, "What do I do?" We were at Adelaide and we had to do something different to get the team past the post. Nathan Astle was opening, and I told him I would live with him getting caught behind, caught at slip, caught at deep third man – but he had to take McGrath away from his "spot". I wanted him to take Glenn on. He worked out the one way he could take him on was to take one step down the wicket and hit the ball down the ground. He hit Glenn for six and after nine overs Glenn had 0 for 54. It didn't change the result, though. While we finished with 254, Mark Waugh got a big score. But in terms of Glenn, we had to take him away from his comfort zone and I was happy to lose two wickets to do that. One thing about Glenn is he could – and would – change if you had a bit of success against him. He'd change his line of attack, especially in a one-day game.'

Steve Waugh, who relied upon McGrath to help drag Australia out of the fire on more occasions than he can remember, acknowledges Rixon got it right – and he is both grateful and amazed more batsmen didn't follow Astle's lead and back themselves by taking the fight to McGrath.

'The only time I ever saw Glenn struggle was when someone took him on,' Waugh says. 'Abdul Razzaq did when we played Pakistan in a one-dayer. He knew Glenn had that mastery of line and length, and, in some ways, that was also a weakness, because as a batsman you knew where the ball was always going to be pitched. However, very few people had the ability – or the courage – to take him on.

'If I was the coach, particularly of a one-day side, I would have told the players to walk at Glenn. Kevin Pietersen did it in the last Ashes series and, while Pigeon eventually got him out, I think Pietersen made his point and showed Glenn could be taken down. As I say, it takes a lot of courage to take someone on in Test cricket and to break the mould. However, Glenn also had the ability to think quickly on his feet, he would always devise a plan and he was smart enough to counteract a batsman who attacked him.'

Border, who was one of McGrath's first 'big' scalps when the bowler was a rookie NSW player, says he can understand why batsmen were loath to bat outside their crease to have a crack at the 'human metronome'.

'You start doing that and that makes him a metre quicker,' he says. 'And he has that ability to bowl 130 and crank it up to 135, which starts getting quick. He's very tall, has a great action, he can crank it up a bit, and he was that good you'd expect he'd pull his length back the metre or so the batsman was batting outside of his crease. There are blokes who take him on and he gets frustrated. He set himself high standards in drying up runs and bowling at fields.'

When Geoff Lawson first met McGrath at NSW practice, the first thing he noticed was that the boy from Narromine kept to himself and didn't say much. However, the Test bowler realised that, in terms of the young skinny bloke's bowling technique, there wasn't much to talk about because it seemed sound.

'You couldn't say to Glenn his hands were in the wrong position — because even early on they weren't,' says Lawson. 'With a bowler like Wayne Holdsworth, you'd spend a lot of time talking to him about technique because he had an interesting technique, but with Pigeon you'd notice nothing too bad. There was no need for him to alter his left elbow or tinker with his run-up. It really was a case of, "Just keep going, mate."

'Underrating isn't quite the right word, but the batsmen didn't see someone tearing in at them and being overly aggressive. Glenn just kept getting people out, which was the bottom line. I attend a lot of coaching clinics, and basically, when it comes to judging a bowler, it's not what they look like, how they talk or even what they think — they're measured by wickets and how they get their opponents out. Glenn gave very few clues away about what he intended to bowl. He looked the same no matter if he bowled a bouncer or a yorker, and it was that sameness that made him so difficult for the batsmen to play. The really good batsmen pick up on cues. They're the ones who know Brett Lee is about to bowl a bouncer because he drops his head a little. People analyse video to look for the cues, they stop-frame the deliveries – and the really good players pick the delivery 90 per cent of the time; the tail-enders have no idea. Pigeon revealed nothing. He didn't change anything, and the fact he could make late decisions when he was going to bowl made him even more difficult.

'He got so few cheap wickets. Dennis Lillee was the greatest fast bowler I ever saw. I watched him play and he was my hero. I played alongside him and saw the pain he went through. The quality of players he played against was tremendous, too. However, when I go through Pigeon's record I think it is phenomenal, and when you try to put it in context with Lillee, Glenn played against a bigger base of Test-playing nations and I think it is fair to say Test cricket has been diluted in certain areas. However, he got the best of the best out: Jacques Kallis, Gary Kirsten, Tendulkar and Lara. As a former player, I look at that record and see he got the best batsmen out and in their conditions. I'm trying to put him on the same level as Dennis, but he's just a toehold under him. It's only just a toehold. And he's like Lillee in that he's a champion in every sense.'

David Hookes, who died before he could sit down with McGrath and thrash out his thoughts and theories, had one last comment. 'Glenn McGrath would be the first bloke I will take a young fast bowler in Australia to go and watch,' he said. 'But as a spectator, I wouldn't pay my ten bucks to watch him bowl; I'd prefer to see a bloke try to get someone out with yorkers and half-volleys and the odd run being scored.

'But the compliment I offer Glenn McGrath is this – he'd be the first fast bowler I'd pick on my side.'

25

Mind Over Batter

Any batsman will tell you that going back to face a bowler who has had success against you is a psychological challenge, and so it will be for me this time around. His success, and therefore my lack of it [in 1997], contributed to England's often poor first innings totals and so to our ultimate defeat . . .

Mike Atherton on facing McGrath before
the 1998/99 Ashes series

The torment was over and McGrath watched through what even he thought at the time were 'strangely sympathetic eyes' as Mike Atherton walked for the last time from centre wicket towards the England dressing-room. In his final Test, in 2001, he was caught by Shane Warne off McGrath for a disappointing 9 at the Oval. His head bowed, each of the opener's steps could have been timed to the beat of Chopin's *Funeral March*. It was a significant moment, not only because it'd be the last time the foes would cross swords, but also because it was the first – and only – time the fast bowler ever felt a slight pang of sorrow for his natural-born enemy: a batsman.

McGrath dismissed Atherton six times during the opener's

last campaign – the 2001 Ashes series – and 19 times in total throughout their careers. There were people who joked that 'Athers' must have woken in the dead of the night howling and shaking after his latest nightmare of a wild-eyed pig hunter from Narromine gunning for him. That day at the Oval, though, McGrath thought it was unfair he'd actually dismissed the man who, at his most dogged, made batting look like trench warfare with such a simple delivery.

'I wasn't bowling all that well,' says McGrath. 'I was bowling gun-barrel straight and the ball kept missing the edge of his bat. He just kept playing and missing. I decided to bowl one straight at the stumps and I couldn't believe it when he nicked the ball and it went to Warnie. All I could think to myself was, "How unlucky could a bloke be?" I actually felt sorry for him. Though, that was the only time I felt that way about a wicket.'

Atherton's problems with McGrath's bowling first made headlines during the 1998/99 Ashes series in Australia, when the media noted the spars between the pair normally ended with McGrath standing with his fist raised in the air triumphant. Former England opener Graham Gooch – who opened for his country alongside Atherton – seized on it as an issue, as did Australian skipper Mark Taylor and a host of others, including McGrath, who turned the screws in a public and purposeful manner.

When Atherton spoke of having a back problem ahead of a Test, McGrath vowed to bowl bouncers at him the next time they met. Before a match McGrath would call Atherton his 'bunny' and would do his best to sow seeds of doubt in his opponent's mind by telling the media how much he enjoyed bowling at him.

McGrath talked the talk, but Steve Waugh loved the fact his strike bowler could also walk the walk.

'We all knew Atherton struggled against Glenn long before it was made into something,' says Waugh. 'McGrath bowling at Atherton was like watching a cat stalk a mouse. He knew he'd get him at some stage, but he had fun with him in the meantime – toss him around in the air before putting him away. He had the mastery of line and length and Atherton had that unusual technique where he'd sort of push the ball outside his off stump. You just couldn't do that to McGrath . . . you couldn't offer him any encouragement in the area. The slips fielders knew it would only be a matter of time before something would happen. Glenn also started bouncing him and had Atherton caught out hooking a few times. Atherton just didn't have any weapons to counter what Glenn delivered.'

When Atherton returned to the SCG as a television commentator during the New Year's Test of the 2002/03 Ashes series, he was adamant McGrath's mind games hadn't affected him.

'I can't speak on behalf of the other batsmen, but his comments didn't prey on my mind,' said Atherton in between commentary shifts. 'I didn't take any notice of it; it was all psychological on Glenn's behalf. The truth is every bowler wants to get the opening batsmen out; every opening bowler with the pill in their hand is targeting you.'

England wicketkeeper Alec Stewart supported his old skipper, suggesting McGrath's penchant for targeting opponents was perhaps a ploy by the Aussie to bring out the best in himself.

'I don't know if it is to intimidate people or to spur himself on,' said Stewart. 'I'll give him this, though – he backs himself well, because more often than not he does what he says. However, I don't think it affects batsmen.'

Graham Thorpe missed Atherton's last Test because of an injury; however, he was in the dressing-room after his old skipper was dismissed. During a stint as NSW's assistant coach in 2006, Thorpe relived Atherton's loud sigh of relief four years earlier when he realised his private war with McGrath was finally over.

'One thing I'll say about Atherton is he was never different in the dressing-room before he went out to face McGrath, and that's why I thought he was always a mentally strong player – because even though this bloke had knocked him over time and time again, you wouldn't have known it until his last game,' said Thorpe. 'I remember speaking to him after the match and he told me that as he walked out to bat in the second innings, it felt like a relief to know he was facing McGrath for the last time. For McGrath to have a very good batsman like Atherton come technically undone was incredible. He could constantly get the ball in the right area, and basically he messed up his footwork.'

While there were batsmen who were reputed to have been 'out' before they even faced a delivery from McGrath, Thorpe made it clear he was not one of them.

'I never had that approach to any bowler,' said Thorpe. 'We came up against some good bowlers in that ten-year span I played. Glenn had some good qualities which allowed him to thrive for as long as he did. One was his accuracy – and there were a few others who had it during that era, including Ambrose and Pollock. If they wanted the ball to land in a certain area, they were bloody good at it. They kept the pressure on the batsmen by doing that. I would have thought there were certain batsmen who would've struggled against Glenn. I played against Glenn early in his career, but something I noticed in 2001 when I came back from a broken hand was that he looked quite an imposing figure at the crease. Over the years he built up and he grew stronger and bigger. He also had greater knowledge of what worked well for him, and that helped.'

In time, one of the media's first questions of the international cricket season was for McGrath to predict who would win the series and to name who his bunny was. His responses never failed to make headlines. His list of targets reads like a who's who of big-time cricket, and his success rate – as the stats below indicate – was excellent.

- McGrath pinpointed Brian Lara for extra attention in 1999. By the end of the four-Test series, Lara had fallen to McGrath on three occasions. (The first time McGrath dismissed the West Indian, however, he'd already scored 213.)
- South African opener Gary Kirsten was in McGrath's sights during the summer of 2001/02, and Kirsten fell to him in each Test.
- McGrath fancied Indian skipper Sourav Ganguly's scalp during the three-Test tour of the Subcontinent in 2001. He bagged him twice.
- Sanath Jayasuriya was described by McGrath as the key to Sri Lanka's batting line-up in the 2004 two-Test series in northern Australia, so he had to be stopped. McGrath trapped him twice.
- In 2004/05 McGrath targeted two Pakistanis, Inzamam-ul-Haq and Yousuf Youhana. He dismissed ul-Haq once in the only Test the Pakistan captain played in, and he sent Yousuf packing once in the three-Test series.
- In the 2005 Ashes series McGrath earmarked Andrew Strauss as his man of the moment. He removed him twice in five Tests.
- In McGrath's farewell Test series, the so-called 'Ashes redemption series', he dismissed England star Kevin Pietersen three times in the five Tests.

'The mind was something I knew a bit about,' says McGrath. 'But the longer I played, the more I developed that side of it, and I realised how powerful it is. The difference between those days I bowled well and those I didn't was if I didn't back myself. And that's why I talked it up in the paper and it is why I targeted players – it was all part of the psychological game. And it is sometimes hard to back yourself during a game. You might feel tired, or there might be a niggling injury. On other occasions you know what you should bowl, but do the opposite – and that always hurt. People have their reasons for not backing themselves. I backed myself because I hated the idea of walking off the field and feeling as though I didn't have the faith in myself.

'The other thing I did, apart from visualising success, was I'd watch tapes of myself taking wickets because it was positive reinforcement. It worked, too. I stopped for a little while until Jane said she remembered when she first came to Australia I often watched my wickets. I started doing it again and it seemed to help. I guess cricket is such a confidence sport that anything you can do to reinforce positive thoughts can only be a benefit.

'I was also lucky in that I can't ever remember having a bad dream about bowling. When I dreamt about cricket, I just bowled the ball I wanted to and I either found the batsman's edge or bowled him out. Sometimes in my dreams I'd bowl the entire team out . . . but I was also fortunate in that I never had any trouble shutting down of a night during a game. Some blokes can't switch off, but I could. It didn't matter if I was batting, either; it wasn't as though I lay awake all night worrying about what awaited me the next morning.'

Express bowler Brett 'Binga' Lee, as he read the paper before the start of a Test series, would see who McGrath had decided to target and learn that Australia was going to win the Ashes, or any other series, in a whitewash. He'd smile and shake his head, but one thing he appreciated about McGrath early in his career was that, like the postman, he always delivered.

'As a team, we found it pretty funny,' says Lee. 'But we also knew there are players out there who risk getting egg on their face by making big statements because they can't back it up. Glenn thrived on making bold predictions, but he could come through. If he said he was going to knock Brian Lara over for 10 runs, well, nine times out of ten he'd do it. He put the pressure on the batsman and not himself. If a bowler said he was going to do this or that and he gets hit around, he'd wish he never said anything to the press, so it's not going to work for everyone. However, it worked well for Glenn and he did it very well. Was the way he dominated Atherton and Lara mental? Big time. It helps, though, when you're bowling at a good pace; when you're as tall as Glenn and have a perfect wrist, especially when bowling at the left-handers. He enjoyed the challenge and I think it put the pressure on the batsmen and not the bowlers.'

Team trainer Jock Campbell, however, remembers muffled groans from some players when they heard McGrath had predicted Australia would waltz undefeated through a series. Yet Campbell always considered McGrath's confidence a strength.

'You'd hear the players read that Pigeon had predicted a 5–0 whitewash and they'd say, "Oh no, not again!"' laughs Campbell. 'He was right about those things more times than not, and I think it intimidated the opposition – and if that is ever proven to be the case, then he has done his job, because international sport is all about confidence and competitiveness.'

That was the view McGrath's bowler partner Jason Gillespie subscribed to. 'I didn't ever feel pressure when Glenn made his big statements,' he says. 'He was asked how many were we going to win by. What does he say? We're not going to win? We're going to lose 3–1? We'll draw? He'd say 5–0, 4–0, however long the series was scheduled to go for. It was Glenn's little way of saying he wasn't going to give away a game – and if you look back on his predictions, he did all right.'

However, McGrath also admits one reason why he was never scared to back himself or make the bold predictions was the calibre of his team-mates.

'I was lucky to have played in an era where Australian cricket was so strong. Every time I walked out on the field, I only had to look at the sides I was in and there were guys like Mark Taylor, Shane Warne, Steve Waugh, Adam Gilchrist, Ricky Ponting, Matty Hayden. Walking alongside them gave me a lot of confidence, because not only did we go out there to have fun, but the thought of losing never entered our minds. We went for the win from ball one – I couldn't help but to think we'd win every series in a whitewash.'

McGrath's foray into the power of the mind extended beyond making his opponents doubt their own ability by airing his thoughts – like a hypnotist in a public forum – on what he considered their weaknesses to be and how those would lead to their demise. When others tried to turn the tables on him and say he was getting old or was too slow, McGrath had too solid a foundation of self-belief to be rattled. After all, that faith in himself had been formed when he was a teenager who had to defy the popular opinion that he couldn't bowl.

'The two things that always held me in good stead were that I knew my game well and I knew myself very well. It helped for me to be successful, knowing who I was; knowing how I worked best and always looking for ways to improve and learn. I always thought I was fairly stable emotionally and mentally. My highs were never all that high and my lows were never all that low. I was always controlled – but other guys had massive highs and the downside was they suffered terrible lows.

'They say we only use between five to ten per cent of our brain capacity, so we really don't know what we are capable of. In time, and I guess it'll be a long time, we'll do amazing things by harnessing the power of our minds. I believe you can heal yourself with your mind – that is very real.'

McGrath put his belief into practice when he injured his ankle and needed a quick recovery to galvanise Australia's bowling attack during the 2005 Ashes series. He had been given by Justin Langer a book to read titled *Zen in the Martial Arts,* which taught Zen principles to open potential sources of inner strength. In its pages McGrath read such things as: 'The mind of a perfect man is like a mirror. It grasps nothing. It expects nothing. It reflects but does not hold. Therefore, the perfect man can act without effort.'

However, of all the book's wisdom, the story that hit home for McGrath concerned the time when its author had used his mind to help heal some horrific injuries as he lay in his hospital bed.

'Before he would go to sleep he'd imagine teams of little men going inside his body to work the overnight shift to help him heal,' says McGrath. 'The concept was while he slept these little blokes would repair the damage. And when he'd wake up an imaginary siren would sound in his head and that was the signal for them to stop work and he took over. It seemed such a great concept, so I applied it – and it worked. The philosophies in the book ring true and they apply to so many areas of life. It was a powerful tool for me. It's about the state of mind and that we are all a product of ourselves. We can blame everyone else for what happens in our lives, but I think we all need to take responsibility for our actions and also for who we are and how we feel, because ultimately we are the only ones who can change it. I think it's true some people aren't happy unless they are unhappy. They whinge and moan about how much they hate things, yet the fear of changing their environment scares them. It comes down to their insecurities, or they lack the courage to change. Basically it comes down to backing yourself. In the book it says the mind is like a fertile garden and whatever you plant in it, be it negative or positive, is what will grow and flourish.

'So be careful about what you think.'

26

Body of Evidence

> He could have problems later on in life, but Glenn
> is one of the lucky ones because he got out of it
> pretty well. He's had ankle problems and the
> odd injury but his back seems good, though his
> shoulder seems dodgy. All things considered he's
> been a professional sportsman for 15 years and
> played over 100 Tests; he's lucky to have gotten
> out of it the way he has.
>
> Jock Campbell, former
> Cricket Australia conditioner

Fitness expert Kevin Chevell stood under a gum tree with his mate Greg Fitzgerald at Caringbah Oval in 1993 watching as the state's best talent contested a 'possibles and probables' warm-up game a few weeks before the Sheffield Shield season started. The one player who captured his attention was a bowler whose skinny frame was grossly out of proportion with his height. Unlike judges before him, Chevell instantly recognised something special in the kid's simple action, even before he dismissed NSW opener Steve Small, and it crossed his mind that there was greatness just waiting to be tapped.

Fitzgerald, a stalwart of the Sutherland club, said the bowler was Glenn McGrath, a country kid whose potential had recently been recognised by the state selectors because they'd included him in the NSW train-on squad. Fitzgerald added that McGrath played for the mighty Sharks and was a nice, quiet young bloke who seemed determined to succeed.

'All I said to Greg was if I ever got my hands on McGrath, I'd make him the best there ever was,' says Chevell, who was then the personal conditioner for Test skipper Mark Taylor and Steve Small. 'I was impressed by his approach, his delivery and his follow-through. It was something you could work on. But what also stood out was he was terribly underweight. I was concerned the rigours of fast bowling would tear him apart.

'I thought of a bowler from a few years earlier, Bruce Reid, a great talent but his body just couldn't withstand the punishment of fast bowling. Glenn looked as if he could have been susceptible to the same problems: constantly prone to injury because of the forces that go through a fast bowler's body. I thought if I could get hold of that kid . . . I would build him up so he'd be so strong and so powerful, and I'd combine that with his unique height and economical bowling action to make him the best ever. I thought I could teach him to be unbreakable and unbendable in mindset so he could fulfil what I thought I saw in him – being as good as, if not better than, Dennis Lillee.'

Chevell was a child prodigy. At 13 he was selected for Bankstown to bowl fast alongside the likes of Test bowlers Jeff Thomson and Len Pascoe. However, he took a detour on the road to cricketing stardom to pursue his other passion: motorcycle racing. He eventually returned to the game and played first-grade in Sydney and then in Perth, where he enjoyed one of his career highlights – clean-bowling South African batsman Barry Richards in a Western Australian Cricket Association club match. Richards, who had decimated the Australian bowling attack during their 1970 tour of the Republic, was so impressed by the delivery that he made a point of shaking Chevell's hand for what he called 'a job well done'.

Chevell knew about fast bowling and about fitness – and while he knew he could make McGrath a household name, he wasn't one for chasing people.

Two years passed before the pair met, and Chevell described their meeting as a match made in cricketing heaven. McGrath had just conquered the West Indies on the 1995 tour of the Caribbean and Geoff Lawson had invited Chevell to train the NSW squad during the off-season.

'At the end of the first session, this quiet bloke came from the back of the group and asked if I could help him,' says Chevell. 'It was Glenn, and when I asked what he was prepared to do to fulfil his dreams he gave the right answer: whatever it took.'

Chevell gave McGrath two weeks to prove he was made of the right stuff – and it was no picnic. He was pushed so hard in what he now laughingly refers to as 'torture sessions' that he found it hard to walk, his muscles screamed for mercy that was never given, and there were times when he was physically sick. But he didn't give up, and that impressed Chevell. At the end of the fortnight's trial he promised McGrath he had the knowledge and the will to make him the greatest fast bowler in the world, but whether he reached that height was up to McGrath.

'I told Glenn I was prepared to do whatever it took to get him there and he could call on me at any hour,' he says. 'That was the agreement. And over the last 12 or 13 years I spent thousands of hours with him.'

McGrath embraced the teachings of Chevell and saw immediate results.

'Kev trained me so hard – pushed me – that I was happy when the international season started because it gave me a break from him, because his training sessions were designed to be much worse than anything I'd experience in a cricket game,' McGrath recalls. 'What Kev taught me was that when you train hard you get stamina, you get strong and gain fitness – but the main benefit is the confidence it gives you. He believed the people who succeed consistently and at a sustained level in any field were those who believed in themselves, because they were the ones who kept it together when the world fell apart around them. That held me in good stead and I was lucky to get his messages in the early days of my career. And he became a trusted mate, someone I respected and someone I listened to, because when Kev spoke I knew it was from the heart.'

Chevell's first concern was to address McGrath's weight. In 1995 he hit the scales at 77 kilos. The trainer knew only too well that cricket is a sport potholed with stories of promising fast bowlers who snapped like dry twigs because they lacked the strength for the relentless job of bowling day in, day out. And he didn't need to look too far for a program to help add bulk to his charger.

'I was like Glenn when I was a kid; I had a lot of talent but I was very, very skinny,' he says. 'I was forever fighting injuries, mainly back problems, and I couldn't accept the fact I couldn't beat it or get around the problem. I was playing for Balmain at the time, and Greg Fitzgerald suggested I do weights with him during the winter because I was too skinny.

'I went to Western Australia, and in my second season there I vowed I'd do something or kill myself trying. I promised myself I was going to be unbendable, unbeatable and unbreakable and that I was going to pick up two yards of speed. I didn't really know what I was doing then – I do now – but I had lots of enthusiasm. I trained every single day for the 180-odd days in between the end of the season and the beginning of the new one, and I picked up two yards of pace. I was 12 kilos heavier, I was faster and fitter, and I had a self-confidence I'd never had before – and I carried that well. And that was when I realised there were more benefits – self-confidence and belief – to training than just physical ones.'

Chevell's plan to pack bulk onto McGrath went against conventional thinking, because it challenged the belief that the more weight and muscle a fast bowler carried, the greater the risk of his losing his natural bowling action and skills. Chevell thought the theory was wrong – and he believes he has proved his point by adding 20 kilos to McGrath's frame over the 13 years they trained together, which helped, not hindered, him.

To achieve their aims, Chevell placed McGrath on a program that he said would not allow him to make good progress like most fitness regimes, but would ensure 'unbelievable' progress. He introduced McGrath to super-foods and insisted he rest well throughout the day, because without that Chevell said no athlete would last under him.

'A lot of times throughout his career he would come to Penrith and stay with my wife and me for many days at a time,' he says. 'We would do our exercise training a couple of times a day, and I would feed him up to five times a day around the clock. He'd sleep during the day and in the evening. I would set an alarm for 2 am, get up and make up a food supplement with oats and eggs and other ingredients, and I'd walk into his bedroom, wake him up, get him to quickly drink or eat it, and he'd go back to sleep. The idea was to help him consume food that would help him to grow and recover more quickly. No matter what I asked him to do – it didn't matter how distasteful it might have sounded to him at the time or how much he might not have wanted to do a particular task – Glenn would do exactly what was asked of him . . . and that sums him up.'

The time McGrath spent with Chevell prepared him well for the rigours and challenges of spearheading Australia's bowling attack for 13 demanding years. The training he was put through was so much tougher than anything he'd experienced in the middle of the cricket oval – and the mental challenge to hang in and complete Kevin's drills under duress taught him how to react to stressful situations. It provided McGrath with an overall toughness and ability to slog through nightmare scenarios when others might have found it so much easier just to curl up.

'It's having a plan and knowing what you want to achieve,' says McGrath of the mental challenge. 'You really have to try to stick to that. It also helps to get into a routine and just keep bowling and bowling. I wore a heart monitor a few times and the data showed it was in the 160–180 beats per minute range. I always thought real fitness was not how fast or far you ran but how quickly you recovered. At my peak fitness I was able to bowl longer spells and my recovery would allow me to still be effective in my second and third spells.

'The one day that springs to mind is the 1999 Test against the West Indies in Barbados because I bowled 17 overs straight. I just kept going. Whenever Steve Waugh said, "This is your last over," I'd take a wicket and get a few more overs. Courtney Walsh and Brian Lara got the Windies home that day, but I bowled 17 overs straight and while it was effective, Justin Langer said I looked skeletal I was so gaunt. But I actually felt fine . . . I was a bowler and I was happy to bowl as often as possible.

'And Jane helped me realise that whatever pain I thought I might have been in playing cricket, it was nothing compared to what other people endure. Sore feet, bad back or whatever didn't compare at all to her battle. People talk about "heroics" on the cricket field, but I know what real heroics are because Jane is that. She was the reason no injury ever seemed as bad as what it may have appeared.'

Brett Lee, who assumed McGrath's role as the spearhead of Australia's pace attack when the Pigeon retired, attributes McGrath's ability to plough through tough workloads – such as his marathon 17 overs in Barbados – to his strong muscles and mind.

'He was so mentally tough,' he says. 'There were times when he was suffering pain in his back or in his ankle but he somehow switched it off. He'd make a joke about it and imagine his little workers inside his body at the injured spot repairing the damage. He believed in that and it worked for him. But he was such an amazingly mentally strong person.'

To be a fast bowler, a person must have an incredible pain threshold, the stamina of a camel and a masochistic streak, because while they might end the day footsore, muscles throbbing, a big toenail hanging off and a lower back that won't stop aching, they return the following day and commit themselves to sheer hell all over again. Jock Campbell describes the fast bowler's lot as one of the most unnatural things the human body can do.

'Fast bowling is so unilateral, it is so unbalanced,' he says. 'Every time McGrath bowled he'd come down on his front foot at over ten times his body weight. When you slow that down to 250–500 frames per second on the cameras that the biomechanical people have, you can see the force that goes through the ankle and see how unnatural it is. The wear and tear on the knees and the back is also highly unnatural – and it doesn't matter how strong or fit or even how diligent the bowlers are, they always bowl with some form of injury because of their workload. Glenn was very strong – he was taught how to train hard by Kevin Chevell, and he liked to train hard in the gym and push himself.

'My job "in season" was to maintain the players' fitness, and in Glenn's case we looked after his strength and power, his speed around the field. Aerobically he was terrific and that helped him bowl all day. The heat is normally the factor that determines how the bowlers perform. While I had no doubt Glenn could have bowled all day, the heat and the humidity make it difficult for anyone to do that. The soreness and the pain stems from the fact they always carry some sort of injury because of the stress on their body. The idea of the recovery session – swimming in a pool, taking ice baths and stretching – is designed to relieve their soreness. Glenn was diligent and adhered to those requirements. He had to – it was the only way he could survive because of the demands on him.'

One year after his retirement, McGrath's early-morning reminder of his cricket career is a limp, courtesy of what he describes as a 'dodgy' ankle. However, he appreciates that there are many former fast bowlers much worse off than him.

'Because I was a front-on bowler, and not a side-on, I used my stomach and side muscles,' he says. 'While that saved me from the stress fractures guys like Dennis Lillee and Brett Lee suffered, I tore my rectus abdominal, my inner costal and my side muscles – the "grunt muscles", as bowlers call them. I had a scan on my back a few years ago and the team's physiotherapist Errol Alcott called it "pristine", because it looked as if I had never bowled a ball before in my life.'

McGrath attributes some of his back's bone strength to good genes. During an osteoporosis-testing program which tested his paternal grandparents regularly over many years, his grandmother's bones were found to be twice as strong as what is considered normal. 'I think that was passed on to me. I think the fact my action was stress-free and my body was aligned also helped me.'

Despite inheriting strong bones, McGrath did suffer wear and tear from his role as the workhorse of the Australian Test side.

'You don't think about the future and the effects fast bowling might have on your body – you just bowl and push through whatever is bothering you at the time. I accepted years ago that there really is no preventative measure from future aches and pains, so I told myself I'd just deal with any problems down the track. However, my shins and knees are good, hips are fine . . . The only problem, apart from a few small tears, was my ankle – and again, that was only due to the workload and the stress of repetitive bowling.'

Chevell fulfilled his promise to chisel McGrath into an unbreakable, unbeatable and unbendable dynamo – and plenty would agree he fulfilled his other vow to make McGrath the best there ever was. McGrath is adamant he could never hope to thank Chevell enough for his behind-the-scenes work, done well away from the limelight and the glories, though Chevell begs to differ.

At Christmas in 2007 McGrath arrived at the Chevell household with a large cardboard box cradled in his arms. When it was opened the hard man choked up with tears. Without a word being said, they embraced. In the box was a glass display case that contained one of McGrath's most prized possessions – his much-loved baggy green cap, the ultimate trophy of any cricketer in Australia. McGrath had engraved on a plaque his heartfelt thanks for all Chevell had done. The fast bowler dismissed his trainer's stream of protests about not being so bloody stupid as to give away what should be an heirloom for his children. McGrath and Jane had spoken long and hard about the gift, and both agreed it was a small way in which to let Chevell know the great impact he'd had on the bowler's life.

'I have no doubt the sessions with Kevin were the reason Glenn performed for as long as he did,' says Jane.

'It was also the best way to express what I feel without having to say too many words,' explains McGrath. 'But Kev is one of the reasons I succeeded . . . he showed me the way by strengthening my body and mind.'

27

Spin + Seam = Lethal

I was very lucky in a way to have played against
Warne and McGrath when they started their
careers because I didn't just play the bloke. I knew
I was up against two fine bowlers, and after a while
you could tell they were great. Their longevity was
great, the accuracy was always there. They could
be containing bowlers if they needed to be. They
weren't too proud to sit in and wait for you to
make a mistake . . .

Graham Thorpe, former England batsman

In the first three years of his tenure as skipper of Australia,
Ricky Ponting slept soundly at night, safe in the knowledge
that regardless of whatever might happen on the field, he had
as his backup Test cricket's most lethal combination: Warne
and McGrath. Their skill and statistics had provided similarly
comfortable mattresses for Ponting's predecessors, Mark Taylor
and Steve Waugh. In the 104 Tests Pigeon and Warnie played
together, they captured 1001 wickets – 513 of those to the
skill and cunning of Warne's leg spin, and 488 to McGrath's
relentless line and length. And in those 104 Tests they celebrated
71 victories and suffered only 18 defeats. Waugh believes they

possessed an 'X-factor' that allowed them to read an opposing batsman's body language and to zero in on his vulnerabilities. For his part, Warne believes Australia was always in control of the moment – and the game – when he or McGrath had the ball.

While the pair are as far apart in manner and appearance as humanly possible – Warne was beset by a series of off-field controversies, had a shock of bleached blond hair and wore an earring; McGrath stalked wild boars for fun, boasted a no-nonsense haircut and desired a quiet life – they 'clicked' as both friends and team-mates, and Ponting watched on with a sadistic delight as the world's top batsmen suffered at their hands.

'You could see the sweat drip off the batsmen, especially if Shane or Glenn had a good strike-rate against them,' says Ponting. 'If McGrath bowled to Michael Atherton, for instance, you just knew Atherton would be absolutely shitting himself. You just know there are certain match-ups when you have a Warne or McGrath in your team. Before we played India in the 2006 ICC Champion's Trophy, I hadn't used Glenn to open the bowling in the tournament, but because I was aware of his great record against Sachin Tendulkar, I knew Tendulkar wouldn't be too keen to bat against him. I let Glenn take the new ball and, sure enough, he knocked Sachin over in the first three overs. I was incredibly lucky, as was everyone else who played with those two guys. Now we have to replace them and that won't be easy.'

During the last Test of the 2001 Ashes series, Warne was fielding at first slip at the Oval. He smiled to himself as he watched McGrath trudge back to his mark to bowl another ball at Atherton, who was playing his final Test. The Englishman's body language against McGrath, allied with his hesitant and clumsy strokes, brought to Warne's mind the idea of water torture. If anyone looked as if he was being slowly but surely sent around the bend, Warne thought, it was the English opener.

'It was the torture technique, the drip on the forehead,' says Warne, recalling his old bowling partner's nagging line and length which brought the best in the business undone. 'It was relentless. Glenn would just keep dripping away. He had an uncanny knack of working batsmen out. Every bowler has a plan, but you need to be able to execute it. Glenn didn't do that just once or twice – he did it so many times, and he changed the face of the game doing it. From first slip I had one of the best views in the house to watch him work the batsman over, and it was brilliant to watch. The power of positive thinking when you have the wood on a batsman can have amazing results: he'll fall to a magnificent catch; the ball that has done nothing all day will suddenly keep low and shoot along the ground or it hits back further than anyone else's; the fifty-fifty LBW decisions seem to go your way. It's amazing what that confidence can do for a bowler.'

What was also amazing was watching the prey's confidence crumble in the presence of his hunter. At the Oval McGrath bowled his next ball and Atherton edged it straight into the waiting hands of Warne. It was the nineteenth – and final – time McGrath would skin his bunny.

Warne says the pair bowled against their opponents so often that they came to know exactly where to bowl. 'The trick was knowing how to execute the plan on the day. I can't recall too many days when I thought to myself that Glenn didn't look too good. As a bowler, you could always sense when a batsman wanted to take the challenge to you, and that was when you had to rise to the occasion. There weren't too many days when

I thought a batsman had got the better of Glenn. There were the occasional days, but overall there weren't too many. And he was very honest. If Pigeon bowled rubbish he'd tell you so, and that says a lot about his character.

'But we had a great partnership. It wasn't as if Glenn and I sat down and spoke about it all the time. We really didn't have to say much; we just knew if I was bowling at one end and he was at the other, something would happen. It might've been a run-out because of the pressure we'd built up, or when someone came on to replace us they'd get a wicket straight away. If a game was getting away from us, I thought we grabbed control back when Glenn and I were brought back on.

'I put a lot of my wickets down to having Glenn McGrath bowl at the other end. I was very lucky to have someone with such accuracy and high concentration levels. Something always happened. I loved bowling with Pigeon. As a friend, he has been very loyal to me – we'll be lifelong friends. Our families get on great and he is a genuine guy, an amazing bloke who has overcome so much in his private life, with Jane, to do well.'

McGrath looked upon Warne as the man born to be Australia's cricket captain. But when circumstances didn't allow that to happen, Warne received what McGrath considers the next best accolade: being considered by his peers as the leader of Australia's bowling attack, the go-to man for answers, advice and inspiration. And Warne was not only proud to carry such a responsibility, but he lifted his bowlers with him.

'I believe there are only two men who have had a real effect on cricket – Bradman and Warne,' says McGrath. 'You might throw Sachin Tendulkar and Brian Lara in the mix, but I think Warne had the bigger impact. He has a passion for the game. You look at what he has done for Hampshire in English county cricket – he's turned the place around.'

And just as Warne feels lucky to have bowled with McGrath, so McGrath considers himself blessed to have bowled at the other end from Warne. McGrath also believes that without Warne he wouldn't have taken as many wickets as he did, and that Australia wouldn't have won as many games as it did during Warne's reign.

'When Australia needed a breakthrough, he'd come through time and time again. We were opposite bowlers, but we were the same in that we could build pressure. People talk about seeing the sweat drip from the batsmen and how they'd sigh with relief when we were taken off – only to play a rash shot and get out against the new bowler because they wanted runs. The pressure was our strength. And while people talk about great bowling partnerships they normally think about fast bowlers working in pairs, but the reason Warnie and I complemented each other was we had good control over the ball.'

Steve Waugh highlights another benefit of the Warne–McGrath partnership, one which helped Australia to dominate the world stage: their bowling partnership was so powerful it effectively allowed an extra batsman to be selected in the Aussie side. That Australia needed only four bowlers when Waugh was at the helm was due to the unique ability of Warne and McGrath not only to attack the batsmen, but to contain the flow of runs. In other words, the two of them could do the job of four men.

'I was lucky because [in both] I had two bowlers in one,' says Waugh. 'They could tie up an end and no runs were scored off them, yet they were capable of taking wickets too. They were both attacking and containing bowlers, and that is very rare. That is why we only needed four bowlers – because we really had six with Warne and McGrath doubled up. The difficult part of the job was ensuring they were happy with the amount of bowling they were going to get, or the ends they bowled from. Actually, the biggest problem was taking the ball off either of them to give someone else a chance! It was sometimes difficult to do that when the tail-enders were in; Glenn and Shane had done all the hard work beforehand and that was sometimes hard to manage. But in saying that, there were far more positives than negatives with those two.

'Glenn just wanted to bowl all the time. He'd never tell you if he was struggling. Every time I'd say enough, he'd ask for just one more go, and it was very hard to say no. Ninety-nine times out of a hundred I'd give in and he'd take a wicket and get another three or four overs on top of that! Some blokes might feel unlucky bowling with McGrath, because when he'd come on for a spell it'd look innocuous but he'd get a wicket. The aura he and Warne exerted meant they put pressure on the batsman straight away. It was as if they'd say, "Oh no, it's Glenn McGrath – or it's Shane Warne – so this is going to be hard." And all of a sudden they'd get a wicket.'

In October 2007, Warne's and McGrath's enormous contribution to cricket was acknowledged by the Sport Australia Hall of Fame's prestigious 'The Don' Award. As well as high achievement, the Don recognises the traits of respect, dignity, courage and sportsmanship, criteria laid down by Sir Donald Bradman shortly before his death. The pair's citation acknowledges the enormous amount of work undertaken by their respective charities, the McGrath Foundation and the Shane Warne Foundation (which raises money for causes that range from homelessness to sick children).

McGrath is proud that the ties that bind him to Warne go much deeper than past cricket glories, awards and time spent together forming strategies that rattled both the egos and the wickets of the world's batting line-ups.

'Warnie is an amazing guy,' says McGrath. 'How he is viewed for what he has done off the field is up to individual opinion, but I stand by him. We've spoken more than ever since we retired and we plan to do plenty more good things together. It's funny: he *is* larger than life and he did me a favour by taking a lot of the limelight off me when it came to the media. He revelled in it and I did it because it had to be done.

'The last cricketer who was like Warnie was Keith Miller – and maybe it's a generational thing, but Miller's so-called playboy antics were celebrated, but Shane copped grief . . . Shane is my friend and those of us who really know the bloke and what he is about can't help but to love him.'

For Warne, taking the skinny newcomer with the nerdy haircut under his wing in 1993 when he first made the Australian team has had numerous rewards as well.

'It has been an absolute pleasure to play with him,' says Warne. 'He was an absolute pest around the changeroom. You notice those things when you're away from the game. When we played and he annoyed us you'd think, "McGrath, can you piss off for a while?" Because he'd squashed a grape in your ear, tied your shoelaces together, signed his autograph on the back of your bat, all those stupid things. But when you've retired and you sit back and think about how much fun it was, you think about those times – the crap you talked as you sat around in buses, the lows and the highs you shared. It was about being a part of a team and the spirit we shared. And when I think of that, it's when guys like Pigeon come to my mind.'

28

Ankle Tapped

Just to set the record straight, it wasn't me who made them play touch football; Pigeon and Haddin were out on the field passing the ball. The coach put the balls around the field as part of the training drills and Glenn trod on one of them, unfortunately. It wasn't that bad . . . only cost Australia the Ashes.

Australian conditioner Jock Campbell on
McGrath's ankle injury in England, 2005

McGrath writhed on the ground in agony from the pain in his right ankle, flopping about like a fish that had just been hooked out of a river. The ankle had puffed up the instant he rolled it on an errant cricket ball placed on the ground for training drills, and the pain was so intense that he immediately believed it was broken.

None of McGrath's team-mates appeared overly concerned by his predicament as he struggled to control the pain. They were doing their own thing. Ricky Ponting and Adam Gilchrist inspected the pitch – on which they intended to bowl if Ponting won the toss – Brett Lee limbered up, and no-one had noticed McGrath's fall.

He clenched his teeth and forced himself to sit up again in a desperate attempt to catch someone's – *anyone's* – eye, but still no-one noticed him. His head fell back to the turf as he succumbed to the waves of pain that washed over him, and his hands covered his face. *'Where are they?'* Perhaps this was the price he paid for being the dressing-room pest, the boy who cried 'wolf' once too often, but McGrath's agony was very real.

'I was passing the football – a rugby league ball – with Brad Haddin to warm up when it went skidding past me; a pretty poor pass by Hadds, which was disappointing seeing as he's the Canberra Raiders' number one ticket-holder,' says McGrath. 'I turned to chase after it and I planted my foot on a cricket ball that had been laid out for fielding training . . . I rolled over, my ankle took the complete force of the fall, and I hit the deck.

'I felt a sharp pain and when I looked up no-one was looking at me. I lifted my head again and shouted for someone to get Errol Alcott to treat me. They wanted to know if I was serious. "Of course I'm serious!"'

Ponting ran from the damp centre wicket with Gilchrist a pace behind him to join the throng of concerned players who milled around the winged Pigeon. The skipper needed to only read the expression on McGrath's face as Alcott prodded and poked the bowler's swollen ankle to realise he'd have to reshuffle his bowling attack.

'The look on Pigeon's face made it obvious he was in pain,' Ponting recalls. 'I think as soon as he trod on that ball he would've known his Ashes campaign was on the line. It broke and his face . . . the poor bloke, it was as white as a sheet; he didn't look good at all.'

Trainer Jock Campbell watched as Alcott commenced work on the ankle immediately. His efforts to help McGrath overcome the injury would only enhance the reputation he'd forged since taking on the job as the team's physiotherapist in 1984.

'Errol's work bordered on miraculous,' says Campbell. 'He worked with Glenn as soon as it happened. He had Pigeon ice the area, make small movements with it and they made steady gains every day. To see both of them working together was amazing, brilliant. I reckon Glenn spent six hours a day, at least, in rehab. It was a massive effort that was very similar to one that got Steve Waugh over a hamstring injury on the previous Ashes tour.'

McGrath's freak injury was a bitter blow to Australia's chances of victory at Edgbaston. Not only had he dominated the English batsmen in Australia's opening Test victory at Lord's by taking nine wickets (5 for 53 and 4 for 29), but many team tactics for the Second Test revolved around him. It was decided, for instance, to use McGrath as much as possible against England captain Michael Vaughan to exploit his uncertain footwork, particularly early in an innings.

Kevin Pietersen, who had established himself as a danger man at Lord's with two half-centuries, was also a target for McGrath. Ponting planned to initially set Warne and Lee in tandem against him because their styles troubled him, especially early in his innings. However, if Pietersen survived the first quarter of an hour, Ponting would unleash McGrath with the edict to bowl wide of off stump. The theory was that this would frustrate Pietersen, whose batting favoured the leg side. The Australians hoped that drying up his quick runs would test his patience and force him to play a rash shot.

But now these plans – and Australia's chances of victory – lay in a crumpled heap in the outfield. The Edgbaston crowd cheering the sight of McGrath being helped onto a buggy only rubbed salt into the team's wound. Ponting sought the counsel of the team's senior players – Gilchrist, Langer, Hayden, Warne

– and Darren Lehmann, who was working in England as a commentator, to discuss whether they should still go ahead with their plan to bowl first. Warne was the only man to advise against it.

McGrath returned to Edgbaston on crutches 15 minutes after play commenced, and he sat with his ankle packed in ice as Australia's bowling attack struggled. The pitch was snail-slow, there was no swing or seam movement, and England charged to 1 for 132 by lunch. Although dismissed for 407 at the end of the first day, England had adopted an aggressive approach and had taken the Aussies on, hitting 10 sixes and 55 fours. Ultimately, Australia would lose the Test by just two runs after Lee and Kasprowicz put on a last-wicket stand of 59. They displayed tremendous courage in the face of hostile fire, withstanding numerous blows from the English pace attack. England's win levelled the series at 1–1.

'It was a gutsy effort by both Binga and Kaspa,' says McGrath of the stand. 'They almost got us home, but Brett did it tough after he was hit on the hand by Andrew Flintoff. He'd been hit on the same hand in the First Test, and it must have hurt. However, he didn't just soldier on, he took the fight to the English and almost did it. We were so proud of Brett and Kaspa.'

In the wash-up of the defeat, there was a school of thought in Australia – and in England, also – that the Aussies might have won had McGrath been in the line-up. It is a possibility Ponting refuses to dwell on.

'If you ask Glenn that, he'll say yes,' says Ponting. 'Look, who knows? You're crystal-balling there. We didn't score enough runs but our second and third bowlers got hurt as well. Warnie had to shoulder a lot of responsibility; we had to use Brett in a way I didn't want to – he's best used in short, sharp spurts, but he had to get through a heavy workload. I had to keep going back to Brett because Gillespie and Kasprowicz were going all around the park.

'Had McGrath been there with his expertise, skill and experience, it could've been a different kettle of fish, but we'll never know. I was going to bowl that morning anyway and I did. If I had've had Glenn that morning, it might have been a completely different story. It was just hard to cover for one of the greatest bowlers of all time.'

Coach John Buchanan, one of cricket's left-field thinkers, also refuses to concede that the loss of McGrath at the eleventh hour cost Australia the Edgbaston Test – and, ultimately, the Ashes, which were won by England 2–1.

'It cost us Glenn McGrath for that Test,' says Buchanan. 'It was hard work for him to come back, and when he did he hurt his elbow and needed to compensate for his lack of match fitness. It didn't cost us the Ashes. Even on that day when everyone said we shouldn't have bowled, well, I did think we should've bowled. We bowled pretty terribly and fielded pretty terribly, yet even with all that we bowled them all out on that first day. I think there were a lot of other factors, but in saying that, I'd hate to see anyone lose their frontline bowler just before a Test.'

The early prognosis for McGrath wasn't good. It was a grade two tear of the lateral ligament and there was associated bruising. Alcott told the press that McGrath also experienced bone abnormalities in his joint. The injury produced swelling, internal bleeding and some loss of motion.

While Alcott refused to elaborate on how long it would take McGrath to recover, it was noted that this injury would normally take up to six weeks to heal. Behind the scenes, though, Alcott informed the Australian team's hierarchy he was confident McGrath would be available for the next Test. While McGrath had torn some ligaments, Alcott explained that the injury could be overcome by strapping the ankle in such a manner that his foot would not twist or rotate when he bowled.

The fast bowler iced his ankle, strapped it and pictured his body healing itself. In the days that followed he lost the crutches, the moon boot and, most incredibly of all, the hobble. McGrath was lucky to have Alcott on his side. He had developed a reputation for shortening recovery times to injuries; in 2004 he'd helped the actor Russell Crowe to recover from a dislocated shoulder quickly enough for him to complete filming the boxing movie *Cinderella Man*. Getting McGrath into a position where he could play seven days after it appeared his tour was over only enhanced Alcott's reputation. 'It almost seemed impossible to believe,' says Ponting of McGrath's rapid recovery.

Although McGrath was able to bowl again, he needed to prove his match fitness to the Australian selectors. It had been three weeks since he last bowled in match conditions, and McGrath was renowned for gaining his fitness and rhythm from grinding through lots of bowling. While he wanted the Pigeon in his attack, Ponting was adamant he should not be picked just because Alcott felt he could play; Ponting needed proof he'd last the distance.

A fitness and bowling session for McGrath was held on the centre wicket at Old Trafford the day before the Third Test. Some reporters felt it was simply an attempt to play mind games with Michael Vaughan, however McGrath backed up the following morning with another 30 minutes of solid bowling. It was good enough for him to regain his place in the attack ahead of Kasprowicz.

McGrath's miraculous comeback was one of the most incredible recoveries from a sports injury people could recall. However, it was tempered by some misfortune when Gilchrist spilt two chances – from Trescothick and Vaughan – and McGrath was denied another wicket when he bowled Vaughan with a no-ball.

Jock Campbell winces when he thinks of what McGrath's ankle endured as he bowled over after over at Old Trafford. 'When Glenn had his ankle strapped it was so badly swollen I couldn't see it – it was like a balloon. He had ligament damage, a sore elbow as well, and it struck me that if the public saw that, if they saw what Glenn and the other blokes went through to get on the field, they'd have huge respect for them. It was incredibly gutsy.'

29

Fast Bowlers' Cartel

The ties that bind cricket's great fast bowlers are their tremendous work ethic along with a level of determination and desire that borders on a form of madness.

Dennis Lillee

There are two factions in the Australian cricket team: the Fast Bowlers' Cartel (the FBC) and the Platinum Club, which is the domain of the batsmen. According to McGrath, a founding father of the FBC, the Platinum Club's members are renowned for quaffing lattes, cruising arcades to buy designer label cardigans, reading stock reports and discussing the Sunday newspapers' gossip columns and social pages. The FBC, says McGrath, eat red meat, drink the occasional beer, hunt feral pigs on his outback property and discuss, among other subjects, the best way to rip the spine out of the world's batting line-ups.

'The Platinum Club – *ha!* The name says it all,' says McGrath, with his tongue planted firmly in his cheek. 'I reckon a meeting of the Platinum Club's members would be a stuffy event. They probably take minutes and put their hands up to speak. While I *do* have friends who are batsmen, they are quite a serious crowd. Fast bowlers like to have a laugh, we're like big kids who joke with one another, wrestle, throw things and play practical jokes. Any quick named in the squad gains automatic selection into the FBC. It's a very proud and quite exclusive club. We have a "No Big-heads" policy and we realise our first commitment is to the good of the team – though I think the Platinum Members have a similar rule.

'I think it also helped – a lot – that we had a winning era. We really supported each other because we were mates, and we were happy when one of the group did very well because we knew what he had to go through to enjoy his success: pain, exhaustion, frustration and heaps of training. There was no sulking or wondering aloud, "Why did he get all the wickets?" It was instead a matter of shaking the successful bowler's hand – and firmly – and celebrating his success as if it was your own. It made for a happy group of bowlers.'

Jason Gillespie, a card-carrying FBC member, said the fact the two factions exist highlights the gulf between batsmen and the bowlers, the workhorses of the noble game.

'Fast bowlers understand the physical side of cricket,' Gillespie says. 'Batsmen appreciate more the mental side of it. I found the beauty of being a fast bowler was that if you bowled a wide or a no-ball, you had the chance to bowl it again. However, if a batsman makes a mistake and snicks one to the wicketkeeper, that's it – his innings is over. If it is a one-day game, that's it.

'I think the advantage of being a fast bowler is that, as you walk back to your bowling mark, you think of how you'll bowl the next ball. You might think, "Right, I want to land the ball to the top of off stump, through to the 'keeper." And you lock that in and run in. The batsman has to switch on and off and focus on every ball and wait to see where the ball is going, how it is bowled. Batting, bowling – it's a different game; you may as well compare apples and oranges, I guess.

'We bowlers can go out and sledge. A batsman, he can't win. He is always only one ball away from being dismissed, so if he sledges and gets out, he looks like a prize goose. A fast bowler can get away with it. You can show emotion, walk off the ground and then have a cup of tea. We then ice up our bodies while the batsmen go out and work. Give me the choice of being a batsman or bowler, and I'll pick being a bowler any time. We work hard out on the field but we get a bit of a break at least.'

But Geoff Lawson, who toiled until his boots sloshed with his own blood, begs to differ. He insists people should appreciate the hell that fast bowlers endure.

'People don't understand what a fast bowler's body goes through,' says Lawson. 'Because it is physically demanding, a bowler has to go through pain. It becomes a mental thing. It was like watching the cyclists in the 2007 Tour de France when [Australia's] Michael Rogers went over the side of the mountain. You could see his brain was saying to keep going but eventually the pain took over the physical injury.

'As a bowler you must get into the zone to bowl 30 overs with blood oozing out of your feet, stress fractures, dodgy knees, all that sort of stuff, because you have to be tough; it is part of the territory. The batsmen stand around in slips chewing gum and sharing a joke, but no matter if the poor old bowler is 0 for 100 or 5 for 50, he has to do the same stuff.

'The mental challenge is significant. You hear people ask why a bowler bowled a bad ball – I tell them it was a mental error first. That is why, to be a fast bowler, you must train so bloody hard and have a good pain threshold.'

THE FBC MEMBERS
by FORMER PRESIDENT
GLENN McGRATH

BRETT 'Binga' LEE: His pace and his athleticism are his strengths. When Jason Gillespie and I were in the team, Brett could just run in and bowl whatever he wanted. There was a lot of talk about how he should be used, this way and that, but I always thought the team should have exploited his express pace – just have him run in and let 'em rip. I saw him as an out-and-out wicket-taker, and that is how he should be used. I thought that because the team always had me or Jason Gillespie, bowlers who could tie the batsmen up and bowl to good areas. For a while I thought they were trying to turn Brett into Jason and me, and I didn't agree with that.

When I bowled back then I always had aggressive fields, but Binga never felt comfortable having two fielders on the leg side, one on the leg side or extra slips. Brett wanted extra protection; that's just the way he was and that was fine by me.

Because some people in the team wanted him to bowl one way and others wanted him to go in a different direction, I don't think Brett was sure for a long time what his role was meant to be. I think he's matured a lot because of the added responsibility that has been placed on him, and it pleases me to see – from the comfort of my lounge chair – that Brett is thriving on it.

Born: 8 November 1976. Debut: versus India 1999/2000. Australian Test player number: 383

JASON 'Dizzy' GILLESPIE: Diz was a great bowler. I think he was probably hard done by only getting 259 Test wickets, because he always had to push uphill and bowl into the wind. He was quicker than me. I think my strength was that I didn't

13 November 1993: Glenn McGrath takes the wicket of New Zealand's Mark Greatbatch, his first in Test cricket.

Photo by News Limited/Newspix

McGrath appeals for a wicket during the Fourth Test of Australia's tour of the West Indies, 3 May 1995, at Kingston, Jamaica. Photo by Shaun Botterill/Getty Images

David Boon leads the celebrations after another Test victory to Australia.

McGrath runs in to bowl against England at Lord's, June 1997.
Photo by Adrian Murrell/Allsport/ Getty Images

McGrath celebrates his eighth wicket in the England innings. He finished with 8 for 38, at the time the third-best figures ever by an Australian bowler.
Photo by Laurence Griffiths/Allsport/ Getty Images

The last wicket of Australia's World Cup semi-final against South Africa in 1999. Allan Donald walks off dejectedly after being run out, as the Australians celebrate a tie that puts them through to the final.

Photo by Ross Kinnaird/Getty Images

Three days later, after defeating Pakistan in the final, Australia is again crowned the World Champion of cricket.

A selection of McGrath's most prized cricket souvenirs.
Photos by Alan Richardson

McGrath meets a six-month-old rhino at Chipangali Wildlife Sanctuary, just outside Bulawayo, Zimbabwe.

Photo by Hamish Blair/Allsport/Getty Images

Sachin Tendulkar of India ducks into a McGrath bouncer and is given out LBW at the Adelaide Oval, December 1999.

Photo by Hamish Blair/Allsport/Getty Images

McGrath is awarded the Allan Border Medal for the Australian Cricketer of the Year, 31 January 2000.

Photo by Alan Richardson

Michael Slater and Justin Langer celebrate McGrath's hat-trick against the West Indies at the WACA, 1 December 2000.

Photo by Hamish Blair/Allsport/Getty Images

England captain Mike Atherton, the player McGrath dismissed most in Test cricket, leaves the ground after again losing his wicket to the Australian. Edgbaston, July 2001.

Photo by William West/AFP/Getty Images

November 2002: McGrath takes one of the most spectacular outfield catches of all time to dismiss England's Michael Vaughan off Shane Warne's bowling.

Photo by Nick Wilson/Getty Images

McGrath angrily confronts Ramnaresh Sarwan during Australia's 2003 tour of the West Indies – an incident the paceman still regrets.

Photo by Hamish Blair/Getty Images

Success at the 2003 World Cup: Michael Bevan, Brett Lee, Glenn McGrath and Nathan Bracken.

McGrath hits out against New Zealand at the Gabba in 2004 . . .

. . . and celebrates his first Test half-century.
Photos by Hamish Blair/Getty Images

Photo by Greg Wood/AFP/Getty Images

*McGrath's best Test figures of 8 for 24 – the second-best bowling ever by an Australian –
came against Pakistan at the WACA on 19 December 2004.*

7	GILLESPIE		3	7
8	HAYDEN			
9	KASPROWICZ		2	4
10	McGRATH	8	2	4
WK	GILCHRIST			

Photo by Hamish Blair/Getty Images

Test wicket number 500, taken at Lord's in 2005: Marcus Trescothick, caught Langer, bowled McGrath.
Photo by Mike Hewitt/Getty Images

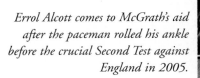

Errol Alcott comes to McGrath's aid after the paceman rolled his ankle before the crucial Second Test against England in 2005.
Photo by Tom Shaw/Getty Images

Above: Four of McGrath's prized trophies and awards.
Below: The most treasured possession of all, his baggy green cap.

Photos by Alan Richardson

Three champions retire: Shane Warne, Glenn McGrath and Justin Langer, after their last Test match, a victory over England at the SCG, January 2007.
Photo by David Hancock/ AFP/Getty Images

A third straight World Cup victory – the perfect end to McGrath's international career.
Photo by Hamish Blair/Getty Images

bowl too quick, so I got more off the deck because the batsman would see the ball and he'd have to play it. The ball would move, but they'd have time to adjust and they'd nick it. Dizzy would bowl quicker; they'd see it, go to play it and the ball would pass them before they knew it. I think he deserved far more wickets than he took.

Steve Waugh had a lot of faith and time for Jason. It was only during the 2005 Ashes tour that things didn't work too well for Dizzy, and he didn't play much for Australia after that. It was thought he was injury-prone, but that was only because he worked very hard.

I'll always remember him as a great bowler and I'm proud we share the record as the leading opening bowling wicket-takers. He was the unsung hero of the Australian team for a long time. Jason had the pace and bounce to worry batsmen. He had that control and he hit good areas.

Born: 19 April 1975. Debut: versus the West Indies 1996/97. Australian Test player number: 370

Tests	Balls	Runs	Wkts	Ave	Best	5wI	10wM
71	14234	6770	259	26.13	7/37	8	–

ANDY 'Bic' BICHEL: His warm-up ball was delivered at the same pace as the ball he'd bowl mid-spell and his last one of the day. He had one speed – and that was 100 per cent. He was a great team player – very enthusiastic – and we nicknamed him 'Barman Bic' because he loved to ply people with drinks after a game. He did pretty well. He was physically strong, but he didn't have the height of Dizzy or me and he didn't have the pace of Binga, so he had to work harder than most to get his wickets.

Bic was one of the reasons we won the 2003 World Cup. He and Michael Kasprowicz are good mates and the unfortunate feature of their careers was that when one of them played it was normally at the expense of the other. He would do anything for the team . . . if he had to hurt himself by diving for a catch he wouldn't hesitate if it was for the greater good of the team.

Born: 27 August 1970. Debut: versus the West Indies 1996/97. Australian Test player number: 371

Tests	Balls	Runs	Wkts	Ave	Best	5wI	10wM
19	3336	1870	58	32.24	5/60	1	–

MICHAEL 'Kaspa' KASPROWICZ: He was a wholehearted fast bowler in what I call the true Queensland style because, like Bichel and McDermott, he worked hard on his feet. Kaspa was another great team-mate. He responded to the challenge of taking on more responsibility during the 2004 tour of Sri Lanka when I wasn't available, and he did it very well. He took 12 wickets at 25.16. He'd also work hard on all areas of his game, like swinging the ball. He bowled in tandem with me when I took my 8 for 38 at Lord's in 1997, and that he was still around to take part in the 2005 Ashes tour says a lot about his durability and longevity. He's had his rough trots through injuries, and I think the fact he always played under pressure because he wasn't a permanent member of the pace attack must've made it hard for him. He was a nightmare to glove to during fielding drills because he threw the ball so hard.

Born: 10 February 1972. Debut: versus the West Indies 1996/97. Australian Test player number: 369

Tests	Balls	Runs	Wkts	Ave	Best	5wI	10wM
38	7140	3716	113	32.88	7/36	4	–

PAUL 'Pistol' REIFFEL: Pistol did a great job for the Australian team. He was in and out of the team as my replacement, but what I remember most about this FBC member is nothing ever seemed to affect him. He was so laid-back I often had to resist the urge to poke him with a stick when we were in the dressing-room to see if he was asleep. He was such an introvert that I was amazed when he became a first-class umpire, because it seemed to go against what I thought was his nature – and he must be doing a good job because there have been suggestions he could one day officiate in a Test. He took over 100 Test wickets, he was a handy batsman, and those who toured the West Indies with him in 1995 remember Pistol for standing up to be counted against the Windies.

Born: 19 April 1966. Debut: versus India 1991/92. Australian Test player number: 352

Tests	Balls	Runs	Wkts	Ave	Best	5wI	10wM
35	6403	2804	104	26.96	6/71	16	2

DAMIEN 'Flemo' FLEMING: The FBC's only true swing bowler, Flemo was very unlucky not to play more than his 20 Tests because his career was hampered by shoulder problems that required surgery. It was a pity because I enjoyed bowling with him. He made an immediate impression in his Test debut against Pakistan in the 1994/95 Test series by taking a hat-trick, only the third person in history to achieve a hat-trick on debut. In 1999/2000 he finished the summer with 30 Test wickets at an average of 22.67. Who knows how my own career might have panned out if Damien hadn't been so unlucky with injuries? However, his time on the sideline allowed me my chance to establish myself as a permanent member of the team. One of my favourite Fleming moments was when he took his 50th

Test wicket, because he yelled 'only 450 more to go' to get 500 wickets.

Born: 24 April 1970. Debut: versus Pakistan 1994/95. Australian Test player number: 361

Tests	Balls	Runs	Wkts	Ave	Best	5wI	10wM
20	4129	1942	75	25.89	5/30	3	–

CRAIG 'Billy the Kid' McDERMOTT: He was different from the rest of the FBC, as he was very stylish and pedantic about the way he laid his clothes out. 'Meticulous' is the word that I think best describes the red-headed fast man. Craig was a great bowler, one of Australia's best, yet I don't think he received the recognition he deserves. He carried plenty on his shoulders.

He made his debut for Australia in the summer of 1984/85 against the West Indies when they were at their terrifying best, and he was one bowler who delighted in giving them a taste of their own medicine with short-pitched stuff aimed straight at their throats. In 1991/92 he was named International Cricketer of the Year. He was a big, strong bloke who knew how to swing the ball. What I loved about playing alongside Craig was that regardless of what happened – even if our batsmen were skittled for a low score – we believed we could do the job and win the game.

Born: 14 April 1965. Debut: versus the West Indies 1984/85. Australian Test player number: 328

Tests	Balls	Runs	Wkts	Ave	Best	5wI	10wM
71	16586	8332	291	28.63	8/97	14	2

STUART 'Sarfraz' CLARK: He's been described as my 'clone' for a long, long time. While he calls it a compliment, I think it is a bit harsh on Stuart because we certainly do things differently. I'm sure he'd like to be regarded as his own bowler – and he should be. Stuart is a confident guy; he's never been scared to let people know what he thinks. He's quite opinionated and is confident about doing things I was not, like voicing his thoughts. He's nowhere near as laid-back as Dizzy or me.

He's also a bit different from the other boof-headed members of the FBC because he's a super-intelligent university student. It is sad he had to wait until he turned 31 before he was given his chance as a bowler, because he has been a quality player. But the advantage is he definitely knows his game – he knows what he has to do and his role in the team is defined. We had similar jobs in the side and I find it hard to fault him in any way because he has handled the step up brilliantly.

Born: 28 September 1975. Debut: versus South Africa 2006. Australian Test player number: 396

NOTE
I haven't included statistics for Stuart Clark or Brett Lee because they are still playing. There have been other FBC members over the years, including Test players Nathan Bracken, Brendon Julian, Simon Cook, Scott Muller, Mitchell Johnson and scores of one-day bowlers. While they were all talented, I have focused on those fast bowlers I played most of my Test cricket alongside.

I believe that over the next 12 months we'll see some new bowlers inducted into the FBC, with the likes of Doug Bollinger from NSW vying for selection. May they long uphold the FBC's spirit of all for one and one for all, not take themselves too seriously, and be proud of their role as the workhorses of cricket. It is a great privilege.

Glenn 'Pigeon' McGrath

30

Under Pressure

Knowing the people they are, I'm not surprised by
the way Jane and Glenn handled it. They're two
fantastic human beings who accept life the way it
is. I think when you have your head screwed on like
those two, you take things in your stride. There'd be
no whingeing, no 'Why me?' Jane is one of those
great people to be around – she has an infectious
smile and manner. No, I'm not surprised they
accepted it.

Mark Taylor, former captain of the
Australian cricket team

'If only man could cry . . .'
So thought Australian coach John Buchanan as he
watched Glenn McGrath's battle to hold everything together
in spite of the pressures he and Jane had lived with for over a
decade. Buchanan's sensitive nature made him different from
most coaches. He encouraged his players to do things like write
and recite poetry at team meetings as part of his holistic approach
to mentoring elite athletes. To help them develop, he needed
first to understand them as humans, not just sportsmen. And
while he worked hard to fulfil his aim, following his retirement

279

the thought played on his mind that he may sometimes have failed to pick up on signals from players who'd screamed for help despite not making a sound. McGrath was one who suffered in silence.

'I believe the role of a coach is to help players and I probably – in my own mind, at least – wasn't there to help some players because I was busy doing other things; or because I hadn't really got in tune with that person, I wasn't able to help them even if they were crying out for help,' says Buchanan. 'The reason I asked players for poetry was to allow me to understand the whole person. It just wasn't about Stuart Law or Ricky Ponting the cricketer. And while the cricket was the most important part of their life at the time, it struck me that if all I wanted to know about them was their cricket, then I really couldn't help them. To help them I had to know their game inside out.

'As for Glenn, the biggest thing he needed to know was I was there if he needed me at any time. He needed to know there was compassion, understanding and every leniency possible. However, because Pidge is Pidge, he kept so much inside and I found that amazing. I wondered what he'd have go through his mind every night he went back to his hotel room alone. How was Jane? The kids? The future? Yet when you'd see him the next day, he'd answer your enquiry about how he was doing with, "Never better, mate."

'If only man could cry. You can't show weakness when you're Glenn McGrath, the country boy, the role model, the bowling template, because everyone looked up to you. Thinking about it, it must have been so hard for him.'

Buchanan wonders sometimes if McGrath's stoicism was a case of an athlete living up to what the public expects a hero to be – the strong, silent type who can perform no matter how badly his body or spirit was injured. Steve Waugh, one of

McGrath's closest friends, admits cricketers do tend to build a facade as a survival mode.

'Glenn was a master of churning out the clichés, but I think most cricketers are like that,' says Waugh. 'We played a game where you learn to put up a defence; brick walls all around them. It is a game where you need to spend a lot of time away from loved ones and on your own; you don't give too much away, because you figure it might be taken the wrong way or seen as a weakness. You keep things to yourself.'

Waugh gained a raw insight into the pressure his mate lived with when he was called to McGrath's room at 5 am during the team's stopover in London on their way to the West Indies in 2003. Jane had a secondary cancer.

'We were at the Gatwick Airport Hotel, not a flash place at the best of times,' says McGrath. 'Jane didn't know where we were staying and she contacted the Cricket Board. I received a phone call from one of the employees just before 5 am and was told to ring my wife. My first thought was to think of the kids . . . I had a million fears as I dialled home. Jane told me that after six years of everything being clear, the cancer was back. It knocked me around. I think there was bliss in being naive when it first happened because it was a case of, "Yeah, we'll beat it." But I knew too much.'

Waugh, Errol Alcott and McGrath decided he should not worry about his luggage – he should head straight to where he was needed most: home.

'He had to return and sort his private life out,' says Waugh. 'He was always positive about his and Jane's situation, though he never said a lot. He never went into detail as to how bad things may have been, but I'm sure behind the scenes it was different. Unfortunately, I experienced a similar thing with Lynette [she needed emergency brain surgery to remove a blood clot in 2006] and you don't let people know 90 per cent of what is happening behind the scenes. It gave me a much better insight into what Glenn's life was about. Jane and Glenn wanted to keep their lives as normal as possible, they didn't want the cancer to rule their lives or overtake it, and that's why he played cricket. I think playing good cricket was important to Glenn because that meant a sense of normality had returned. I think cricket was his break from reality – he could go out and do his thing and forget about everything for a while. I believe that is why he played so well – his time on the field gave him a clear focus.'

Playing cricket was an outlet for both McGrath and Jane. Apart from allowing him to gain satisfaction from taking on the world's best, it also allowed Jane a focus other than her illness. McGrath realised the cricket field was not the place to take out any emotion or aggression for the hand fate had dealt him and his wife – although there was no doubt that the pressures at home contributed to his brain explosion when he rejoined the team during the 2003 tour of the West Indies. His sledging of batsman Ramnaresh Sarwan ended up in a wild-eyed, expletive-ridden stand-off.

'A few people asked if I ever took my frustration out on the batsman, but I didn't,' McGrath says. 'Cricket was an escape for Jane and it was for me. It wasn't a place to go out and bowl bouncers at batsmen to feel better about myself. Bouncers and aggression weren't going to help Jane. Bowling bouncers wasn't going to help my team. The truth about cricket is you need to stay in control to do well.'

Ricky Ponting prides himself on being able to recognise when a player is in need of some respite from the physical and mental grind of their sport. According to Ponting, however, McGrath was unreadable.

'He made it clear to us when he needed to be rested,' says Ponting. 'I can spot things clearly and early and I know when things aren't right with most guys in the team, but Glenn never gave that impression at all. It was only when things got to their very worst that we realised something was up with Glenn. I remember when we played a series against the South Africans at the Telstra Dome in 2006, and he just packed his bags and went home when Jane got sick.

'I always found it remarkable how he could separate his cricket life from his personal life. We all talk about how hard cricket is when we're away from home and travelling around the world, but when you get something else on your plate as well it makes life a hundred times harder. To Glenn's credit, he'd always answer that Jane was going great when we'd ask. I think deep down Glenn knew we realised that wasn't right, but we respected his approach because that is how they wanted to deal with it. Jane and Glenn were ultra-positive all the way. I think it is a credit to them both – Jane especially – how they have handled it. She is obviously an incredibly tough person who has been through some incredible stages and phases in her life.'

Jason Gillespie is one of McGrath's most trusted friends, yet he realised early on that McGrath wanted his – and Jane's – privacy to be respected.

'He didn't have to say anything,' says Gillespie. 'When guys had personal problems they handled it differently. Some guys will sit down in the bar and chat to a mate, others shut their door to be alone. All of us appreciated what was going on in his life and we'd say that if he ever needed a chat, we were there to listen. There was the occasional chat over a beer, but we knew when she was hurting and when he was hurting. He remained upbeat and I think a reason for that was because Jane is such a positive influence on Glenn.'

Warren Craig recalls McGrath's first reaction to helping Jane fight the good fight as being quite simple and innocent.

'Obviously it was very traumatic,' he says. 'From Glenn's perspective, his view was that if you have a situation in front of you, you assess it and do whatever must be done to fix it up. That was probably a bit naive in the early days. In Jane's later bouts he knew a lot more about what they were dealing with, but that idea to "fix it" remained his philosophy.'

In Craig's view, McGrath and Jane have a very similar approach: 'Once they've recovered from the initial shock, they sit down, close ranks and seek out the people they need to talk to and work out a strategy. Once they have their plan, they get on with life; that has largely been how they have coped with it. They have never allowed the cancer to be something that would beat them.

'From a cricket perspective, Glenn has taken time out when it was needed. When Jane was first diagnosed he took time off so they could work out a strategy. When Glenn felt everything was under control and the plans were all in place, he returned to cricket. Jane has always been of the view that when Glenn is playing cricket, things are normal. He's just taken it head-on. Ever since I've known him his attitude has been, "There is a solution."'

While Shane Warne is adamant his friend displayed a rare strength and character not to allow life's battle to overwhelm him, he is certain it took plenty out of McGrath.

'What he had to go through with his private life – Jane and being on the road away from home – took its toll, I have no doubt about that,' he says. 'Every time we saw him in the dressing-room or at the hotel or on a bus, he was always upbeat and positive about everything. I like to think that I was there for him when he needed support, because I appreciated all the support he offered me at various times. Jane, Glenn – how strong are they as a couple to have gone through all they have? My hope for them is they grow old together because they deserve it.'

Trainer Jock Campbell says he knew Jane was not doing so well when he didn't see McGrath at training. However, he admired the fact McGrath never lost his sense of humour, when it would have been easy to snap.

'When Glenn came off the field after a bad day or a decision went against him, he'd yell, "There's no justice in this game! No justice!" We'd laugh. No justice? Five hundred Test wickets, house on the water, a beautiful wife – and believe me, he's punching above his weight with Jane, because he was hopeless with girls as a young bloke – beautiful kids, great car. Yeah, he's right, there is no justice,' Campbell laughs.

'His family obviously means the world to him. He's a very loyal bloke and I think that showed in the West Indies when he had the blow-up with Sarwan. That was more through frustration at what had happened to Jane than anything else. It affected him, even though he wouldn't allow himself to say anything because he is such a positive bloke. There were times during the West Indies tour in 2003 when we could tell he would definitely have preferred to have been home with Jane.'

While McGrath is viewed by thousands of cricket fans as the epitome of determination no matter how great a challenge may be, he and Jane created a foundation that would eventually provide thousands of women afflicted by breast cancer with hope. With Jane as its driving force, the work by the foundation would surpass anything McGrath achieved on the cricket field.

31

Foundation of Hope

There's so much that individuals can do for themselves, especially young women, who are told time
and time again that breast cancer is not going to
happen to them. They're the ones with careers and
families, and they are the ones we are losing. It
saddens and angers me because it needn't happen.

Jane McGrath, founder of the
McGrath Foundation

Something concerned Jane as she pondered life in the
tranquillity of her back yard a fortnight before Christmas
in 2007. Was she really defined by her illness? Was she simply
'Jane McGrath, breast cancer survivor'? After all, her life was
so much more than that. She'd travelled the world, met and
married the man of her dreams, migrated to another country,
and was mother to two healthy, happy and beautiful children.
Weren't those things just as important a part of the package of
her life as her health battle? She also wondered aloud why she
lived and others died.

'Of course she's more than a breast cancer survivor,' says
Tracy Bevan with a mischievous giggle. 'She's also Jane McGrath
– the cricketer's wife!'

As well as heartily confirming that Jane certainly is more than *just* a breast cancer survivor, Tracy's answer also provides an insight into the frustration cricketers' partners experience when they're introduced at functions simply as so-and-so's wife or girlfriend, not an individual in their own right.

'I have told Jane that there's a reason she was diagnosed with breast cancer and pushed into the limelight because of it,' says Tracy. 'It's to warn people about this disease, and Jane can do that because she's strong and she's courageous. It's because she can give people inspiration and hope. It's not fair, I know that. But my beautiful best friend who found a lump in her breast when she was only 31 proves it can happen to anyone at any age. She is their wake-up call, because if someone like Jane – who might be seen to have a wonderful life – can get it, then anyone else can too, regardless of their age, their skin colour or who they are.'

Being thrust into the realm of celebrity was hard for Jane. There were numerous public intrusions into her life as the state of her health became fodder for gossip columnists. The lowest point came when a photographer sold to a newspaper shots of Jane dropping the children off at school. This side of the media was uncharted water for both her and Glenn – and they loathed it.

'I didn't like it,' says Jane. 'Worse still, there is no control over it – the gossip writers write what they want to regardless. Sometimes it was hard to go to the shops because people would want to talk about *it*, even if it was to offer their best wishes and support. They were well intentioned and I appreciate that so much, but it's also nice to not have to think about it. After Belinda Emmett died, her husband, Rove McManus, was swimming in a waterhole in Queensland and someone asked if he was Rove. He answered, "Not today." And I understand totally what he meant.'

Emmett, a dear friend of Jane's, was diagnosed with breast cancer when she was only 24 and died eight years later aged 32. She, too, was on Jane's mind that day she sat in the back yard. Perhaps Tracy was right. Maybe, Jane thought, her purpose – as draining as it could sometimes be – was to act as a wake-up call for women to be conscious of an insidious illness that creeps quietly and unannounced like a monster. It was because Jane had learned through her own experience that breast cancer could happen to *anyone* – from any town or country – that she had created the McGrath Foundation in 2002. Her aim had been to raise money to help fund research into the disease that had been causing such upheaval in her life.

In 2003, however, when Jane was diagnosed with a secondary cancer, her perspective changed. She came under the care of a breast cancer nurse – and the depth of the woman's understanding, compassion and care was a great comfort.

'She was someone I could unload all my frustrations and emotions on; she could answer my questions and understand my concerns. She was such a great support,' says Jane of the specialised nurse. 'She allowed me to become Jane McGrath the mother, wife and the friend, not just a breast cancer survivor, and that was important to me.'

Jane's positive experience with the breast-care nurse was a defining moment for the direction of the McGrath Foundation because it gave the charity a focus and direction. One thought that had distressed Jane as she slowly but surely regained her strength was how hard it would be for women in remote or rural areas to cope with the personal and physical devastation of breast cancer, an illness that strikes one in eight Australian women. She felt an empathy as she imagined their feelings of isolation as they waged a life-and-death battle in the shadows alone.

'There is no support network for them,' she says. 'They have to pay to travel to their nearest city for treatment, pay for accommodation, and those costs – on top of everything else – add an extra burden on them. It's not fair that people outside the metropolitan areas are at such a disadvantage. Anyone with breast cancer has enough to cope with. Our aim was to pay the wages of breast-care nurses to be based in the country, because that was something that could make a difference. The nurses not only support the patients but they coordinate care for the women and ensure they are fully informed about what is happening to them – and that their physical and psychological needs also are looked after. It is so important, and I thought that was what the Foundation could do to help: we could place breast-care nurses in rural and regional areas.'

Tracy Bevan was called upon in the McGrath Foundation's formative stages to add her energy and drive to ensure it would succeed. Apart from being the person Jane sought out during the Ashes tour in 1997 when she thought something was wrong, Tracy had been through many life experiences with Jane. They'd even gained their Aussie citizenship together in a ceremony at Darling Harbour in 2002. Jane knew Tracy was someone who'd go the extra yard to help the Foundation achieve its aims to help and educate.

'The Foundation is very important to me,' says Tracy, who is now general manager of the McGrath Foundation. 'The motto of the Foundation is "*Together* we can make a difference" – and it has. The Foundation has helped so many women, but it was also something I could do for my best friend. This was one way I could help her fight breast cancer. There's not a single day that goes by without me thinking about her. Certain things happen and I know Jane would be able to relate to it because she's like my sister, but sometimes I don't call because I don't want to bother her.

'The Foundation was also Jane's way of giving back to Australia, because she loves the country and the people. But it is also tremendous in that I go to a function and meet amazing women. I am told they were diagnosed with breast cancer 25 years ago; they've been in remission five times but they are still here. And I ring Jane and tell her that, because that's great news. It gives her hope and inspiration. And it inspires me, too.'

The Foundation started by funding the cost of a specialist nurse at the St George Hospital, the facility where Jane was first treated. The first thing Jane, Tracy and Glenn discovered about their new project was that it was an expensive ambition – $300,000 was needed to fund a breast-care nurse over a three-year period.

Initially, pieces of Glenn's cricket gear – such as boots and shirts he'd worn in Tests and One Day Internationals – were used to help get money in the can. McGrath's sponsor New Loan was so inspired by the Foundation's aim that it pledged to donate money for every wicket he took and each run he scored. Try as he might, however, McGrath would never put New Loan in danger of bankruptcy with his batting exploits.

Soon other sponsors such as Ingham's Chickens, Elders, Masterfoods, Mars Snackfood (Australia), Intimo, Crabtree & Evelyn, Inspa, Edelman, Relax, Today Network, Lexmark and even the English football club Altrincham helped the cause by throwing their corporate muscle and generosity behind the Foundation. Their reasons were easy enough to understand: they were moved by the small organisation's effort to fight a big battle.

The McGrath Foundation. It soon became a rallying cry and people from all over Australia offered to help. Two hundred employees from Cumberland Industries Filpac raised $2200;

students at Newhaven College in Victoria raised $10,000 through a series of fundraisers; one of Australia's oldest and most prized flora festivals, Bowral Tulip Time, nominated the McGrath Foundation as its charity, and radio personality Alan Jones encouraged people to dig deep at the Tulip Time gala dinner; the Mittagong RSL donated $2 for every old bra donated to the 'bra barrel' located in the club; Twenty-six of Australia's 'hottest' footballers from the AFL and NRL posed in the Foundation's 'Naked For a Cause' calendar, while McGrath, Michael Bevan and English cricketer Alec Stewart played in a Sports Legends versus Celebrity All-Stars match hosted by the Altrincham Football Club in northern England, where the gala dinner raised $60,000 for the Foundation.

Pigeon's team-mates offered their help too. Adam Gilchrist wore pink gloves in the Test at Adelaide in January 2008 when he announced his retirement from the international cricket arena. Fast Bowlers' Cartel member Brett Lee donated the proceeds of a book – *Childhood Heroes*, written to encourage young boys to read – to the McGrath Foundation.

After the federal election in 2007, the new Labor government made good on a pledge by the previous government to put $12 million towards helping the McGrath Foundation achieve its aims. For Jane and Tracy and those who had volunteered their time to make the Foundation a success, it was a sign that they were being taken seriously.

McGrath has been praised by those who monitor charities for his 'boots and all' involvement with the Foundation. He attends functions, even when Jane is unable to, and constantly promotes the Foundation and its aims and values. However, McGrath is adamant that the reason people have thrown their wholehearted support behind the charity, regardless of whether they're battlers or corporate high-flyers, is because of Jane. He is convinced that the nation sees in her not only a fighter but also someone who is not scared to have a laugh at herself – as she did with Andrew Denton in 2004 on *Enough Rope*, his popular ABC TV interview show:

Denton: So you had a prosthetic breast, is that right?
Jane: Yeah.
Denton: And how does that work?
Jane: It was tricky at times. It'd fall out. Washing the car, it fell into a bucket one day. And that was, you know, not the best thing to happen.
Denton: Thank God you weren't at intersections washing windows.
[Audience laughter]
Jane: Yeah, I could never do that. The career path was . . . couldn't follow that one . . .

And the public could cry – if not with her, then *for* her – as she told the *60 Minutes* reporter Charles Wooley about her initial thoughts when a doctor located a secondary cancer on her hip in 2003.

'My first thought was the kids,' she said. 'I just . . . I couldn't breathe for those few seconds and I've just gone, "Oh the children! The kids need me." And I thought, "Right, I am just going to do absolutely everything in my power to be rid of this, once and for all." And I was – and am – so determined to do it. There'd be nothing on this earth that would take me away from my kids.'

Jane became for many the human face of breast cancer, a point that has been reinforced for Tracy on many occasions, at fundraising breakfasts and functions throughout Australia, including in Albury–Wodonga on the NSW–Victoria border.

'That was where we placed our first regional nurse,' Tracy says. 'What really made its impact was how grateful the community was that they had a breast-care nurse. You can't appreciate their gratitude unless you see it for yourself, and it is so lovely. We had 350 people turn up – and there was also a waiting list – to the Pink Breakfast one Saturday morning . . . The way the community responds does make a difference.

'We had a dinner in Wagga and 450 people turned out in support. I think what appeals to the people who support the Foundation is that it's tangible, they can see how the money is being used and the organisation is growing.'

The Foundation has since placed a nurse in Queensland in the Wide Bay area, where 65 women a year are diagnosed with breast cancer. It has employed two part-time nurses in honour of Belinda Emmett in Bega and Moruya. There's a McGrath Foundation nurse in Western Australia and plans to include the Northern Territory in the scheme. The Foundation has funded three nurses at the St George Hospital, but in July 2006 they were integrated into the hospital system. This meant the community would still benefit from their skills and Foundation funds would be freed up to use elsewhere.

The triumph of the Foundation is not only the love and strength that it was built on, but the support it has given to women with breast cancer all over Australia. The following testimonials from breast cancer survivors acknowledge the impact the Foundation's nurses have had on their health and well-being.

> From day one, when we first went to our surgeon, you have been invaluable to us. You have been available whenever we've attended cancer care sessions and are always available on the phone or

email to ask questions. Your counselling skills and your in-depth knowledge with the ability to answer questions cannot be replaced, in our opinion, as we cannot always contact our doctor.

Elizabeth Nelson

The McGrath breast-care nurses were a tremendous support to me during a very difficult time. Their kindness and compassion were very important during this stressful period of my life.

Patricia Williams

Alison Szwajcer [a McGrath breast-care nurse at the St George Hospital] helped me through the darkest period of my life. She came to see me prior to my surgery to offer support and to answer any questions I may have had. It was so nice to know that I had support at a time when I had so many questions and was scared to death of what lay ahead. She was a Godsend to me. So you see, if it wasn't for the Foundation and Alison, I would have been floating in a sea of despair.

Kristen Kasparian

Jane and Glenn McGrath were granted the clarity to take nothing for granted in life at a time when they stood to lose everything. From their experience they not only forged an unbreakable bond, but they provided hope and inspiration to so many others. For the women whose lives have been touched by the McGrath Foundation, the couple's commitment to the charity supersedes anything the world's most successful fast bowler achieved on the cricket field. To them, McGrath is simply a nice bloke and the husband of Jane – a mother, wife, friend, traveller; a person of great strength, dignity and compassion; the founder of a charity which offers hope and support to strangers; and, yes, a breast cancer survivor.

32

To Sledge or Not to Sledge

I reckon he'd be a reasonable bloke, Glenn McGrath, because he couldn't sledge. He had no idea, so that tells me a lot. Lenny Pascoe is a good sledger, I'm a good sledger and we aren't good blokes. Based on that, he'd be a good bloke, I reckon, Glenn McGrath.

Former Australian Test bowler Rodney Hogg
when asked to rate McGrath as a sledger

The voice of reason urged McGrath to put his baggy green cap calmly back on his head and return to his fielding position on the boundary. But the voice of treason was louder and angrier, and it promised to give McGrath a sense of immediate satisfaction as his blood boiled in his veins: *'Go get him – he just insulted Jane!'* McGrath would live to regret the mad seconds that followed as he pointed his finger and ranted and raged under the blazing Antiguan sun.

The picture of McGrath towering over the smaller batsman Ramnaresh Sarwan was beamed around the world. McGrath thought it made him look like such a bully that he cringed every time the scene was replayed on television. The fallout from this regrettable moment had such a profound effect on McGrath that he briefly considered walking away from cricket.

'After what happened with Sarwan I came close to giving it away,' he admits. 'I felt so bad. I don't really want to go into what was said, I was in the wrong state of mind. It was regrettable and I apologised to Ramnaresh for it. It still hurts to talk about it now. The days that followed were terrible. I kept to myself and I couldn't stop thinking about what I'd done. No matter how hard I tried to tell myself it was okay, I felt really disappointed with myself because I'd let myself down.'

It was a hot day. The West Indians, with Sarwan leading the way, were chasing down the record 418 runs they needed to win the Fourth and final Test of the 2003 series – and each scoring shot threatened to deny Australia a historic 4–0 whitewash in the Caribbean. As McGrath prepared to bowl at Sarwan, the scoreboard showed his previous two overs had conceded 21 runs, and he looked pained as he gripped the ball. He had joined the tour late, having returned home when the team was in transit in London to be with Jane on hearing she was diagnosed with a secondary cancer. After a few weeks at home, he had returned to the Caribbean at Jane's insistence – 'I just wanted life to carry on as normal,' she says. McGrath, however, found himself questioning the wisdom of being in Antigua while his wife recovered from radiation treatment.

He began his run in.

After Sarwan dug a ball out and ran a single, McGrath looked in his direction and, according to a team-mate, asked, 'What does Brian Lara's cock taste like?'

It was a tired line, aimed at annoying the in-form batsman. However, Sarwan's quick-witted response would be posted on internet chat sites faster than a Brett Lee delivery.

'I don't know – ask your wife.'

Under normal circumstances, McGrath would have accepted that he'd asked for it. But with Jane at home sick, all he heard was an insult – and he saw red. While a little voice pleaded for him to ignore it, something just wouldn't allow him to let the slur go unchallenged.

McGrath pointed his finger in the face of a bemused Sarwan, and his team-mates heard him rage: 'If you ever fucking mention my wife again, I'll fucking rip your fucking throat out!'

Jason Gillespie watched from afar as the scene intensified, not knowing how the confrontation would end. 'Oh geeze,' he thought. 'Sarwan's cracked open a hornet's nest here.'

At that point umpire David Shepherd interjected to defuse the volatile situation. McGrath let him know the batsman had said something unsavoury about Jane and stormed off to his position in the field, with an angry West Indian crowd jeering him from the stands. Worried that McGrath might be hit in the back of the head by a bottle, Steve Waugh sent Matthew Hayden down to field in his place. As Sarwan tried to work out why McGrath had reacted in such a way, Justin Langer reprimanded him.

'I didn't hear the first part of the exchange,' says Langer. 'All I heard was for Glenn to ask his wife something, and that annoyed me, especially after what Glenn and Jane had been through. I blew up, I told him he was out of line – out of order – to bring Jane into it. There is a gentleman's agreement about sledging – you don't make it personal. As it turned out, Sarwan had no idea of Jane's problem and he was quite apologetic about that.'

Following the incident, Sarwan kept a cool head and guided the West Indies to a historic and well-deserved victory. Gillespie was pleased to see that Sarwan and McGrath left the drama on the paddock as they sat and talked for an hour together in the dressing-room.

'They were drinking rum and coke and there was no issue there. They shook hands, had a laugh and got on with it,' says Gillespie. 'We all knew he wasn't referring to Jane's illness.'

In the aftermath of the incident, captain Steve Waugh was criticised for not intervening in the exchange. He received a phone call from the chief executive of the Australian Cricket Board, James Sutherland, demanding he do something about the behaviour of his players. The Australian public said they felt 'ashamed' by what they'd seen. Waugh, however, countered that too much was made about an unfortunate incident that involved a player under enormous personal pressure.

'The bottom line was Glenn came back two matches into the tour,' he says. 'Jane had obviously decided she was going okay and she encouraged him to return to the team so life would seem as if it was back to normal for both of them. I think, to be fair, Glenn was short of a bowl – and he was worried about what was going on at home and that maybe he should have stayed there. There was a culmination of things: him not bowling well, what was going on at home, and a batsman who was frustrating him. He exploded.

'It happened so quickly that I didn't see it until it was all over. We were crucified in the wash-up, all of us. There were extenuating circumstances. It didn't look good and it wasn't right, but you had to be compassionate about the situation. Sarwan was quite clever and he probably got one up on Glenn with his quick comeback. I think we all have situations where life seems tough, but unfortunately when Glenn had his, a few million people were watching.'

The incident prompted a flood of letters to the press. *The Sydney Morning Herald* published over 40 letters from the public and none supported the Australians.

The ICC match referee, Mike Procter, was criticised for

appearing to endorse the stand-off by saying it was unnecessary to take action against McGrath or Sarwan because umpire David Shepherd had stepped in at the right time.

'Australia has always played pretty tough cricket,' said Procter. 'I don't think anyone wants them to change the way they play. Sometimes people like to knock the people at the top. They are a wonderful side and play in the spirit of the game.'

Critics of the so-called 'ugly Australians' – the Australian cricket team – saw Procter's remarks as an official endorsement of the players' freedom to act as they pleased, all because they were a champion team.

The timing of McGrath's brain explosion had an unfortunate irony; it came just three weeks after the Australian Cricket Board met in Bowral to discuss its 'spirit of cricket' initiative, one of James Sutherland's pet projects. The initiative was to be built upon four solid pillars of the game: boosting participation at the grass roots; enhancing the game's image commercially; cricket's rich history; and the conduct of the current players. So Sutherland was ready to vent his spleen to Waugh down the phone, telling him to bring his players into line and to take a look at the way his team behaved when things didn't go its way.

When Sutherland was asked by journalists whether McGrath was justified in his response to Sarwan's comment, he bristled: 'I don't think that there was a defence forthcoming in the circumstances.'

Jane McGrath stood by her man. When she heard what sparked McGrath's rage, she thanked her husband.

'I said thank you for defending me,' she says. 'I would hope any man who loved his wife or his partner or his children would react in a similar way. I was annoyed by the way people reacted to it. The umpires and ICC didn't take any action because they understood what was happening in our lives. It made me angry and upset to hear the media say, "Who does Glenn McGrath think he is?" No-one mentioned why he may have reacted the way he did.'

Warren Craig knew there was a problem when he woke at 5.30 am and saw ten messages on his mobile phone.

'What's happened?' he thought as he sat bolt upright in bed. From that moment, he was bunkered down in his office for a week. He cancelled appointments and was bombarded with calls from the media wanting either a comment or, better still, an interview with his client.

'People expect fast bowlers to be fiery and aggressive, so commercially speaking the Sarwan incident didn't have an impact on him,' he says. 'Media-wise, it was the longest an incident involving Glenn dragged on and there was some obvious public flak. Once the issue about Jane surfaced it put a lot of things into perspective. I think people understood circumstances came into play, and what I found was that the people who knew Glenn understood and they stood by him.'

While McGrath did receive calls of support from home, he felt hunted and hurt over the next few days. He refrained from letting people know the core of the pressure he was under. He was loath to be seen to be using Jane as an excuse, and he didn't want Jane to think her illness was having such an effect on him because he feared that would have a negative impact on her. While people in the West Indies seemed to forget the blow-up quickly, it was huge news in Australia for a week – and McGrath was gutted to realise the poor light in which he'd been cast.

'Maybe I shouldn't have been in the West Indies; maybe if Jane hadn't been sick it wouldn't have happened; why didn't I just keep walking? They were the kind of thoughts going around in my head,' says McGrath. 'It wouldn't go away. The difference in our sizes looked terrible. I spoke to Sarwan and he was really good about it. He told me he wasn't aware Jane was sick and he offered an apology, but I told him it was me who needed to say sorry. But an incident like that doesn't just happen and then go away, it plays on your mind because you've let yourself down. And then when you hear from home that you're considered a disgrace . . . it really plays on you. I was angry with myself. I had no intention of making excuses but I did look at why it happened.'

Sarwan, who went on to score a century to help the West Indies to a record-breaking three-wicket victory, took some of the sting out of the story's tail when he informed the media he and McGrath remained on friendly terms.

'We appreciate each other's friendship,' he told the brigade of Australian journalists.

Four years earlier, again in the Caribbean, McGrath had been involved in another well-publicised controversy when he was accused by Brian Lara of spitting at a batsman. The enraged Lara accused McGrath of spitting at West Indian opener Adrian Griffiths after he'd bowled the last ball of the session. He struck a nerve: McGrath was not only furious that the West Indies skipper would think he'd do such a thing, but he'd already had a conflict with Lara in the previous Test when Lara had shoulder-charged McGrath as he completed a run. To prevent McGrath from exploding with fury at Lara – who was waiting to give the bowler an old-fashioned verbal spray – Errol Alcott had dragged and pushed him into the Australian dressing-room at the end of the day's play.

Lara filed a report to match referee Raman Subba Row. While McGrath was eventually found not guilty of the charge, he was fined $3000 when Subba Row ruled spitting of any kind on the field would not be tolerated.

'Lara said I spat at his batsman, which wasn't true,' says McGrath. 'Griffiths was a good five or six metres away from me when that happened. I wasn't looking and I spat on the ground as I turned away to head back to our room. It was such a load of rubbish, there was nothing to it, and the camera angle Lara based the complaint on – over Griffiths' shoulder – distorted what really happened. It made it appear as if I spat at him. However, the side-on angle proved I was about six metres away and there was nothing to it.

'To spit at someone in the West Indies is a terrible insult, just as it is in Australia, but I think Brian saw it as an opportunity to let some emotions out. In the previous Test he shoulder-charged me when he made a run and it annoyed me because nothing was said – you can't run into an opposing player – and it seemed to me as though there were double standards at play. He ran into me and nothing was done about it; I spat on the ground and he made out I targeted his opener. When I walked off the field he caught me unawares when he started on me, because I hadn't even thought about spitting on the ground. He was just into me, and I returned serve. It was getting fiery and Errol grabbed me and pushed me into our room, because he'd noticed all the Windies team had started to come out to see what all the commotion was about and he didn't want any trouble.

'I tried to go back outside to continue it, but the team management refused to let me leave and all but locked the door. It was a joke. And I couldn't believe the match referee gave the claim credibility by investigating it, and I was dirty on Brian for quite a while. His actions made bowling to him more interesting for a little while after that.

'I saw Subba Row at the World Cup opening ceremony and when he asked something along the lines of whether I'd forgiven him for what happened, I couldn't bring myself to say anything to him. I did something I've never done to a person before: I just turned my back and ignored him. I wouldn't have been able to afford the fine if I said what was on my mind!

'Of the two incidents, the Sarwan and the spitting, I regret Sarwan most of all because that was my doing. It was a tough time and what hurt was knowing I was in the wrong. I was always conscious of the way athletes like Tiger Woods and Roger Federer were viewed by the public. They're admired for being able to control their emotions and the way they handle themselves. I tried to be like that . . . I wanted to be like a robot and not get affected by things – and I'd actually think about it before a game, not that I got in trouble every game. But I was human. When I'd get in trouble, it'd be for a big blow-up and it was as though that got it out of my system for another 12 months.'

McGrath was branded one of the bad boys of cricket because he was perceived as a serial 'sledger' – someone who tries to unsettle an opponent by ridiculing them with cutting comments. In South Africa it is called 'chirping'. Americans refer to it as 'trash talk'. When Jane McGrath would be watching cricket on television and she'd see her husband mutter under his breath as he stormed back to his mark, she realised it looked bad. However, she also knew what he was saying – and it had nothing to do with the batsman not knowing his father or other similar insults.

'A lot of it was Glenn talking to himself because he'd bowled a delivery that didn't go the way he wanted it to, and the stump camera would pick up his reaction. And I suppose people could interpret it however they wanted,' she says. 'I hear people talk about sledging and they say it is bad, but my own view is I think it is good. I think it is good for the game. I like people showing aggression on the field because it shows they're passionate; it's about winning and everyone wants to win.'

Brett Lee, acknowledged as one of the sport's nice guys, supports Jane's claim that a lot of the abuse McGrath was believed to have dished out to the opposition was actually self-flagellation.

'If you saw Glenn mumble a few things when he was walking back, the chances were he was hopping into himself and not the batsman,' Lee says. 'He rarely said anything to a batsman, and if he did, it was said to be funny, to make the batsman laugh. He was for having fun out there. He played his cricket in the best way.'

Nathan Bracken listened to McGrath unload on England's Kevin Pietersen during a practice game before the 2007 World Cup and found it hard not to laugh as McGrath looked at the batsman and held his ribs, feigning injury.

'During the Australian summer, Pietersen charged Glenn in a one-day game,' Bracken recalls. 'It was as if he was saying, "I don't respect you," to McGrath – a silly move – and he ended up with broken ribs for his trouble. In the warm-up game Pietersen said something to Pigeon and it was on. He said things like, "Do your ribs still hurt when it gets cold?" And all of us thought it was funny.'

Whether or not McGrath's reputation as a heavy sledger was unjustified, his Test captains, Mark Taylor, Steve Waugh and Ricky Ponting, say that what the myth-makers forget to mention is that McGrath wasn't very good at this so-called Australian artform.

'I would never call Glenn a good sledger,' Mark Taylor says. 'He was one of those guys who weren't hard to read. If anything, he was a fierce competitor who loved bowling. I lost count of how many times he said, "One more, just give me one more," every time I wanted to take the ball off him.'

Steve Waugh concurs. 'He didn't say a lot. He wasn't the cleverest of talkers out on the field, and I don't think he'd mind me saying that. You could see when it was going to happen. Generally the signs were that he'd tug at his collar and he'd say a few things to himself. The only time I saw Glenn get disturbed was when he wasn't bowling well, rather than worrying about what the batter was doing. It was when he wasn't bowling so well that he'd take it out on the batsman – and when he sledged, it wasn't all that incisive, or hitting the mark, or putting the batsman off. Their reaction was to shake their head and look as if to say, "What are you doing that for?"

'Not many of the Aussies were big sledgers. We were very encouraging of one another and sometimes it got misconstrued; though there were times when blokes did get frustrated and they'd say the wrong thing. However, we weren't worse than others.'

Ponting believes the media has dramatically overplayed the sledging issue: 'I think now, with so many cameras trained on the players in the field, if you're seen to open your mouth or say something to an opposition player, it's considered sledging. I'd say 95 per cent of the time it isn't the case. There is a bit of banter between players on the field, but it is all pretty tame stuff. I think Glenn is as responsible for a lot of the . . . *tame* stuff as anyone else. Some of the so-called sledges I've been told about and in games I've played are absolute crap.'

Graham Thorpe is another who thinks the sledging side of the game is overplayed in the media. A former England youth football representative, he thought cricket was placid when compared to the threats of violence he received on the football pitch.

'Playing football helped me in terms of dealing with any sledging on the cricket field,' Thorpe says. 'You're totally in control of it. But in football you'd play against guys who'd turn around and threaten to break your leg in the first five minutes – and who knew, maybe he could? When a guy has a cricket ball in his hand, he might threaten to hit you in the head with it, but you're in control of that.

'Warnie and I would have a bit of banter early on. As for Glenn, I could tell when he was having a bit of a grumble at himself or there'd be a bit of a glare. I always knew he was in his zone and he was just trying to put me under pressure, but I was in my own zone. I always thought the Subcontinent teams were worse. It's a bit of a myth, sledging.

'People say it's an underhanded tactic – and I know of some players who played against Australia who thought that – but I always found the competition was fair. I never felt wrongly intimidated. I didn't mind the wind-up stuff occasionally, because it would test you. I remember when I played the Aussies at Edgbaston when I was 24. Ian Healy stumped me after I heard him say, "Watch this selfish prick go for the red-inker," and I charged Warne. That was the only time in my career that happened, because I'm a quick learner. I was wet behind the ears then.'

McGrath concedes sledging is a part of cricket. He thinks many of Australia's opponents are so preoccupied with the prospect of being sledged that they overlook other elements of Australia's play. In a similar vein, Merv Hughes says that sledging accounted for 25 per cent of his wickets, because he liked to get into the batsman's head and 'jumble' their thoughts.

'I was never a big sledger, not as big as people may have wanted to believe,' McGrath says. 'I think Steve Waugh had the right philosophy when he said they called it "Test" cricket because it's five days of tough, unforgiving international cricket which challenges you mentally and physically. The weak don't last. And from what I've learned, the least of a player's problems is a bit of niggle.

'I've said it before, but I believe the Australian game is an aggressive one and, while that might not make us the world's favourite team, it at least makes us the side everyone wants to watch – if not play.'

33

Bodyline and Language

McGrath, stop making a c**t of yourself.

Sign-off to a letter from an elderly man
who was critical of McGrath appearing
to swear on the field

The ball was pitched on a line outside off stump and Australia
A batsman Matthew Hayden stepped away from it to give
himself room to cut Glenn McGrath's delivery square. The ball
sped past the fieldsmen and Hayden felt great satisfaction to
see it crash into the advertiser's sign for four. He jogged slowly
between wickets, his eyes fixed on where the ball finished its
quick journey. And that was when he smashed into *something* –
bloody McGrath, who stood in the middle of the pitch with his
hands on hips also watching the ball. The Queenslander didn't
appreciate it, as McGrath soon discovered.

'I didn't know Matt, he didn't know me,' says McGrath with
a grin. 'He thought I'd barged him on purpose and he growled
a few threats at me – "If you ever do that again, you so-and-so,
and I'll do this and I'll do that." He was right behind me and
breathing down my neck, so I pushed him away – it was a
decent enough shove – and we got on with the game.

'The Australia–Australia A games were always good, tough

cricket. The Cricket Board introduced them into the triangular series in place of a foreign team and it was competitive, because the A players wanted to get into the Aussie team and we had to keep them down. We won all our games, but they were always close. What also made playing against Australia A tough was that they were the underdogs, so the crowd always got behind them.'

ICC match referee and former New Zealand international John Reid demanded McGrath and Hayden attend a meeting straight after the match to explain themselves. McGrath noted that Hayden looked very relaxed as he turned up with a beer in hand. He was certain that Hayden shared his view on the matter: it was a nothing incident.

'The first thing Reid said was Matt could get rid of the beer because he wasn't on holiday,' remembers McGrath. 'It turned out Reid didn't have the authority to dish out any punishment, but he made it clear he would either have fined or suspended us if he had. We were put on notice. After the meeting Matt and I shook hands and became mates. Jane is now godmother to his daughter. I was always of the impression I got on well with Reid, but I received a surprise in 1999, just before the World Cup, when I heard he'd told a few people that if Warne or I stepped out of line during the tournament he'd wipe us out. I was shocked. As I said, I thought we got along.'

Had David Hookes – and not Reid – been in that meeting room, there is every chance he would have congratulated Hayden for barging into the bowler. While Hookes found McGrath to be what he called a 'good bloke' on the tour of the West Indies in 1995, by 2003 he admitted there were aspects of the bowler's on-field persona that grated on him. One was what he called McGrath's tendency 'to stand, hands on hips, in the middle of the pitch' when things didn't go to his liking. He referred to it as the 'angry teapot' stance. The other was what Hookes called McGrath's almost divine belief that the batsmen had to run around him. These traits annoyed the former Test batsman so much that he even raised them as issues for the ACB to investigate. Hookes, however, insisted his complaint wasn't lodged to land McGrath in hot water; he was merely campaigning for batsmen to be allowed the same right as fast bowlers to show some emotion when they were frustrated.

'I don't like Glenn's "teapot" action,' said Hookes. 'He gets hit for four and he walks back to his mark shaking his head. It's probably a habit for him now and he probably doesn't even realise he's doing it. However, a batsman *is* allowed to hit a four; a batsman *is* allowed to hit a good shot or even a lucky shot. If he plays a lucky shot, tell him he's a lucky so-and-so and walk back to your mark.

'But this teapot attitude and shake of the head – and Glenn is one of many bowlers who do it – I think it is very unfair. When a batsman is given out when he's not out, he might stand there for quarter of a second, throw his head back, mumble something as he walks off – and he gets fined 25 per cent of his match fee. Glenn McGrath and many bowlers do that six times a day. What is the difference? It gets under my goat. Look, I'm *happy* bowlers react like that, but batsmen should be allowed to as well. It's incongruous bowlers can do it six times a day.'

McGrath does not agree with Hookes' 'teapot' accusation and regrets that fate denied him the chance to debate it with the left-hander.

'I knew Hookesy, admittedly not all that well, but I knew him,' McGrath says. 'When people form a perception or an idea, you wish they'd come and talk to you about it to hear your side of the story, so they don't just have a biased point of view. I try to look at things from both sides; obviously it is hard to do that when you are emotional. I guess when someone works as a commentator, they have a greater opportunity of keeping their job by generating controversy. I respected Hookesy's commentating and enjoyed listening to him. But I would have loved to have talked to him about those points he raised.

'The teapot, shaking my head: I did that only because I was unhappy with the ball I bowled,' he says. 'You see a batsman play a shot he's unhappy about – he doesn't hit it properly or whatever – and you'll see he walks around and shakes his head. It's exactly the same thing. I wasn't getting stuck into the batsman because he hit me for four, I was hooking into myself. I hadn't bowled the ball where I wanted it to land; it was just a sign of frustration. It wasn't the same as a batsman getting out and going off. If a batsman plays a bad shot, he stands there shaking his head and gives himself a bit of a serve. If a batsman gets out and carries on, it's exactly the same as a bowler reacting to an umpire giving a batsman not out when he thinks he should be dismissed. I really think Hookesy was off the mark with what he said, and I'm sorry to think we'll never get to debate it.'

Hookes was also critical of the 'new age' batsmen for allowing bowlers to call the shots. He cited McGrath's tendency to stop in the middle of the pitch and make the batsmen run around him as something he would never have tolerated during his playing days – he'd have followed Hayden's lead in that Aussie A game.

'I think this generation of bowlers is lucky that they're playing in a subservient era of batsmen,' said Hookes. 'What Glenn does really badly, and he's got away with it for ten years, is when he gets hit to fine leg, for example, he has it in his heart to have the batsman run around him. This is a reflection of the [current] batsmen's attitude to bowlers, because I know he wouldn't have got away with it against a Viv Richards, a Gordon Greenidge, an Ian or Greg Chappell, or Ian Botham and Sunil Gavaskar.

'Now, if he'd done that to me, I *may* have conceded he'd stumbled. If he did it a second time, I would have said loud enough for the umpire to hear, "If you do that one more time, I'll wrap this bat around your ankles." Then I would have said to the umpire, "Did you hear what I said?" Glenn would have gone, "Waah, waah," in a silly way and his NSW mates would have yelled out with him. But I would have said to the umpire, "If he gets in my way again, I'm going to hit him in the shins with my bat, and you understand that I have told him." They [the umpires] would have sweated and panicked, but he wouldn't have done it again. So, the game has reached [the stage] where Glenn can do that and it's weak to think the world's batsmen have allowed him to do that.'

McGrath, however, says he was permitted under the rules of the game to stand his ground.

'I was entitled to keep the same line I ran, and that's all I did,' he says. 'So, it was up to the batsman to go around me. It's interesting coming from a batsman's point of view. I think Viv Richards said that if we had played against one another and I ran in front of him during the follow-through or if I changed direction, he'd have run straight through me. And now I learn Hookesy would've smashed me around the shins with his bat! But that's the way it was. I didn't stand in front of the batsmen intentionally, but I *did* intentionally stand my ground, because bowlers are entitled to do that.

'I have no problem to think David may have raised things as an issue for the Board to look at; that's all fine, as long as it gives a fair perspective from both the bowler's and batsman's view. However, I am concerned that picking and choosing different parts of the game and having a go from a personal perspective can be . . . *tough*, if not a little unfair. I don't mind as long as it is across the board, that's why the "teapot" and my shaking my head was pointed out, because I'm a bowler. It is interesting because batsmen do it and they get away with it.

'When a batsman is out, he can go and release his frustrations and emotions in the change room. A bowler has nowhere to hide and when things go bad, the chances are his day will only get worse. Though it can get better, because he can bowl a heap of rubbish all day and finish at the end with two or three wickets to make it a great day. A batsman can look a million dollars playing one shot and get out the next. That's the difference between the batsman and the bowler, and we'll argue both cases until we are blue in the face.'

Some of McGrath's behaviour in the early stages of his international career angered some purists enough to send him critical letters, while others aired their disapproval on talkback radio. He clearly remembers the spidery writing of an elderly man who described in his letter the salad days of his youth, when he'd join thousands of others at Sydney's Hurstville Oval to watch St George as Don Bradman batted and Bill O'Reilly bowled for the club. The correspondent noted that Bradman was a gentleman and declared that McGrath was not, because he swore too much on the field. The man had never met McGrath and the fast bowler was amazed a stranger could form such a strong opinion on him based merely on what they saw.

'I should have followed Merv Hughes' lead and kept all the hate mail I received and based a book on that, because there was some lively stuff,' says McGrath. The elderly critic who remembered Bradman as a gentleman but condemned McGrath for possessing what he called a 'foul mouth' signed off with the remark: 'McGrath, stop making a c**t of yourself.'

'As soon as he put that there, he lost all credibility,' says McGrath. 'That letter annoyed me because I knew it wasn't me. But he was someone who'd never met me, he had no idea of the person I was, yet he felt the need to write me an abusive letter. It would always get under my skin, but I found if I waited a while and calmed down, I'd think it didn't matter. The person they saw as me wasn't me.'

McGrath does not swear much in general conversation, but he did when he was with his team-mates or out on the field: 'I did find in the team environment and sometimes out on the field there were plenty of times where I'd use blue language. I think that's an Australian thing: when you're with the boys, you slip into it. I went into the dressing-room during the SCG Test against India in 2008 and I let fly with a few, as did the players, and then I realised my son James was with me. I thought, "Oh, no!" And while I didn't quite cover his ears, I was mindful of my tongue.'

Like many sportspeople, McGrath discovered athletes carried a higher level of expectation than most other people in Australian society – and his behaviour was mostly exemplary. After all, he wasn't a big drinker, he abhorred drugs and didn't smoke. He signed autographs, posed for photos with fans, offered aspiring pace bowlers his hard-earned tips of the trade, and provided the media with his insights on aspects of the game. And very few athletes have matched his level of commitment to charity work.

'We don't ask to be role models, but my approach was just to be myself,' he says. 'I couldn't do any better than that. I refused to go out of my way to be something I wasn't. I do think athletes need to be given a bit of leeway, because we are still human and we're going to make mistakes, though most of us don't go out to cause problems. My only advice to any athlete on the job of being a role model is to be yourself.'

But Jane was often left feeling shattered to think people who'd never met her husband judged his character solely by what was written about him in the paper – or said on the radio or shown on television. Didn't the world know he was her knight in shining armour? she'd wonder. Didn't they realise he was the man who didn't bat an eyelid when she'd offered him an 'out' in the early stages of their romance and she was diagnosed with breast cancer?

'I've never had to defend him, as far as I'm concerned,' she says. 'And because of the relationship he has with me, most people think he's Saint Glenn, anyway. They know what we have been through is bigger than cricket. It was frustrating to hear things over the years, but I love him more than anything else in the world . . . he is a great and loving husband and father and man. He has an incredible strength and a great capacity for compassion; it's a shame if there are people who didn't – or don't – see that.'

However, in this age of celebrity where athletes have profiles that rival those of movie stars, McGrath has long appreciated that the public's perception of many high-profile sportspeople is based on how they're portrayed by the media, even if the reports are based on nothing more than unproven rumour and innuendo. And he is adamant the media must accept responsibility for the way athletes and other people in the spotlight are viewed by the public.

'The one thing that has worried me about the media is that some of the people in that industry comment on things they know very little about,' he says. 'However, many members of the general public form their opinion from what is in their articles. In many ways, I'm as qualified to write an in-depth article on what it's like to walk on the moon as some blokes are to write on cricket – and their word is taken by a lot of the public as gospel. I didn't have any trouble with journalists, and I never minded criticism, but the critics or journalists lost me when the facts they used to support an argument were wrong.

'I found that when you'd ask one or two of them why their story went to print the way it did, they'd blame the editor or someone else back at the office. Rather than do what a few other blokes did and "wipe" certain reporters, I kept an open line of communication because I thought that was one way to help enlighten them. I do think credit must be given to the cricketing public who really know the game and see through the poor stories. It annoyed me when people who had no idea about cricket would say a certain player was a disgrace and deserved to be sacked, yet they had never watched a ball get bowled in their life.'

Sports psychologist Gavin Freeman, who worked with Australia's 2006 Winter Olympics team, says many members of the public live their lives by taking 'ownership' of those athletes they cheer – and loathe.

'Look at the reaction when Ian Thorpe retired – it was almost a case of, "How dare he?"' says Freeman. 'People are basically selfish. Some live their lives through their favourite athletes and others define all that is wrong in the world by another athlete's actions. If a fast bowler puts his hands on his hips and is perceived to be mouthing abuse at a batsman, they mightn't like it and a negative reaction forms when they watch or talk about that cricketer. The cricketer in question might be the nicest man in the world in his everyday life, but those people I'm referring to fixate on what they perceive to be an aggressive, negative image. And when an athlete does something they don't agree with, they really turn.'

While Mark Taylor identifies McGrath's tendency to wear his heart on his sleeve as a reason he may have upset people over the years, he says it wouldn't be fair for him to be remembered as anything but a champion.

'You just knew when he wasn't bowling well,' says Taylor. 'You knew when he was getting frustrated. Through his career, he was one of those players who walked the fine line between disappointment and dissent. And that is exactly what you want from your fast bowler – you want him to walk that line but not to cross it. You want them on the edge. You want them to give their all, all the time, but when something goes against them you don't want them to lose the plot. It's not easy, but I think Glenn handled it well. Occasionally he jumped that line, but as captain I could understand. I think people should know Glenn McGrath is a lovely bloke. It's a tough line to walk as a fast bowler: to get yourself fired up and to do what your country wants you to do in terms of your cricket. It must be so hard to be smashed by a bloke you thought you had just got out, but the umpire says no. I think most people understand that.'

Geoff Lawson knows firsthand what Taylor means. He also laments the fact an individual's entire sporting career can be defined by what people see on a television screen. Fast bowling, he explains, is as much about spunk as it is about speed. However, Lawson says it'd be impossible for anyone outside the fast bowlers' union to understand the reasons for the aggression, the surly expressions and the body language.

'Bill Lawry [Channel Nine commentator and former Test captain] used to say I looked as if I hated being out in the middle, but I loved every second,' Lawson says. 'I loved the game. I was intense; I had a job to do. I was a fast bowler, so I hated the batsmen – I had to get them out. People who view any sport through their TV set get a narrow view of what goes on in a game. If a player takes 5 for 40, they'll think he shouldn't be shaking his head and slapping his cap back on his head when he gets it back off the umpire. But that was just Glenn. On the field he might have appeared a bit snarly, but you need to be that. I think 99 per cent of people play sport like that.'

If McGrath loathed bad calls by the umpire or the batsman enjoying some good luck, the spectators who tried to give him grief when he fielded on the boundary discovered he would not tolerate fools. During the 1997 Ashes tour of England, he gave a group of English spectators 'the bird' when they offered mock compliments about his bowling after he'd taken some punishment from a local batsman.

'Most of the time I would have a bit of fun with the people in the outer,' he says. 'Even the Barmy Army in my last summer was great — we swapped banter and it was all light and breezy. But those blokes in 1997 were absolute pains in the backside. I didn't appreciate their sarcasm and I let them know it. There were also a few families sitting around them and they were using terrible language — it wasn't right.

'England would get to me because while most of what they sang and chanted was quite witty, they would also go a step too far and sing things like you were a paedophile. It was sick, absolutely sick, and that would annoy the crap out of me. It was pathetic, and I'd look at those people chanting that and wonder how they could say that. There were also some people who thought that because they'd paid their price of admission, it was their right to abuse you.

'You change as you get older, and probably towards the second half of my career I realised that if the crowd wasn't giving a player a hard time, it meant they didn't respect him; they thought he had nothing, you weren't worth worrying about. The English were generally good-humoured, but no matter what they said in their songs, Australia normally had the last laugh on them because we were so successful. Any of the boys could pretty much ask them for the series scoreline – "Australia is winning 3–0, right?" – and it'd really hurt them. However, I am certain it would've been so much tougher to cop a lot of what they sang if we were losing.'

While the Australians had long agreed to adopt a turn-the-other-cheek approach to the abuse from the crowds and not to retaliate to any fans in search of trouble, McGrath found it impossible to follow that edict during a one-dayer at Wellington in 2005.

'I had trouble with a security guard,' he says. 'Balloons kept coming onto the field and because they had the Silver Fern on them – the Kiwis' national sports emblem – I thought it would create diplomatic dramas if I jumped on them to burst them; it could've been considered an insult. So I gathered them up and handed them to the security guard nearest to me – he wasn't a New Zealander but he *was* a smart-arse, because he threw them back on the field when I turned my back so I'd have to pick them up. He called me a wanker when I told him off and I saw red. *That* was it.

'It was a very close game. Binga was bowling and I had a choice to make. I could either ignore the bloke or I could give it back; I chose to give it back. I hopped over and asked the other security blokes to get rid of him – that the bloke was a jerk. I turned and ran back to my fielding position and as my foot landed on the field, the ball was hit my way. I was travelling at pace and as I charged in, the ball went over my head for four. It wasn't good. Punter called me straight over because he wanted to know what the hell was going on down there. He thought it was someone else's fault that I was caught out, but I took full responsibility. Adding to the problem in that game was that Simon Katich had also copped it – but from the crowd – and he gave it back to them.'

The Australians ended up winning the one-dayer by 10 runs and McGrath was named Man of the Match. After the game, the media wanted to know what had happened. McGrath regrets that in their subsequent reports the press misrepresented the incident, this time in his favour: 'Unfortunately, the way it was written up in the papers made it sound as if the crowd had given me grief. But that wasn't the case at all and it's a point I stressed to the reporters. I had no problem with the Wellington crowd – they were great. The problem stemmed back to a security guard who wanted to be a comedian.'

Ricky Ponting refuses to accept the edict of media managers and spin doctors that says 'to hell with what the mob thinks' when a high-profile person's character is attacked. Ponting is clear in his belief that natural justice says a person should be acknowledged for who they are – and not judged by the image of them manufactured in the often ill-informed public arena.

'Glenn will be remembered as one of the all-time greats of cricket,' says Ponting. 'But he will also be remembered by some people as a player who was pretty feisty, sledged a lot out on the field, and in general seemed a pretty angry person. But that's not the bloke I know; it's not him at all. I think it will be disappointing if a lot of players are remembered in a way that is not necessarily true. Glenn has his charity, the McGrath Foundation, and through his and Jane's efforts it is doing a great job of helping to fight breast cancer. He puts a lot of time into that. Most of the guys in the Australian team consider themselves to be in a position to try to help however we can, and it might be going to schools, interacting with younger people or doing our bit for charity.'

Ponting thinks McGrath's retirement will bring a fuller picture of him to the public domain. 'People will start to learn a lot more about him and some will be surprised, because it'll go against the grain of some opinions.'

34

The Stubborn Foe

I can't help but feel we'll beat any challenges
which might present themselves in the future.
We're a team.

McGrath on his and Jane's resolve
to beat cancer, 2000

Jane sat in the local optometrist's chair to have her eyes tested.
She expected to learn that the 'wavy shimmering' she saw in
front of her eyes was little more than Mother Nature pointing
out it was time to wear spectacles.

'I'd turned 40 and thought that it was time to get glasses,'
she says of the appointment in February 2006. 'As part of the
test, I was to press a button when I saw a dot cross the screen
in front of me.'

The optometrist was bemused, saying it was strange to find
an entire area on the test left blank. It indicated there were
moments when Jane hadn't seen the dot at all, and that was a
concern. When the optometrist suggested Jane see a specialist,
she felt a familiar chill that scared her because it revived many
dark memories.

'I had a flashback to when I had my first mammogram,'
she recalls. 'I remember thinking, "Oh no, this is it . . . it's
happening again."'

Jane left the optometrist with tears running down her cheeks. Before she phoned her doctor, Jane called Glenn, who was in Melbourne preparing for a one-day international against South Africa. While Jane tried to be brave and resilient by saying everything would be fine, the tone of her voice betrayed her and McGrath realised there was a problem the moment she started speaking.

'I went to bed, but at about 11 pm I woke with a terrible feeling,' McGrath says. 'I knew I'd be going home.'

An MRI scan confirmed Jane's worst fears – she'd need to wage a third battle with the stubborn old foe. This time though, it was in the form of a brain tumour, two centimetres in diameter. Cricket Australia officials would cite 'personal reasons' for McGrath's decision to pull out of the game two hours before the first ball was bowled. By nightfall he was at Cronulla trying to digest the dreadful news that the cancer had returned.

'I was in a state of disbelief and horror,' says Jane. 'I think the only thing worse than breast cancer and then a secondary cancer is learning you have a brain tumour. The brain tumour was the unknown.'

McGrath, Jane's rock, had fears of his own. 'I think it was because I knew a lot more about cancer than I did when Jane was first diagnosed that it hit me hard,' he admits. 'And it hit even harder because . . . well, we didn't expect it.'

A brain tumour – the location forced Jane to face her own mortality. She thought about her latest situation and went into an emotional meltdown. Yet she somehow managed to keep her head above the waves of despair by grasping on to her creed that the cancer and its ally – the mind-numbing fear that accompanied it – could not be allowed to overwhelm her.

'You have to take charge,' says Jane. 'You must get on with it. Move forward.'

Things were grim, though. A member of a group of medical professionals Jane calls her 'pit crew' warned that any operation might have a permanent effect on her eyesight. Apart from the threat of blindness, he added, there was also a risk that she would not survive the operation.

And there was the simple fact that Jane did not like the idea of someone cutting her head open.

Just as Glenn's skipper in 1997, Mark Taylor, had put Jane in touch with Dr Chris Hughes when she was so devastated by the need for a mastectomy that she considered death a better option, now Steve Waugh shone some light amid the gloom. Waugh, also a former skipper, and McGrath's best man at his wedding, put Jane in touch with a doctor he was certain would be able to help.

He gave her the phone number of Dr Charlie Teo, a renowned neurological surgeon. Once Dr Teo learned where the tumour was located, he offered Jane some greatly appreciated hope.

'Charlie said it wouldn't get me,' says Jane. 'He said it was just another of life's hurdles and he could help get me over it. He did say that where the tumour was located made it a risk because it was impinging on the visual cortex [the part of the brain that receives visual input from the retina], but he wanted to see the scans. He hoped he could remove it.'

After examining Jane, Dr Teo declared he could operate. She still had reservations about the procedure, but another conversation with Steve Waugh helped her decide to be rid of the tumour once and for all.

'Steve said if it was him, he'd be there,' Jane says.*

McGrath was convinced the operation was a better option

* Six months later, Dr Teo would be required to perform an emergency operation on Waugh's wife, Lynette, to remove from her brain a blood clot the size of a peach.

than hoping that radiotherapy would make it slowly disappear. Like Jane, he saw the operation as a swift and definite step, and that appealed to him.

The toughest job for Jane was to tell her children she needed an operation. She did not want to frighten them, but she didn't want to lie to them either. Jane chose her words carefully as she told James and Holly that her eyes were blurry and she needed to go to hospital for them to be fixed.

Jane was gripped by a deep-seated fear the following Monday morning as she waited to be operated on. She was terrified she might wake up blind and never see the faces of Glenn or the children again. She started to cry and began to doubt the wisdom of her decision. Yet her inner courage refused to let her run. Her inner voice demanded she go through with the operation and beat the tumour.

Still, she sobbed as Glenn walked beside her and held her hand while the hospital orderlies wheeled her towards the operating theatre. As McGrath looked down at his wife, he felt the familiar pangs of hopelessness he detested. 'The hardest thing for me is the fact Jane has had to fight the actual battle on her own,' he says. 'It's hard to be on the sidelines thinking I'd gladly do it all on for her if I could . . . but I can't.'

Both found it almost impossible to loosen their hold on one another's hands. McGrath, who'd needed to summon all his courage on so many occasions to help Jane, almost didn't have enough to leave his wife's side so she could have the operation. It was a desperate and sad time.

'You have to have faith,' says McGrath. 'You have to believe everything will be fine . . . any other thought can't be an option. Never.'

Dr Teo performed the delicate operation through a small hole drilled in the back of Jane's skull. A scan confirmed he'd cut away the tumour. When Jane woke, she felt as if the weight of the world had been lifted from her shoulders, and after telling Glenn she felt great, it crossed her mind to ask if she'd missed the latest episode of *Desperate Housewives*.

The operation was a success, but the aftermath – the loss of her hair as a result of a fortnight's worth of intensive radio-therapy – left Jane in a debilitating state of depression. She didn't want to get out of bed, and for once the idea of 'starching up' and getting on with life didn't resonate.

'It was a tough time,' recalls McGrath. 'It was so tough watching Jane experience depression. She is such a positive person, I think it hit her harder than most. All I could do was offer her as much support and care as she needed.'

Jane's parents had travelled to Australia to offer their support and love before the operation. Her mum, Jen, remained to help the family get by. Yet Jane's depression was rooted deep, and she credits Errol Alcott with finding someone who helped her to finally break free of the dark fog that had engulfed her.

Jane phoned Alcott on what she recalls as a 'bleak' Sunday, not because of the weather but because her back hurt. When Alcott saw how fragile Jane was, 'on the inside and out', he suggested she contact Kate Turner, a yoga and meditation specialist. Kate agreed to go to the McGraths' house because Jane felt awkward about leaving the safety it offered her from prying eyes. Jane even wore a beanie around the house because she feared the sight of her baldness might frighten the children. She was wrong. When she summoned the courage to show James her 'look', he didn't scream. He laughed and urged her to put the beanie back on before giving her a loving hug. Holly vowed to never, ever have her hair cut so short.

Their innocent attitudes only added to the brightness that had re-entered Jane's life through meditation and yoga with

Kate. 'I felt as though I could open up to Kate,' she says. 'When we did our yoga I felt happy – really, really happy – but I felt like I was going to cry. While I felt great, there'd be these tears of emotion. It was deep-rooted emotions coming out. It was a turning point, because from that moment I felt myself getting better.'

Part Three

35

Beginning of the End

James McGrath made his cricket debut on Saturday in an under-8s game in suburban Sydney, but his dad wasn't there to see it. Glenn was on a plane to Malaysia to play in a tri-series against India and the West Indies, a tournament he described as being far from the biggest he's played in.

The Herald Sun, 12 September 2006

Adam Gilchrist and Glenn McGrath were in a car returning to the Australian team hotel after visiting Matt and Kel Hayden's place in Brisbane before the First Test of the 2006/07 Ashes series. Both men felt as if they were a million miles away from their respective families and homes. McGrath, aged 36, had hours earlier told the media he felt good enough to play until he was 40 – but that was in response to jibes he was part of a *Dad's Army* outfit which contained too many players on the wrong side of 30 to be a serious threat to England's hold on the Ashes. What annoyed McGrath most of all was that former Australian fast bowlers Geoff Lawson and Jeff Thomson had joined Ian Chappell in throwing barbs his way.

While McGrath respected and understood everyone's right to an opinion, he found his fellow quicks' input hard to take.

'But those guys always questioned my form heading into a new season. I knew I was closer to the end of my career than the start, but I still believed I was contributing. It had always been my intention to step down if I figured I'd passed my use-by date. And they should have known that. Guys like Courtney Walsh and Richard Hadlee bowled until well into their late thirties and they continued to produce. However, I found that the older I became, the quicker they were to point out it could be my last series, which was frustrating.'

McGrath was stung by the apparent lack of faith – and his declaration that he still had a few good years left in him was his ultra-positive response. However, during the car trip back to his hotel, the fast bowler's thoughts weren't with the knockers but with Jane and the kids. He'd recently started to think often about the amount of time he'd lost with them due to his commitment to cricket, and the all-too-many magic moments he'd sacrificed as a father and husband weighed heavily upon his mind. He'd previously steeled himself from such thoughts by believing playing cricket was 'what I did', but cracks had started to appear in that protective barrier and they threatened to destabilise everything.

While the idea of retiring hadn't taken root, the factors that would soon lead to it began to mount. And it had to happen. While Jane had faithfully documented on video and digital camera such things as friends' birthday parties and other outings, McGrath found watching James' and Holly's lives unfurl on a television screen or laid out in a photo album a poor substitute for living their experiences of wonder and delight. He missed the other fatherly duties as well, like being close by to comfort his children after they'd had a nightmare or when they tripped and scraped their knees.

In the lead-up to the summer of 2006/07, McGrath had

spent eight months at home recovering from an ankle problem. During that time he had been enchanted by family life and doing normal dad things. He drove his children to school, fished with James, marvelled at Holly's imaginative stories and spent invaluable time with Jane. However, bliss came to an end when McGrath had the tough job of sitting James and Holly down to explain it was time for Daddy to return to work – to contest the DLF Cup in Malaysia, a triangular one-day series which involved the Aussies, India and the West Indies. The looks of disappointment on their faces were clear in McGrath's mind as he opened up to Gilchrist in Brisbane. He remembered how, as he tried to convince his children that everything would be all right, his own eyes started to sting.

'When I was growing up, my parents were around 24/7 and my grandparents were only down the road,' he says. 'While you don't think about it as a kid, you realise as you grow older that there was a lot of comfort in knowing you have the support of a parent or grandparent nearby. Through cricket, Jane had pretty much been a single parent. I could be anywhere in the world at any given time; my parents were 500 kilometres away and Jane's were in England. While she has plenty of good friends who'd do anything for her, there was no family network and although she never complained, I know it was tough on her . . . it'd be tough on anyone.

'I know it was hard on the kids, too. They'd go to things where the other kids had their fathers, but James and Holly's father was away most of the time. In the eight months I stayed at home, Holly became a real Daddy's girl and James liked having me around to do things like kick the footy and play backyard cricket. I was concerned when he started bowling leg spin, though. Concerned, because you might've noticed those spin bowlers are a different breed.

'Those thoughts were on my mind when I spoke to Gilly in the car. I was expressing things I would normally keep private and it really surprised me to hear myself saying them out loud. It was one of those things you wouldn't do too often, because I think if you went on about those things on a regular basis it could create a negative environment. But on that particular day, talking openly to Adam made me feel as if I was ridding myself of a great weight. I never really spoke about the personal stuff to the guys because I thought it might be considered a sign of weakness. Perception is everything: I was a member of the all-conquering Australian cricket team and people form a picture of you – and deep down you try to live up to it. However, what I realised from talking to Adam was that I wasn't the only person who felt the way I did . . . and that helped a lot.'

Gilchrist was amazed to hear Pigeon open up. In all the years he'd known McGrath, he'd been reserved and resilient. While surprised by his team-mate's candour, he kept quiet and allowed McGrath to bare his soul. What struck Gilchrist, though, was that the big bloke could quite easily have been reading his own mind.

'Well, I echoed Glenn's thoughts,' says Gilchrist. 'It was probably not just Glenn who felt that way, but the entire Australian cricket team.' Gilchrist acknowledges the extent to which the team members helped each other, but this was mostly related to cricket.

'Ask any bowler about Glenn's impact and I know they'd say Pigeon helped them a lot, that he led by example and he was happy to lead the discussions about cricket. But I think we could do more for each other in regard to our emotional state; issues that relate to family and friends and the loneliness of long tours. I'm not sure if Pidgey – given that what he and Jane endured was played out in public – was a little bit cautious about how much information he divulged. That came back to his personality.

'After our conversation, I made it a point of asking how he was going because I began to understand the frustrations he felt at being away from his family, especially the kids. We don't get the time we lose back. I always felt as if I wanted to grab Glenn and get more out of him after that chat and to let him release what was on his mind, because he kept so much to himself. I guess that was the style of the guy. He obviously endured extraordinary private moments and situations with Jane. We all have our own things, but some find it more difficult to deal with than others. I think Glenn dealt with his in an admirable way – an amazing fashion, actually.'

Being a long-distance dad and husband wasn't easy. McGrath was grateful for Jane's efforts not only to run the house and care for the kids but also to keep the connection between James, Holly and him 'alive'. She never allowed the sun to set without letting the children know how much their father loved them. It was an exercise that spared McGrath the devastation an Australian rugby league player experienced when he returned from the three-month Kangaroo tour of Great Britain and France in 1986. When he returned, his children – after 12 weeks of kissing a photograph of their dad while he was away – walked straight past him when it was time to say goodnight and kissed the glass frame on the dressing table. The footballer vowed on the spot never to tour again. And he didn't.

Thankfully, McGrath never experienced anything as crushing. While the emotion he carted about was heavy, it wasn't guilt. It was loss. One such moment of loss was when James played his first game of cricket in September 2006. As his son measured out his first steps to bowl in an under-8s game, McGrath was on tour in Malaysia. He was torn. It was vital he played in the DLF Cup to prove he was ready to take part in Australia's quest to regain the Ashes later that summer. It was no secret to McGrath that some at Cricket Australia doubted whether he could come back. Despite the fact he was fighting for his future, he would've given almost anything to have been sitting alongside Jane and Holly and offering his son some encouragement.

'Jane sent me constant updates from the ground via text messages,' says McGrath. 'The kids play 20-over games and each player gets two overs of batting, bowling and keeping. They share it around, which is a great idea. James took two consecutive wickets and was then involved in a run-out from his third delivery. A team hat-trick – not a bad way to start cricket. I couldn't allow myself to get emotional. A long time ago, when I'd think about the problems of being away from Jane, and then the kids, I'd told myself, "This is what I do" – and I focused on cricket. When I was in Malaysia, I told myself the time would come when I'd be able to attend every game James played. Also, when I was with the kids, I'd make it a point to make the most of the time we had together. We cricketers only get a certain amount of time to play at the top level and we have to make the most of it while we can. However, it was getting harder.'

Surprisingly, Jane was always happy to see her husband leave. However, her joy at the sight of him packing his kitbag stemmed not from being happy to be rid of McGrath, but because it was a sign her health was good. McGrath had made Jane's health his main priority early in their relationship and he'd ruled himself out of tours to stay by her side whenever she was ill.

'If ever I thought, even for a second, that something was not right with Jane, I would not have gone,' says McGrath. 'She was always my priority. I would've stepped down from a tour in a second – and I did that on a couple of occasions.'

Jane had stopped going to the airport long before because their emotional farewells had become fodder for the prying lenses of television cameras to show on the evening news and for newspaper snappers commissioned to fill space in the morning papers. Even members of the public had made that last, desperate embrace at the terminal awkward because of their impulse to capture anything that resembled celebrity on their mobile phone cameras. So the McGraths said their goodbyes at home and the taxi ride to Mascot seemed that little bit lonelier and a lot tougher for it.

Jock Campbell left the Australian team in 2005 to start his own personal training business by the beach at Cronulla. He helped McGrath maintain peak physical condition as he recuperated during his eight-month break on the sideline. However, a number of what Campbell called 'tell-tale' signs led him to conclude the great bowler was primed to draw stumps.

'Glenn didn't actually come out and say he was going to give up,' says Campbell. 'He dropped a few hints that the time was coming, but I didn't expect it to come as soon as it did . . . I thought he might've taken a little bit longer. He said he'd had enough of going to the gym and would prefer to do outdoor training. He was a bit stale, so we did a lot of outdoor stuff. We didn't worry so much about the weights. Pigeon seemed like someone at the end of his tether. While he trained hard, I sensed Glenn was doing it tough.'

Despite calls by critics that McGrath was too old to spear-head the Australian bowling attack, he felt relaxed and in control during the countdown to the 2006 Gabba Test. However, Ponting read the reports bagging McGrath and the so-called 'pension-aged' members of his team with a feeling of utter contempt. While he played a straight bat in the public arena in response to what he considered low blows, the words stung.

'We may have said publicly that we didn't care what people said or thought, but of course we cared,' he says. 'Deep down it was an insult to all of us. The selectors didn't pick the team because of names; they selected the 11 best players to represent the nation. If that meant one was 36, or another aged 37, so what? My only concern about Glenn going into the Ashes was whether he had enough bowling under his belt after returning from injury.

'We were always conscious of whether he had enough bowling. He was pretty rusty in Malaysia, so we tried to pump a lot of bowling into him to get his workload back up there. The fact that NSW had no first-class games when we returned didn't help his cause, because he needed time to get his rhythm back. And he needed his rhythm for a number of reasons: firstly, to get his pace and everything else right; secondly, to get a bit of bounce and rip into the wicket; and thirdly, for his own confidence. Everyone had written him off going into the First Test.'

McGrath responded brilliantly to the challenge by tearing through the English batting line-up on his way to taking six first-innings wickets; it was his twenty-ninth five-wicket haul in Test cricket and his tenth against the old enemy. Statisticians also noted that the match, played in humid conditions, was the hundredth time McGrath and Shane Warne had played alongside one another in Test cricket. As he walked from the field holding the ball aloft in recognition of the Brisbane crowd's enthusiastic applause for a job well done, McGrath theatrically grabbed the bottom of his back and faked an old codger's limp. While some interpreted it as a swipe at his critics, it was nothing more than a show of McGrath's humour, anything to give his team-mates a belly laugh.

'I took 6 for 50 and it hit me to take off an old man,' he says. 'The boys thought it was hilarious. I wasn't having a go at anyone or being disrespectful, I was just having a bit of fun. With the columnists, especially the former cricketers, I'd often wondered if they wrote things about players being too old, or whatever, just to create headlines or to help the team. I never really cared what the critics said, unless it was a former Australian player having a crack. I was never a big fan of that because it always seemed wrong. It's a path I certainly won't be taking in the future.'

Rather than use his return to gloat at the expense of his detractors, McGrath used his moment in the sun to pile praise on his greatest supporter via his *Sunday Telegraph* column.

'To get six wickets after being out of the Test arena for the best part of a year is one thing,' wrote McGrath. 'To do it with my wife, Jane, in the grandstand was another. Yesterday was Ladies' Day at the Gabba, and what I achieved by taking six wickets was as much for her as anything else I have done in the game.

'It was great for Jane to be there and it was a big thing for her. It was virtually her first big appearance in public since everything that happened in the past year [a brain tumour operation]. All I hope is she enjoyed it as much as I did. I knew where she was sitting and I made the effort to acknowledge her after I got my five wickets.'

Australia humiliated England by 277 runs in Brisbane. While McGrath could afford to bask in the accolades he received for a job well done, what he didn't realise was that the end of the line was so much closer than he ever could have expected.

36

Stumps

He had a great competitive streak. Glenn would never give up – he was never beaten. That, I would think, reflected his best attributes.

Shane Warne

McGrath felt the hint of a smile flicker across his face as John 'Buch' Buchanan earnestly spoke to him in private not long after Australia's six-wicket win over England at Adelaide in the 2006/07 Ashes series. The grin wasn't an expression of happiness – it was one of disbelief. It also helped to hide the annoyance building in McGrath as the national coach mentioned such words and phrases as 'retirement' and 'picking the right time to go'.

It had been a hard Test for McGrath – apart from finishing the first innings wicketless and then scarcely being used in the second, he'd made a life-changing decision before setting foot on the pitch on the opening day's play. While McGrath respected Buch, the last thing the fast bowler wanted to hear that evening was his philosophy on knowing the right time to hang his boots up and devote himself to family life. In any case, they'd already had that conversation a few months earlier during the tri-series tournament involving Australia, the West Indies and India in

Malaysia, and McGrath had found the topic just as distasteful then. However, he couldn't help but think he'd proven himself since that first chat by contributing to Australia's triumphant ICC Trophy campaign in India and the First Ashes Test victory at Brisbane.

By McGrath's own admission, the Adelaide match was far from his finest moment as an international cricketer. He had started on the wrong foot, so to speak, courtesy of a heel injury that threatened his place in the starting line-up. A pancake-flat pitch that offered neither team's bowling attack any favours in the first innings didn't help either. McGrath had finished the first innings with 0 for 107, Brett Lee took 1 for 139 and Warne 1 for 167. Stuart Clark, the so-called 'McGrath clone', was the pick of the bunch with 3 for 75. So despite finishing wicketless, McGrath was prepared to argue that his effort did not warrant the dreaded 'tap on the shoulder' from his coach.

Buchanan told McGrath it might be time to consider giving cricket away. 'As he spoke, I tried to work out where he was coming from. He always seemed to do things for a reason, so I don't know whether it was John's way to motivate me or whether he really believed I risked ruining my reputation by being dropped from the team, *if* my performances warranted that. Maybe he was worried to think I was one of those blokes who wouldn't know when to retire. It seemed pretty funny to me and I smiled.'

McGrath had staggered his approach to the 2006/07 season and he was progressing according to plan. 'I knew exactly where I wanted to be at certain stages of the summer and I was at that point. And Buch knew that, because I'd told him – and the media – about the stages; but here was the coach of the team telling me I should think about retirement. He said I should consider all the things happening at home – Jane, and the kids growing up, all that sort of stuff. Well, that seemed funny too because no-one knew about what was going on at home better than me.

'The chat was all part of being an older member of the team, and while I didn't take it personally, I thought it was a ridiculous conversation. The funny thing – if you could call it that – was that Buch had no influence on my decision at all. I'd decided before Adelaide it was time to retire, but apart from Jane and Warren, I hadn't told anyone else. I went home for a few days after the Brisbane Test and it hit me then that it was time to pull stumps. Jane didn't want to dare believe I was serious. I was.'

As Buchanan continued to talk about the need for the game's most successful fast bowler to think about how much longer he expected to play, McGrath didn't let on that he'd already made his decision. He instead allowed Buchanan to speak, and the longer he did, the more McGrath silently screamed in his head.

Buchanan, a former Queensland Sheffield Shield player, had a different approach to coaching, because he liked to think outside the square. He was believed to have once intentionally placed his team's match plan and notes under a journalist's hotel room door because he wanted them published in the paper, the idea being that it would play on the opposition's minds. He quoted from Sun Tzu's *The Art of War*; he encouraged his players to write – and read – poetry at team meetings; he wanted to understand his players as men, not just athletes; and he believed the team needed to appreciate that he was their rock. He was also very successful, enjoying a 77 per cent winning record as a coach.

McGrath had initially tried to work out where Buchanan was coming from. 'What annoyed me was that when I reminded

John I'd taken six wickets in the first innings at Brisbane – which, as I pointed out, was only one Test ago – he replied that was expected of me, so it didn't really count. That stung. It was "expected" for me to get six wickets, but if I took none – as was the case in the first innings at Adelaide – I was finished. I was annoyed. A few hours earlier, I'd been walking around Adelaide Oval with my mates celebrating a good win, and now I was being told it might be time to retire.'

The onslaught continued the following day when the chairman of selectors, Andrew Hilditch, took McGrath aside for a conversation that echoed Buchanan's sentiments. When Hilditch had taken over the chairman's role from Trevor Hohns in April 2006, he vowed not to spare the axe if ever he felt it was necessary to wield it. His edict that 'there are tough decisions to be made' was reflected in comments – which made for cold and clinical reading in the nation's newspapers – Hilditch gave when asked about the future of ageing team members such as McGrath, Warne, Langer, Gilchrist, Martyn and Hayden. Yet when 'Digger' Hilditch looked McGrath in the eye 'for a chat', it was painfully obvious he felt uncomfortable.

'I don't know if Buch had spoken to him or if Cricket Australia thought it was a conversation I needed to have, but I listened to Digger,' says McGrath. 'He started out by saying he wasn't sure whether he should have the conversation because I'd probably come out and prove them all wrong. But we had it anyway and the message was basically that if a change needed to be made to our bowling attack, it would be me. I understood that and I told him that was fine, because I felt I still had a lot to offer. I also said I couldn't see why there'd be any need to change a winning team. I could see he didn't look happy about having to deliver his message – but I was fine; I'd made my decision. I didn't tell him either that I'd already decided it was time to go. I didn't want John or Andrew to think they had put the seed into my head, because it was my decision.'

When McGrath phoned Jane to let her know of the turn of events, she felt angry. A few days earlier, when he had 'warned' her it was time to pull out the slippers and rocking chair, she'd been ecstatic at the promise of a normal family life at last. However, she felt bitterly disappointed that Buchanan and Hilditch had felt the need to point out to her husband that the finish line was in sight.

'I was furious for Glenn's sake because, as I've said before, I love him more than anything else,' she says. 'He had worked just as hard as anyone else in the side and I thought, if anything, John Buchanan's comments were like waving a red rag at a bull. I had seen him train so hard in the gym with Kevin Chevell that he vomited because he was pushed and pushed. But he'd keep going. Glenn played the game because he loved cricket. Yes, the monetary side of the game has afforded us a beautiful lifestyle, but at the end of the day, Glenn played because he loved it. And I loved watching him play – it was always special – and the reason I loved watching him was because it was his passion. But the negative feedback he received, it . . . frustrated me, because it showed disrespect to Glenn and all he had achieved. It angered me because there seemed to be no fair reason for it.'

Buchanan admits it was not easy to take McGrath aside for the dreaded talk. It was a tough job – something he accepted as part of the loneliness of his office. However, he also believed not to go through with the talk would be unfair to both McGrath and the team.

'It is obviously very difficult to do,' says Buchanan. He notes that there were several aspects to the issue, one related to McGrath himself and the other relating to the team – and the needs of individuals and teams don't necessarily match.

'In terms of the individual, you try to put yourself in their shoes and understand as best as you can where they are at and what they want to achieve. For someone like Glenn, I always thought it was important for him to leave the game with his dignity, after seeing some other people have that opportunity taken away from them. I thought it was important to try to provide the players with another perspective; in other words, when someone is caught up in things, it is sometimes hard to see what the best course of action is. As the coach, you always try to do the right thing from the individual's point of view, even though that might be a hard decision for them to make at that stage.'

From the team's point of view, the bottom line was always that 'no individual was bigger than the team – no matter who they were'. But as Buchanan points out, certain individuals can become key players in a team, with influence far beyond their own contribution as bowler, batsman or fielder. 'The way these players prepare to play can influence what they take out onto the field. While it might not be necessarily visible to the general public, it is to the team. On a day-by-day basis it might not make a significant difference, but if you stack those days together over the months it will have an impact on the team. And that is something a coach and selectors consider all the time.

'The beauty of Glenn was he could handle that type of talk. He was also at the stage of his career where he would have been having [similar talks] with the selectors, the coach or a friend, or even a team-mate. I think he'd have had those conversations with himself over a period of time. I think everybody reflects on their career and wonders where it is going, how they'd like it to go and those sort of things. He'd always listen. While he might not always have agreed with everything, he at least listened and was able to explain where he was at and what he thought. It was never a problem to address difficult things with him.

'It was always going to be his call. It was just about me bringing [retirement] to the forefront and letting him deal with it from there. The coach has a role to play in those discussions – but the person who ultimately had to have the major conversation was Glenn himself, and he did it all the right way.'

Adelaide was always going to be a tough assignment for McGrath. The day before the Test started he was subjected to a fitness assessment because of his crippling heel problem. The 'fat pad' on his heel was badly bruised during the Gabba victory, and a blood blister that formed in the area made it extremely hard for McGrath to walk around the dressing-room, let alone to go for broke at training. The Australian team physiotherapist, Alex Kontouris, knew before he landed in South Australia that McGrath's heel would probably need some attention – only a few days earlier Kontouris had had to anaesthetise the veteran's heel to enable him to finish the Brisbane Test. And when he did examine McGrath's foot in Adelaide, it looked grim. He also noticed that the bowler grimaced in pain when he stood on it.

'Glenn was depressed because his heel was pretty bad,' says Kontouris. 'The feeling was he wouldn't play, and I think Ricky went back to the hotel wondering who'd replace Glenn. While the rest of the team left the ground, Glenn and I stayed at the oval to work on his heel. I taped it up and played around with it, but nothing seemed to work.' Kontouris then tried taping the heel using a method Errol Alcott used on McGrath for a similar problem a few years earlier, and the effect was amazing. 'Glenn said 95 per cent of the pain had disappeared and he jumped up and down a couple of times to prove it had worked.'

McGrath returned to the nets, where Troy Cooley, the team's bowling coach, and a selector watched closely as he bowled five overs. While he did his best to exude confidence and cool, McGrath was worried as he ran in to bowl – worried that if he was stood down, it'd mean the end of the baggy green line for him. Those cryptic words Craig McDermott had asked him all those years ago, before McGrath made his Test debut against New Zealand, had finally come to pass.

'Are you nervous?' McDermott had asked.

'Nope, not really,' the rookie had replied.

'Don't worry. It will get worse the more you play.'

McGrath hadn't understood what McDermott had meant at the time, but his message was gradually revealed as McGrath grew older and came under harsher scrutiny from the media and those who could make or break his career. In the lead-up to Adelaide, one English columnist joked that maybe McGrath's boots should be placed in the South Australian Museum in the same display case as the 500-million-year-old fossils found in the mountains north of the city in 1948.

McGrath had walked a tightrope for the previous few seasons. He was aware the selectors had wondered if it was perhaps time to inject new blood into the Australian bowling attack. The names of young guns Shaun Tait and Mitchell Johnson had been bandied around as serious contenders for McGrath's berth.

In the nets in Adelaide, facing at an undefended wicket but under harsh scrutiny, McGrath gripped the ball, ran in and did his best to bowl well.

'I was basically faced with the scenario where if I was ruled out of the Test, my career was over. Even after Alex wrapped my heel the first time, it still hurt. However, I remembered how Errol Alcott wrapped my heel the last time it happened and

I asked Alex to try to copy his technique – and it worked. It alleviated 95 per cent of the pain and I was ready to go.'

After his bowling effort, the quick felt good and conducted an impromptu press conference for the journalists who'd hung around to watch the session. He declared himself fit and ready to roar; it was a prognosis Kontouris was happy to agree with.

'Glenn was definitely concerned and anxious that he might be ruled out of the Test,' says Kontouris. 'However, my job is to give an independent assessment of the player's health and whether or not he can play. That is all I can do. The selectors pick the team, I let them know if they're fit or not. I was confident Glenn could get through the game. I thought that if he needed an injection, it wouldn't be until later in the match. You'd be reluctant about giving a bowler with the problem Glenn had a painkiller before the first innings, because it would be asking for trouble with a possible infection. I thought if it flared up in the second innings, the injection would get him through just as it did in Brisbane.'

Steve Waugh, who'd made an emotional exit from Test cricket two years earlier, was aware McGrath's future was in the balance in the lead-up to the Ashes. Waugh believed his friend had been there – and had survived – enough times not only to know what he needed to do to prove himself, but also to appreciate how best to handle the pressure.

As Waugh says, as every cricketer gets towards the end of their career, there are times when they're not sure how they'll play – whether they'll be good enough. 'But you find something deep within. If Glenn was honest with himself, I think he'd agree there were times in the last couple of years of his career where he would've asked himself whether he could come back. He was good enough to keep going. But I played a game with him just before I retired and, to be brutally honest, it was like watching a kid of 17 or 18 trying to make his mark, because he looked uncoordinated and the balls weren't coming out. If someone had seen him bowl that day, I'm sure they would've thought there was no way he could possibly come back. That's why I think it was such a great example of sheer determination and courage for him to return. I'm sure he would have thought he was past his best, but to Glenn's credit he came back and bowled better than ever before.

'There were moments when I was still in the team when there was a decision to make between Glenn and Brett and we'd back Glenn. Pigeon would never let us down, either. He would churn out the performances. If ever I saw Glenn was struggling, I would just tell him to believe in himself, to back himself. I realised that whenever he returned from an injury, he'd try too hard – he'd bowl too quick. I'd say to him to bring it back a bit and to ease himself into it. I backed him because he was a champion, and champions like McGrath come through.'

The heel injury revived unwelcome memories in the Australian camp of the previous Ashes series, when McGrath had rolled his ankle on a stray cricket ball during the team's warm-up before the Second Test. It proved the pivotal moment of the series. With McGrath out of action, England went on the offensive to turn their First Test drubbing into a Second Test victory – which launched their celebrated series win. However, history wouldn't be repeated in Adelaide. McGrath was named in the team.

But not long after England won the toss and elected to bat on a featherbed pitch that would harvest 1490 runs by the Test's end, McGrath's boots began to cause him grief. 'I'd asked for new bowling boots in the lead-up to the match and they hadn't arrived, so I wore my old ones out onto the field even though they were gone. A back spike broke, which placed extra pressure on my heel, and the pain was distributed over a wide area. I was in pain and I left the field during the first session. It had reached the point where I intended to ask if I could borrow someone's boots because I felt the pinch. It was my lucky day – my new boots were waiting for me in the rooms. I couldn't believe it. And what was even more incredible was the fact they'd been delivered only a few minutes before I left the field.'

McGrath felt heartened by what he saw as a good sign, but his return to the fray became a tough slog under the South Australian sun. England had no trouble making the ground's quaint old scoreboard tick over. When they were only three down for 450, the harsh reality of elite cricket hit Stuart Clark – who'd played only a handful of Tests – between the eyeballs.

'One thing I'll say about Glenn McGrath is he never played the game for the money,' says Clark. 'If you did, you'd hate the job because on the days you don't do so well it can be rough. Take Adelaide: England three down for 266 at the end of the first day's play – that is a long, hard day; that is what I call a slog. Cricket is a superficial world, in the sense that most of the time you stay in five-star hotels, people do everything and anything for you . . . but those kind of long, hard days really challenge you.'

As McGrath baked under the sun the idea of retiring seemed the right one. 'Retirement is a funny thing,' he says. 'I always thought I'd play for as long as I wanted. I'd always say to the media I had a few more years left in me, but that was me being ultra-positive; to say anything else would be a negative. After Brisbane I thought it was time. But Adelaide . . . I don't think it was really a decision, it was more a knowing. I think Adelaide was a process I had to go through; it confirmed my decision and I was happy with it.

'In the important parts of my life, when I've had to make a choice between A or B, it was always *bang* – the decision is made, that's what I am going to do. I was focused on a thousand international wickets – and that goal drove me – but all of a sudden it didn't mean as much. I'd probably made that decision subconsciously before Adelaide. At Adelaide it was 3 for 260-odd at the end of the day. England had played well. It was a flat wicket; it was just one of those days. You'll always have good days, you'll always have bad days. I had often wondered about the time to retire. I figured there would be a right time to go or a point where people might view me and say, "Oh yeah, he played too long."'

McGrath stood to lose financially by calling it a day. However, he disputes the suggestion that the lucrative Cricket Australia contract money was a consideration when he was deciding his future.

'You think about that after you've retired,' he says. 'But being paid wasn't the reason I played. That was secondary. I enjoyed my time in cricket – I knew what I wanted, I was proud of what I achieved and I made some great friendships that will last for a long, long time. The money side was never an issue. You obviously get used to a certain lifestyle and you don't want that to change when you retire.

'What I would do when I retired entered my mind. I thought about the future and figured there'd be a chance to do corporate work and to spend more time at home. The overriding thought was that I'd had enough of playing cricket and wanted more time with Jane and the kids. The two things I was going to miss were being out there in the thick of it, and my team-mates. I realised I'd played for as long as I wanted and figured I would only let myself down if I played on.'

When McGrath sought Warren Craig's advice, his manager

had McGrath's reputation and legacy in mind when he spoke from the heart.

'I think the only two people who realised he was seriously considering retirement were Jane and myself,' says Craig. 'When he asked for my thoughts, I answered it firstly as a friend and then a manager. As a friend, I said I thought he was going out on top of his game and it would have been disappointing to think he went out on a down note, though that's not to say that would've happened had he played on. Someone once told me you're better off going out a year too early than one too late, and I think that rings true.'

Craig believed it was a good time to go out. 'It was midway through the Ashes, the World Cup was coming up, there were no big cricketing events for a few years. It was unlikely that Glenn would be around for the next World Cup. I had seen other players go out on a downer and it tarnished their image. Human nature is such that people remember the things freshest in their minds. In terms of the corporate world, as Glenn's manager I had no doubt that if he retired after being dropped, the media and fans would have said he played too long – it would have had a negative impact on his post-cricket image.'

Shane Warne had intended to bid farewell at the end of the 2005 Ashes tour of England, but the home team's victory forced him to delay his retirement. The players knew he planned to retire at the end of the 2006/07 series. So when McGrath decided it *was* time to bow out, he gave his bowling partner a call as a matter of courtesy.

'Pigeon rang me and said, "Mate, I don't want to spoil your party, but I want to retire as well." My response was, "If you want to retire, retire." I didn't want Glenn to worry about what I was doing. I told him it would be a pleasure – a real honour, actually – to walk off the SCG with him after our last Test. I felt happy to be able to do that.

'Retirement is a funny thing. I was happy with what I achieved. Unfortunately, in this day and age there is so much involved with playing sport at the top level. If it had have been a case where Glenn and I could just rock up the night before a game, we might have been able to play for another year or two. However, when you're away from your family to attend meetings, training camps, recovery sessions and all the rest of it, it just becomes too hard. Our families needed us. I'd dedicated nearly 20 years to the game, Glenn 15. It was a long time.

'It was an amazing ride. The journey was unbelievable. We didn't lose too many series; we won more games than we lost. I was just happy. That's it. I was moving on. Glenn was the same. He didn't get too emotional when he told everyone; he was also happy with what he did and achieved. There was no point getting sad.'

McGrath certainly didn't feel sad. But with the series still 'live' heading into the Third Test in Perth, he and Warne saw a need to maintain a strict control over their announcements.

'We agreed we didn't want it to be about us,' says McGrath. 'We wanted to make sure we'd won back the Ashes before we made our announcements, because we felt the coverage could be an unwelcome distraction for the team. We won in Perth, so we felt more comfortable about announcing our decision.

'It actually worked out well for Cricket Australia, because there's a view that dead rubbers aren't exciting. I think with Warnie and I announcing we were going to retire, then Justin Langer – and Damien Martyn had of course gone – I think we made the last two Tests exciting, you could argue even more so than the previous three.'

When McGrath's team-mates found out he was retiring,

it affected them to think that – apart from losing two of the world's all-time great bowlers – their 'family unit' would also be torn apart. Apart from the impending departure of Warne, McGrath and John Buchanan, Damien Martyn had retired – via text message – earlier in the series. Adam Gilchrist, who himself would play only one more season for Australia, had lost count of the number of times he'd wondered whether McGrath could fight back from yet another setback.

'In the final years of Glenn's career there were people always suggesting his time might be up,' he says. 'He battled injury and there were all too many times when I thought it was going to take a remarkable effort for him to come back, but he always proved me wrong. I admired how he constantly overcame the adversity he had to endure. During his last summer there were some outstanding prospects in Shaun Tait, Mitchell Johnson, Ben Hilfenhaus, all playing in the one-day version of the game. I guess the pressure was nothing new to Pigeon – there were always new blokes waiting in the wings. Still, I think Glenn must have been looking sideways and over his shoulder in that last series. He had to prove to the selectors, to the captain and the guys around him – and himself – that he could go forward.'

Langer, the opening batsman who approached cricket like a prize-fighter boxing for a title, felt nostalgic when he heard of McGrath's decision. It made him think of his own 'mortality' as a Test player. He soon announced his plan to retire on the eve of the Fifth and final Ashes Test in Sydney.

'Those blokes I played with – Steve Waugh, Ricky Ponting, Matthew Hayden, Adam Gilchrist – I'd stand shoulder-to-shoulder with all of them without frigging blinking,' he says. 'And McGrath, Glenn McGrath, was one of them. When you say that about someone and mean it, I don't think you could give a bloke a bigger compliment. I would have fought in the trenches with him. But it had to come to an end.'

McGrath's biggest problem soon became managing the retirement. Once the media gained a sniff of McGrath's plans, it became a mission for every journalist to nail the story. Television cameras, photographers and journalists kept vigil outside McGrath's house, and they were not welcome. Jane caught one photographer hiding behind a bush in their back yard. McGrath says having their house under media surveillance was harder for Jane than it was for him. And although he might have hoped they'd respect the privacy of his home, he knew that was never going to happen. 'At the time I got hot under the collar and thought I'd do this and that and complain – but by the next day I just moved on.'

McGrath and Warne hatched a plan that would see the spin king make his announcement before the Melbourne Test, while McGrath would front the media before Sydney. But the speculation and hearsay about McGrath's retirement became too great and he didn't want to lie to the press and the public. 'I had always been upfront with the media about things and I didn't want to end my career ducking and hiding or lying. It seemed as if the best way to get rid of the attention was to address it.'

As had been the case for most of McGrath's career, Warren Craig fielded the media requests and enquiries. He played a straight bat to the first few calls but, not wanting to comment or to lie, it soon became easier to turn his phone off. His in-box was full after 45 minutes.

'I knew the media well enough to know Glenn's retirement was obviously a big story, and that they were going to do whatever they could to get it,' he says. 'And that was fair enough – that is the way the game is played. They try, we resist. We only really ever resisted in regards to Jane's health, because that was a private matter.'

With any other story about McGrath during his career, Craig had been prepared to speak to the media. But when it came to a matter as weighty as his retirement, it was up to McGrath, not Craig, to tell the story. So when speculation about McGrath's farewell to arms began to mount and Craig's phone went berserk, he realised they couldn't keep it secret for much longer. At a sponsors' function on the Central Coast before the Melbourne Test, Craig told McGrath that keeping his retirement quiet wasn't going to work. 'Glenn agreed and we decided to bring his announcement forward to before the MCG Test. Though even when he flew down to Melbourne to talk to Cricket Australia about his decision, he refused to confirm anything at Sydney Airport when he was stopped by journalists. "Retirement? What retirement?" was all he'd say. It was done with a grin and it was pretty funny.'

On 23 December 2006 – a few days after Warne had announced his time had come – McGrath faced a battalion of cameras and journalists. But not everyone crammed into the room was armed with a notepad or microphone. Gilchrist sat at the back, listening in as McGrath declared his journey had reached its end.

'I'd always felt an affiliation with Glenn because we came through the ranks together,' Gilchrist says. 'I wanted to be at his press conference because I wanted to hear what he had to say. It was a part of his life over and I couldn't help but think he did it in a way that was befitting of a champion.'

While Warne decided to say farewell in the MCG's plush dining room, McGrath settled for the workmanlike surroundings of the ground's indoor nets. There were no tears, no choked voice or philosophical statements. He started in typical fashion and made light of what some might have considered a solemn occasion.

'I must say I'm a bit disappointed. I thought there would be more people here, seeing Shane's press conference the other day,' McGrath joked.

McGrath stressed his retirement was unrelated to Jane's health. He told the media he was comfortable to leave then, knowing there were plenty of bowlers ready to step in and take over his role. He said Warne's role in the team would be harder to fill. However, the Aussie warrior who had long prided himself on mastering the mental side of the game left the crowd wanting more when he was asked to name his best English opponent.

'Tough one, isn't it?' he said with a chuckle.

37

Tears and Cheers

He is one of the all-time greats, and if there was a
fast bowler I had to pick in my team to take the
field any day of the week, it would be McGrath.
If I was given a choice from every other country
or every other era, it would be Glenn McGrath,
hands down.

Ricky Ponting, captain of Australia

Glenn McGrath never walked taller as a member of the
Australian team than he did on the morning of 2 January
2007 as he led his team-mates onto the Sydney Cricket Ground
for his grand farewell. Tickets to the Test were the hottest items
in town. Near the ground, SCG members of all shapes and
ages lined up along Driver Avenue before sunrise to secure a
seat for the game that would see the end of an era – and three
magnificent playing careers. McGrath was followed onto the
field by Warne and Langer while their team-mates waited a
respectful few seconds before joining them.

The rousing applause and cheers from the Australian-
flag-waving crowd – and England's Barmy Army – added to
McGrath's sense of honour, and he felt chills race up and down
his spine. Despite the mix of emotions swirling around in his

head, McGrath had wits enough to scan the grandstand to try to catch sight of Jane and the kids. This, he thought to himself amid the din of the crowd, was as much his family's moment as his own.

Jane was overwhelmed by pride at watching her husband make his entrance. Many thoughts flooded through her mind as well: of how much she loved him; of the impact he'd made on cricket and the lives of those who follow the game; of the fact she never read the rule book she'd bought before watching him play for the first time at the WACA. Most of all, though, she was happy her children were with her.

'It was emotional and that was nice,' she says. 'I was happy James and Holly were old enough to realise it was a special occasion. I remembered the times when they were babies and I'd try so hard to amuse them so I could stay and watch the cricket a little bit longer, but that was always impossible. What did I think about? I thought I won't have to worry about what to wear to the Tests any more. And I also realised we didn't know what would happen next . . . we didn't have a clue. But most of all I was very proud for Glenn. I was so, so proud he called time on his own terms. That meant so much.'

As Jane beamed, McGrath was stunned that the crowd reacted the way it did. He felt humbled because he'd never seen himself as any different from the people who were now saluting him – and Warne and Langer – with a standing ovation.

'It never entered my mind that the crowd would be so emotional,' he says. 'Their warmth was really something, but I never thought they would go out of their way for me. I always considered myself a normal person and never looked at myself as being any different to anyone else. And while I shared the moment with two champions in Warnie and Lang, I was humbled.'

The first morning of the SCG Test had always promised to be an emotion-charged occasion for McGrath and his family. The initial reaction from the Sydney crowd – of warmth and respect – set the tone for the days ahead. And McGrath soaked up every second of those few steps onto the hallowed turf. He had planned to do so because he wanted a picture that would last in his mind. It surprised him, because he had never been one for nostalgia. Even when McGrath left his home town of Narromine to try his luck with Sutherland, it didn't occur to him to take a sentimental journey and look at the landmarks of his childhood to sustain him during the time he'd be away. He was a young man in a hurry then, with no time to dwell on what had been. The future and the great things it could offer were what excited him – and he raced off in a cloud of dust to meet it head-on. McGrath was still a young man of 36 when he strode onto the SCG for the start of the Fifth Test of the 2006/07 Ashes series, but he was mature – and he was indeed farewelling a true love.

In the days leading up to the match, McGrath sought out Ponting to ask to be granted the honour of leading his teammates onto the SCG. He'd seen what it had meant to Warne in the Melbourne Test and it moved him.

'I expected to play a few more games at the SCG during the one-day series but that was my goodbye to the Test arena, and the little things that never seemed to matter in the past suddenly became very important to me,' he says. 'I guess it hit me: this was the end. One thing that struck me as I prepared for that last match was how quickly the time had passed since my first SCG Test 13 years earlier. It was against South Africa and Andrew Hudson was my first wicket. I dismissed him LBW. As I drove into the SCG I wondered: where on earth had the time gone?'

Ponting always intended to offer McGrath the chance to lead the Australian team into battle. He deserved it and the crowd deserved the chance to salute him. The Australian team, despite its reputation for thick skins and sharp tongues, places a lot of importance on individual achievements and moments. In the team huddle before a match, various players' personal milestones are mentioned to give the team an extra reason to lift their game another peg and ensure the match will be remembered for all the right reasons.

On 2 January 2007, Ponting looked around the huddle and reminded the players it was a special game. Three of their number – and their coach – were about to end careers that coincided with Australia's greatest cricket era. However, he urged each man to play on skill and not raw emotion. Ponting did not want the retirements to distract the team from the business of winning the SCG Test. He demanded a 5–0 whitewash – to make history and to exorcise any ghosts that may have still lingered from the 2005 series.

Buchanan was urging the same thing. Some of the players believed the coach had tried to switch them on by declaring before the match that England's star batsman Kevin Pietersen was a selfish player. Ponting believed Buchanan had attacked England's most dangerous batsman to ensure the Australians focused on the job, not the retirements. It appeared he wanted to ensure that a confrontation took place. But there was never a danger that McGrath would approach the Test in any other way.

'My biggest fear throughout my career was the idea that I could walk off the field not having backed myself,' he says. 'And that was with me in that last game. I didn't want to be in the dressing-room after either innings thinking to myself, "I wish I had have done this or that." Not backing yourself in cricket means you know what you *should* do but do the opposite.

'The other thing I was aware of, even at the death, was not to over-analyse everything. Any fast bowler will understand the thought-process: "I bowled this ball, he'll expect this as a result of that, so I will do this." At the end of the day, you have to ask yourself, "How the hell do I know what that guy is thinking? I'm not a mind-reader." I didn't want to run the risk of building a plan around what I *assumed* an English batsman was thinking . . . I thought of all those things because it made me realise that while it was my last game, it was still a game I'd be judged by.'

McGrath, the big-game hunter till the end, took two key wickets on the first afternoon. He had Pietersen caught by Hussey for 41 when he tried to charge a ball and hit it with the splice of his bat rather than the full face. While some might have considered Pietersen's plan to attack the game's most successful fast bowler to be a sign of disrespect, McGrath merely licked his lips in anticipation.

'That was the way KP played,' says McGrath. 'It didn't matter to him what situation his team was in. On one side of the coin, he was coming at me and trying to make me change my game plan. On the other side, he set himself up a little bit more and the danger was he'd put his team-mates under extra pressure if he was dismissed. I thought he had a good game plan. It had been successful for him, but it became a little bit too predictable and I felt as if I had the edge over him at the end . . . I knocked him over a few times in the Test series.'

McGrath also knocked him over – literally – during a one-day match in Melbourne a few weeks later. Pietersen again charged the paceman, the ball smashed his ribs and he fell to the pitch like a sack of potatoes. As the South African-born England player lay on the ground writhing in agony, McGrath had to restrain himself from commenting. 'I'd told Pietersen a few balls before I hit him that he was getting a bit too predictable, but his ego wouldn't allow him to listen.'

One run after Pietersen's dismissal in the Sydney Test, McGrath struck again, uprooting the stumps to claim Ian Bell for 71. The two rapid-fire dismissals gave the Australian attack the momentum it needed to rip through England's tail. The tourists tumbled from a healthy 4 for 245 to be all out for 291.

Fighting to salvage some pride, England had Australia pinned down in its first innings at 5 for 190. Only an impressive rearguard action by the Aussie lower order – Gilchrist (62), Warne (71) and Clark (35) – allowed Australia to reach 393. McGrath also enjoyed a better farewell innings than Bradman's duck in the last innings of his career. Unlike the greatest player ever to wrap his hands around the handle of a bat, McGrath managed to dig out each of the three balls he faced.

McGrath's afternoon spell on day three was inspiring. After a series in which his future – and viability – had been openly questioned, he struck back. His 13 overs into a strong breeze conceded a measly 22 runs. Ponting could see the pressure build on the English batsmen, who were desperate to score runs, and it didn't surprise him to see the wickets tumble at the opposite end. Old foe Graham Thorpe, at this time a batting coach for NSW, had no trouble putting aside his loyalty to England to admire what he called a brilliant return from a player who'd been written off.

'The most satisfying time of my career was returning to the Test team when people thought I was washed up,' Thorpe says. 'I would imagine Glenn finding it frustrating that he had to prove himself all over again when he'd played 10 or 11 years at the top. He must've thought, "Heck, don't people know I'm a good player?" . . . I would imagine his last 18 months would have been a very satisfying time for him, considering what he went through.'

McGrath bagged Pietersen again, in the first over of the fourth morning. His dismissal went according to the script the Aussies had prepared. They realised he would be keen to score his first runs of the morning as quickly as possible, so McGrath bowled a good length, aiming just outside the off stump. Pietersen jabbed at McGrath's third delivery and was caught behind by Gilchrist for 29.

McGrath had already taken two wickets when he started his twenty-first over in the second innings. He felt a sense of gratitude towards Ponting because he'd made a point of allowing McGrath (or Warne down the other end) to wrap up the innings.

'As soon as England was nine wickets down, Ricky brought Warnie on at one end and me from the other,' McGrath says. 'It was a sign of respect and the gesture meant a lot to both of us.'

Tail-ender James Anderson had poked and prodded at a number of deliveries, and it frustrated McGrath to watch edged balls fall short of the slips fieldsmen and to have his appeals for LBW turned down by the umpire. As he prepared for his last few deliveries in Test cricket, McGrath put himself in Anderson's boots and he formed a plan.

'Tail-enders are lucky even to see the ball, let alone the bowler's hands and what he is going to do with the rock,' he says. 'He'd been playing his shots so I decided to come around the wicket. For the last ball of the over I decided to try a slower delivery, and I remember thinking to myself the instant I released it that the ball came out perfectly. Anderson went through with the shot and realised too late that the ball was a lot slower than he'd anticipated. The ball dropped, it hit the perfect length and he just scooped the ball. It went up, Huss caught it and I was ecstatic. A wicket with my last ball in Test cricket! If a genie had've granted me just one wish for that game, I would've been selfish and asked for a wicket off my last ball.'

High in the grandstands, McGrath's mother, Bev, and sister, Donna, were crying with pride – and with some sadness that it was all over. John Howard, the prime minister of the day, was sitting just two seats away from Donna and told her he was proud to see tears in the eyes of Glenn McGrath's little sister. Bev thought of all her eldest son had achieved and endured, and felt a great surge of pride.

'He became the world's best fast bowler and that wasn't an easy thing to do,' she says. 'He did it well, too. I was always proud of Glenn and the way he conducted himself.'

As McGrath and Warne were applauded from the field, McGrath gave Jane his trademark thumbs-up. Channel Nine's cameraman captured Jane's smiling response as she mimicked her husband's gesture – a thumbs-up in return.

Warren Craig also smiled as he watched his client – and dear friend – walk towards the Australian dressing-room. 'It was day after day of emotion. Most people who know me will tell you I'm not an emotional person, but I felt very proud. It was such a strange sensation. I'd been involved with someone for so long and once again it wasn't business, it was just great to see him finish on such a high note. I think the fact Shane and Justin were retiring added to it. As an event it was very special and it was exciting. A lot of people asked if Glenn was a sentimental bloke, but he's very much a realist. His philosophy is you go through stages of your life and then move on. He'd always said his life was on hold when he played cricket. I figured once he finished his commitments with the Australian team he'd just get on with the rest of his life.'

Steve Rixon and Tom Iceton were in the crowd to fly the flag for Sutherland. Rixon – who, in McGrath's view, could never hope to know the impact he'd made on the bowler's life – felt he had to be there.

'I was there like everyone else: to pay tribute to what had been an outstanding career,' Rixon says. 'In terms of doing much for Glenn, I was the Johnny on the spot. He was just another kid who came through the club and he made the most of some wonderful opportunities. He had been a pleasure to be around. He didn't play a lot of cricket for Sutherland. He didn't play a lot for his state. However, he played a heap at the most important end . . . and he did it well. That day, for me, was about McGrath and what he had done for Narromine, Sutherland, NSW and, of course, Australia. It was a great moment – you live those moments. There'll be a lot of great players who will retire and never receive the ovation Glenn received. I won't say those blokes haven't earned the right, but people liked what they saw in Glenn McGrath and I loved that we weren't scared to express how we felt about him at the very end.'

The last innings of the Test started with Australia requiring 46 runs to win. As Langer approached for his last stint at the Test crease, the English team formed a guard of honour. 'It was a class act,' says McGrath. 'That said a lot about the England team and it was all good.' A large crowd had turned out to the SCG to be a part of the last hurrah, and when Hayden and Langer had scored the required runs and the battle was over, Ponting did his best not to let the cameras or the public see he was bawling like a baby.

'Gilly was sensible,' says Ponting. 'He wore sunglasses out on the field so no-one could see he was crying. I bawled. I bawled my bloody eyes out – and I did my best to keep clear of the media so they didn't pick it up. I was overcome by a sense of loss, in that we'd lost four players [including Martyn], and with what we had achieved by winning the Ashes series 5–0. We had all dreamt about it; we had all worked so hard to give ourselves a chance to achieve that aim. When the winning runs went through covers, it felt so good to have Matt Hayden and Langer out there, the two warriors who'd won us a lot of games.

'When I ran out on the field, it hit me that would be the last time I'd be out on a ground with McGrath, Warne and Langer. I gave Langer a massive hug. There was also a touching moment when Matt Hayden and John Buchanan got into a long bear hug. It was a sad time, but we'd been through one of the most exciting times of my career. It was over.'

Gilchrist says the fact Australia had avenged the loss of the previous Ashes series laid to rest a lot of ghosts, but the victory summoned to the surface a number of emotions. 'That day was *everything*. The emotion of 2005 came through in all of us . . . all the frustrations of that tour. And we didn't just win the Ashes back, we won them 5–0. It was a total demolition of the England team and it stamped our dominance over them. We lost the three guys and Damien Martyn. It was a whole load of emotion being expressed.

'We also felt very lucky to have been a part of a great era of cricket with the guys. I certainly considered that one of the great highlights of my career: to have played alongside Shane Warne and McGrath. They were two of the best ever at what they chose to do in life. Not many people can say that. As I looked at Glenn, Shane and Justin, I figured that my own career was also being reined in. It hit me to try to remember the moments that mattered with people like Pigeon.'

After the match the two teams shared a final Ashes drink in the dressing-room. Donna gained entry into the inner sanctum where she collected autographs from the big names, like that night in Parkes all those years before, when her brother had represented Dubbo in a Country Cup game. Later in the day, the players and their partners would party on James Packer's luxurious yacht until the early hours of the morning, toasting old battles, past campaigns and the future.

From an incredible day of emotion and sentiment, McGrath carried one special memory. 'I was so happy Jane was there – she made it even more special. And being able to walk around the SCG with James and Holly . . . that was magic. It was one cricket moment the three of us lived together. That is something, as a father, I will never forget.'

38

SCG Magic

The fact everyone had the awareness of what was happening; that it was Glenn McGrath's last over; it was the last ball and they were never going to see him at the SCG again was amazing. The way everyone rose to their feet to applaud him for that entire over brings a shiver to my spine just to talk about it . . .

Cricket NSW chief executive and former
Test bowler Dave Gilbert

Brad Hodge was fielding at deep mid-wicket on the SCG boundary in the second one-day final of the 2006/07 summer. At 6.52 pm the 40,000-strong crowd erupted. Until that moment, it had been a frustrating afternoon for everyone, with play interrupted by rain on several occasions. However, that was forgotten for the final over of England's innings as the mob stood to clap and cheer when McGrath was handed the ball to bowl his last over in front of *them*, his home crowd. A sixth sense warned Hodge to stay on his toes; he knew McGrath's luck – 'arse, not class', as the likes of Ponting and Gilchrist described it – would ensure something happened. Hodge had taken a brilliant catch off McGrath's bowling to dismiss Ed Joyce early in the innings and he didn't want to be caught napping.

'I think the whole team would've thought exactly the same way as me. You could bet your house a catch or a run-out would be on in Glenn's last over,' says Hodge. 'It was going to happen – you just *knew* it – and I'm sure that like me the other blokes would've wanted to be ready for it.'

McGrath realised the crowd sounded louder than normal as he walked to his mark, but the reason for the fuss was initially lost on him. He figured maybe someone had beaten the boredom during the rain breaks by drinking a skinful and now they were streaking. However, the crowd's applause grew louder and louder with each of his strides towards the bowling crease. McGrath felt annoyed when Paul Nixon drove his first offering for a single.

Ponting – who'd watched in horror at the Cricket Academy all those years ago when McGrath had produced a small, sharp knife and thrown it 'Jim Bowie-style' into the cereal boxes he'd lined up – ran the ball over to talk to McGrath. In a different situation the skipper might've wanted to tell him to bowl to a certain field or try a special delivery, but on this particular evening that didn't seem overly important. Instead, Ponting wanted to ensure his old mate appreciated that the cheers and the goodwill flowing from the crowd were their tribute to him.

'We'd seen it before with Steve Waugh in his last Test, when people flocked to the SCG because they wanted to share the experience,' he says. 'It was the same for Glenn. And if he says he thought the people were clapping and cheering because there was a streaker on the field, he's playing it down – I can tell you, he knew the applause was for him because I told him. We all knew it from the opening delivery of that last over because we looked at each other as if to say, "Listen to this." I could see he was moved by what was an incredible gesture.'

It took a few seconds for Ponting's message to register with McGrath. 'It was a shock, a real surprise that the crowd would do that for me, because not for a second did I think they would do something like that,' he says. 'When I look back on that memory now, it still affects me. I am sure if you spoke to Gilly he would talk about the emotion of the moment, and it was very emotional. I might have shown my frustration, my anger and aggression on the field, but I was pretty reserved with the other stuff. I guess I've always thought I'm not really all that special. I figured I was good at what I did, but it didn't go much deeper than that . . . but to think back to that game, I realise the emotion from the crowd was really amazing.'

Liam Plunkett scored two runs from the second ball.

Brad Hodge wasn't the only fielder who was on the alert. Left-arm opening bowler Nathan Bracken had endured plenty of unwelcome stick from yobbos about his long mane of blond hair as he patrolled the 'cow paddock' in front of the old Hill area. They'd spent most of the afternoon telling him to 'go get a haircut' or to 'buy a bloody comb', but they were now yelling support for McGrath. The gesture was so overwhelming Bracken had to force himself not to start clapping as well.

Bracken was struck by the spontaneity of the crowd's response to McGrath. 'No-one from Cricket Australia or the SCG Trust jumped on a microphone and said, "Guys, it's Glenn McGrath's last over, so make it count." A few fans rose to their feet and started to clap. Others followed their lead and within seconds the entire crowd was up on its feet applauding him. It must've sparked billions of goosebumps around the ground because I was covered in them! I've read of how greats like Bradman received that kind of ovation, and while it struck me at the time to stay alert and not to stuff up any chance that might come my way, I took the time to appreciate what was happening around me, because I doubt whether I'll ever see such an outpouring of emotion from an Australian crowd again. At one stage I thought Adam Gilchrist yelled something out to me because he was looking my way, but he hadn't. He was looking at the crowd and absorbing the scene; when he caught my eye he simply opened his arms in disbelief, and the expression on his face said it all – he couldn't believe it.'

Fans in the crowd remained on their feet, still applauding wildly, as McGrath charged in again – and as Gilchrist crouched back down into position, he found himself having to resist surfing the wave of sentiment that was welling up inside him. Gilchrist remembers it as an extremely emotional occasion. 'I felt a synergy with Pigeon because we debuted together for NSW all those years ago against Tasmania at the SCG. While we weren't the two closest team members – he had closer mates among what he called the Fast Bowlers' Cartel – I always felt an affiliation with Glenn because we came through together. The way the SCG crowd responded that day was special, and I remember feeling happy for Glenn . . . happy because it was a farewell truly befitting a champion.'

It had been a different story in Melbourne. McGrath's Sydney farewell came hot on the heels of a final at the MCG – on McGrath's thirty-seventh birthday – he would have paid to forget. *The Sydney Morning Herald*'s Peter Roebuck described the bowler's demeanour well: 'McGrath seemed as cheerful as a farmer whose tractor had broken down.' The downward spiral had started when Andrew Flintoff bowled him for a second-ball duck. McGrath had later taken a catch at mid-on to help dismiss Ed Joyce, but with England on the verge of disaster at 3 for 33, he dropped a sitter from Ian Bell when he was on 18.

Bell went on to score 65. Adding salt to McGrath's wounds, Bell hit him back over his head for six. McGrath was then involved in a botched run-out of Andrew Flintoff when he was in the early stages of what ended up to be a match-winning stand of 74. The MCG crowd gave McGrath a standing ovation as he left the field with 0 for 53, but no-one dared sing 'Happy Birthday'.

After the Melbourne game, some wondered whether his effort there would scuttle his chances of making the World Cup tour. A few correspondents thought McGrath then suffered the 'indignity' of Gilchrist keeping up to the stumps in his final home match at the SCG. But Australia's 'keeper was adamant his positioning had nothing to do with the sun setting on McGrath's career. It was a ploy designed to force the England batsmen to remain anchored to the crease, part of the evolution of one-day cricket. As Gilchrist points out, with batsmen trying to charge the bowlers to put them off their line and length, the wicketkeeper is forced to come to the stumps. He says standing up to McGrath in his last game at the SCG 'wasn't a sign he was over the hill or that his pace had dropped so bad he couldn't get it down there. It was instead a case of him trying to tactically get the pace off the ball; occasionally he'd bowl a quick one and I'd have to try to deal with them.'

Plunkett pulled the third ball of McGrath's last over high for another two runs.

Up in the Brewongle Stand, Jane, Dale McGrath, his mates Ben and Jock, and Warren Craig watched the last over from the Cricket Australia box. There was not a dry eye among them.

'I was watching Adam Gilchrist and he had stopped and was looking at the crowd in what I can only describe as amazement,' says Craig. 'I think that best reflected how spine-tingling a moment it was. The recognition by the crowd that it was Glenn's last over began to build up from the moment he was thrown the ball, and it was such a spontaneous thing. Nothing had been planned . . . I don't think anyone could ever hope to plan such a thing.'

The fans clapped until their hands stung, but Plunkett still managed to hit the fourth ball for a single.

Former English Test batsman David Gower, whose career had finished before McGrath's, took time out from his commentary duties to give an insight into how his countrymen viewed the man from Narromine.

'He hasn't [so much] been a thorn in England's side over the years as the whole damn tree,' he lamented. 'For England, playing against him is like being dropped from a great height onto an acacia tree with no clothes on at 40 degrees Celsius – not a pleasant experience. He's been an absolute pain in the bum.'

Nixon hit two from the fifth ball.

McGrath looked towards Nixon as he prepared to deliver his last ball in Sydney – *the last throw of the dice*. While he'd been humbled by the crowd's reaction, he put it aside to summon what Jane has described as his amazing powers of concentration to give everyone what they wanted – a wicket from his final delivery.

'Just before I started my run-up, I thought of what a dream it had been to take my last Test wicket with the last ball of my over at the SCG,' says McGrath. 'Apparently the commentators were saying I'd saved the wicket for my last ball. I thought to take a wicket with my last ball in one-day cricket at the SCG would be a fairytale. I planned to bowl a yorker, but I bowled what was maybe the worst ball ever; it was a *shocker* – a slow full toss on leg stump. However, I believe in fate . . . I believe you create your own destiny and I also believe things like bowling the worst ball imaginable happen for a reason.'

Nixon lashed out at the delivery and it flew towards Brad

Hodge in the outfield. In the short time the ball took to reach him, some people wondered how on earth anyone could cope with the pressure the Victorian was under.

'I could feel the anxiety and the pressure on me because it was the big finale to Glenn's career at Sydney,' says Hodge. 'But I also knew it was always going to happen, that it was going to be a case of, "What could go wrong in his last game?" And the ball came straight to *me*. It had been really noisy throughout the over while the crowd farewelled him, but there was a period there when it went really, really quiet.'

Hodge's eyes were like saucers as the ball soared towards him.

'I knew I was going to catch it,' he says. 'I *had* to catch it. It was pretty much the fairytale ending for such a wonderful career. It was so perfect that I realised nothing could go wrong in that instance. But I was still pretty nervous sitting under it, actually.'

As Michael Hussey looked on, he couldn't help but wish he was in Hodge's shoes – but not because he doubted his team-mate's ability to perform under pressure. 'I would've loved to have been that one position around from where I was in the field, to have been standing where Brad was, because it would have been a great honour to take the catch for Pigeon's last wicket on his home ground,' says Hussey. 'The farewell was unbelievable. It was great to be there and to share the moment. And while I was thinking "I wish that was me" as the ball flew towards Hodge, I knew there was no way he was going to spill it.'

McGrath, however, held his breath as the scene unfolded before him. He accepted that *how* he'd finish his international career at Sydney was now in Hodge's normally safe hands. He took nothing for granted – after all, McGrath had dropped a sitter during Australia's defeat in the first final in Melbourne, and he'd been battered by the press for it.

'So the ball was in the air, and while you never like to celebrate before the catch is taken, I got ready. I watched and I hoped,' says McGrath. 'The build-up to the last ball was incredible, because I couldn't believe the crowd would stand and clap me the way it did. I spared a quick thought for Hodgey as the ball was in the air, because I know how tough those high catches are. People watching on think they're easy, but so much goes through your mind from the moment it leaves the bat and goes to your hands. There's that little voice screaming in your head not to drop it. But I really wanted Brad to catch it because, apart from the fairytale, I also thought it would be the perfect way to finish for the crowd. I liked the idea that they might get something back for what they did in that last over.'

The ball fell down towards Hodge's hands, and the instant he snaffled it his heart started to beat again.

'It went straight to me. It was a big thing to get the last wicket in Sydney and it came straight to me,' Hodge says. 'Once it was in my hands it felt great.'

Geoff Lawson called that last over for ABC Radio. He had predicted the odds were with McGrath to get a wicket, but it was the emotion-charged farewell from the fans that made a lasting impression on him.

'I love the game and I am moved by the little things people do,' he says. 'Players' last matches don't often do that much for me, but McGrath's – that was simply outstanding. Sometimes as a player you don't realise how much the fans feel for you. I've only realised that in the years since I've retired. You find out that people liked the way you played. It's great.

'As a player, you acknowledge your fans, you appreciate them, but I think you don't understand how much you become a part of their lives. As a fan, I remember sitting in the old Bob Stand at the SCG with a mate from Wagga during the 1974/75 season, and I remember *hearing* John Edrich get hit in the ribs. I watched Thommo bowl side-on and I couldn't see the ball! I remember thinking to myself, "These guys are gods!"

'And Pigeon is a legend in every sense of the word. He's won games, he's been gutsy with the bat, athletic in the field. He cussed himself a lot but he had a great respect for the sport. The people who watch the game take all that into account. It gets people in the heart and the recognition he received was special. Okay, you get paid well to play the game, but the recognition from people who follow the game is the ultimate reward, and that day in Sydney they certainly recognised Glenn for all he'd done.'

McGrath, who finished his 10 overs with a respectable 2 for 41, was mobbed by his team-mates after Hodge took the catch. The crowd was delirious.

Australia lost to England that night when the Duckworth–Lewis method was implemented to reset the run target after more rain. The Australians couldn't reach the revised total of 187 runs from 27 overs, finishing at 8 for 152. McGrath did not have to bat. It was the first time in 15 years the home side had lost the annual tri-series trophy finals. While this provided their critics with ammunition to suggest Australia's upcoming World Cup defence was in tatters, McGrath's team-mates were bitterly disappointed to think the defeat had somehow let him down.

'It was such an unbelievable occasion and it was just a shame we couldn't win that game,' says Ponting, summing up the feeling of his entire team. 'A real shame.'

McGrath stayed in the dressing-room a little longer after the game than normal. He enjoyed a few quiet drinks with his team-mates and the opposition, and he enjoyed the fact Dale and his mates from the bush were there to savour the moment.

'I didn't want a big fuss made about me after the match,' says McGrath. 'We were headed to New Zealand to play the Kiwis in the Chappell–Hadlee Series and then there was the World Cup. After the game I packed up my kit, a few more people than normal came into the dressing-room, and that was it. I was really disappointed we lost – it was a bit of a sour note. But I guess in the big picture, that farewell from the crowd at the SCG – it was something, wasn't it?'

39

Heavyweight Champions
of the World

The All Blacks of cricket.

> Former New Zealand skipper Stephen
> Fleming's description of the Australian team

The detachment of Royal Barbados Police Force officers who remained at Kensington Oval hours after Australia beat Sri Lanka in the 2007 World Cup Final appeared agitated as they looked at their watches for the umpteenth time. Their shift was over; they were weary and wanted to go home. The Aussies yahooing and celebrating made it clear, however, that they weren't working to a deadline. They'd created history, becoming the first team to win three consecutive World Cups – 1999 in England, 2003 in South Africa and they'd now defeated all-comers to waltz through the West Indies undefeated.

The team's spirit was high as the squad linked arms and formed a tight circle on another victorious battlefield. As they stood mid-wicket, Gilchrist asked his mates to share their most special memory of the World Cup, and one by one the players and support crew spoke of the image they expected to relive in the years to come. The squad was getting drunk on a potent combination of sentiment and the local rum, but it helped the team to forget that the final had ended in pitch-black and farce.

McGrath had extra reason to whoop it up. After a summer in which his viability as a member of the World Cup squad had been publicly debated by commentators and sources close to Cricket Australia, he'd taken 26 wickets – the most by a bowler at any World Cup – and he had been crowned the Player of the Tournament. McGrath's 71 World Cup wickets (achieved between 1996 and 2007) was the greatest haul by any bowler and 16 more than the second-placed Wasim Akram. More importantly, though, his farewell to arms was at last complete, and his final duty as an Australian player was to lead his team-mates in their victory chant: 'Beneath the Southern Cross'. As he prepared to belt out his rendition of the song, the police officer in charge stormed towards the group and ordered them to leave the ground. Their shift was over and everyone – World Champions included – was going home.

Ponting appealed for 'two more minutes' to sing the 'bloody' (or a word to that effect) song, but the law enforcer wasn't prepared to compromise. Team members would later shake their heads in bewilderment as they spoke of how aggressive the sergeant had become when he'd ordered them to leave. 'Frothing at the mouth' was one description. The flashpoint occurred when the officer shouldered Ponting to prove he meant business. When the cricketers moved forward to protect their skipper from any further harm, the two policemen armed with submachine guns braced to meet them. Outraged by the Aussies' reaction, the sergeant threatened he'd make arrests if the team did not leave the field immediately. McGrath could imagine the message he'd send home to Jane: 'In Barbados lockup. Visiting day is Thursday. Bring the kids.'

'They were angry because their shift was about to end

and they wanted to get moving,' recalls McGrath. 'We only wanted a few more minutes to sing the song, but the situation became volatile and it didn't seem worth the drama. However, when the officer dropped his shoulder into Ricky we moved in because we didn't know what was going to happen next. It was all annoying, all very petty, but we didn't allow it to spoil what had been a terrific team effort. We went through the World Cup undefeated and we won the final convincingly. The way the police handled the situation was a real shame, but we could see no reason to antagonise them further. It was wisest just to go back to the hotel.'

The Australian team's security detachment, two high-ranking Caribbean police officers, defused the situation by ordering the officer who'd instigated the trouble to 'stand down'. It was an unfortunate – but perhaps not surprising – postscript to a World Cup branded by some observers as the worst sporting event ever staged. Apart from massive scheduling issues, tickets priced beyond the reach of the average West Indian, and lopsided matches between the game's superpowers and battling minnows, the seven weeks of the 2007 ICC World Cup will be forever remembered for the suspicious death of the Pakistan coach, former England batsman Bob Woolmer.

On a less dramatic scale, but serious all the same, the Australian team management contended with a new phenomenon: 'stitch-up photos', when people purporting to be supporters would try to capture the players in compromising positions. One newspaper published photographs of some stars enjoying drinks with female supporters which were left open to the reader's interpretation. On another occasion a fellow dressed in an Aussie shirt grabbed Andrew Symonds in a headlock at a nightclub while his mate stood by with his camera at the ready. It appeared the motive was to enrage Symonds and hope he'd react in a way that would stir up controversy. Rather than be sucked into their 'sting', Symonds headed straight back to the team hotel. If this was cricket in the new age, 'old man' McGrath was quite happy to be getting out.

The Australian team returned to their hotel and gathered around the swimming pool. After clearing his throat, McGrath bellowed the words that should have been delivered at the ground. Fortunately, none of the other hotel guests were bothered enough by the war cry to phone the police, but it signalled the beginning of what McGrath recalls as the mother of all parties and father of all hangovers. The players drank rum and beer through the night and through to the following morning. In between sips of the local liquor, McGrath thought of how his approach to his final World Cup campaign differed from his previous three and he couldn't help but smile.

'My attitude was so different,' he says. 'In every other series I always focused on what I wanted to achieve – and that was basically to take as many wickets as possible – and how I was going to do it. I went to the West Indies keen to help the other bowlers however I could: spending time with them, talking to them and encouraging them along the way. And it was funny, because rather than being fixated on reaching my personal target, I was more excited by the other guys getting their wickets. My approach was that if I took some, great, but if I didn't and the other guys grabbed them, well, that was tremendous. I felt a bit like a school teacher who was happy to see his students get top marks. But the funny thing was, after I relieved myself of the pressure to take wickets, they came so much more easily. I took one in my first over on six or seven occasions, and normally they were within my first two or three deliveries.'

Queensland's Shane Watson – long identified as an integral part of Australian cricket's future because of his ability to open both the batting and bowling – described being taken under Pigeon's wing in the West Indies as a time his eyes were opened to many new and exciting things. He not only returned from the Caribbean with a World Champion's medal, but, courtesy of the team's most senior player, with insights into life.

'I spoke to Glenn a lot about cricket – bowling and the ways to approach certain situations – because I knew it was going to be my last series with him and there was plenty I wanted to ask him and plenty to learn from him,' says Watson. 'I was lucky to be able to sit down and talk to him about a variety of things, like life and personal situations. I was having trouble with my calf muscle over there and I was amazed to hear him talk about what the mind could do and its ability to help the body heal. Glenn spoke about his own experiences and how he dealt with them, which was incredible.

'I considered myself so lucky to have a guy like him pass on that information to me. Though from the first time I met him, Glenn was always generous in providing advice. He was one player who would sit down and talk to you for as long as you wanted if you had questions. What struck me about Glenn was he has been through an amazing amount of things throughout his life, but he gained an understanding for the situations he confronted because he thought about them and learned from them.'

Perhaps the greatest lesson McGrath impressed upon Watson, a player he has earmarked for a great future, was to leave *nothing* in the tank – especially when no-one offered him an ounce of hope of coming through in a tough situation. For Watson, whose career was punctuated by a series of injuries and bad luck, it was a message he grasped.

'If you listened to the critics before the World Cup, Glenn was supposedly past it,' he says. 'Yet he finished as the World Cup's Player of the Tournament. It was incredible, and it reinforced to me how great he was. I had no doubt he'd have a glorious finish and it showed what a champion he is. I thought it was so awesome he finished that way. If anyone could have written the script for Glenn's goodbye, they couldn't have done it better than the way he played it out. He deserved that script because of the wonderful person he is, and the bowler he was.'

McGrath's final throw of the dice proved the folly of writing off a champion, especially one who'd fought so hard for any gain early on. After doubting McGrath's ability to make it through the summer's big three series – the ICC Trophy, the Ashes and the World Cup – Buchanan openly admits McGrath proved him wrong, and that pleased him.

'Even when Glenn got through the first two challenges – the ICC Trophy and the Ashes – I still had my doubts about his ability to play on the wickets in the West Indies during the World Cup, because we believed they would aid the batsmen because they lacked pace and the grounds were small,' Buchanan says. 'What I found interesting about Glenn was that from the time I joined the side, the selectors always seemed to be saying, "This is the end of Glenn McGrath." There was seemingly something always wrong with him. However, while he was with the team Steve Waugh seemed to always be able to find the right words; he knew how to spur Pigeon along. That was a constant theme throughout the time I was with the team, that notion there was a problem or that he'd lost a yard of pace. But did he go out at the right time? Yes, I think he did.'

While the Australian team wanted to send McGrath off a winner, squad member Stuart Clark admits there was no pact or vow to retain the title for Pigeon in the countdown to the final.

'We all knew his career was coming to an end – because basically he wouldn't let us forget,' Clark laughs. 'We'd get the countdown at practice: This is my fourth-last training session, this is my third-last training session. I remember just before the final we warmed up and because it rained we had to do it all over again. I remember that because he was unhappy: Glenn thought that was all behind him, and a few of us actually found it quite amusing it wasn't his last session.'

But no-one in the Australian team found the final hurdle of their World Cup triumph amusing, because it ended in confusion, chaos and darkness.

Australia finished their 38 overs (reduced due to rain delays) at 4 for 281, thanks to a whirlwind 149 by Gilchrist. Under the Duckworth–Lewis method, Sri Lanka needed to score 283 to win, but with 18 balls remaining they needed an improbable 63 runs to win the crown. When the batsmen accepted the umpire's offer to leave the field because of the light, the Australians believed the game was ended. They danced around the ground embracing one another.

However, the party came to a shuddering halt when umpire Aleem Dar advised Ponting that he and his team would need to return the following day to bowl out the remaining three overs. He also told the ground staff to nail the on-field logos back into place. The players were stunned and the groundsmen were put out by having to do what they thought was more unnecessary work. The Aussies argued that 20 overs was all that was needed to constitute a game, and they'd passed that. The officials, however, countered that the rule applied only for rain – not bad light.

No-one could believe the madness of what was unfurling, but then Sri Lanka's Mahela Jayawardene struck what McGrath described as a 'blow for sanity' when he volunteered to bat out the remaining overs to end the game that night. McGrath, like each of his team-mates, accepted the offer as a gesture of tremendous sportsmanship – one that shouldn't be forgotten in the years to come. In the spirit of goodwill, the Australians bowled their spinners Michael Clarke and Andrew Symonds because the batsmen would have been exposed to physical danger had Ponting introduced pace. It was gentlemanly, but it was an edict that denied McGrath his final over.

'Ricky had planned it so I would bowl the last over of the game, but it wasn't to be,' says McGrath. 'It didn't matter too much, because by playing in the pitch black I figured I had *really* experienced everything cricket had to offer. The final was incredible. I was fielding on the boundary and it was like night. They put the lights on in the grandstand, but they were like spotlights and blinded us. They had to turn them off and it was so dark I couldn't see who was bowling, let alone the ball. I don't know what I would have done if a catch came my way.

'But we won and there was a lot of emotion. When I walked around the SCG with Holly and James after my last Test, it crossed my mind that maybe I was setting myself up for a big fall by going to the West Indies because I thought it'd be very hard to better that moment. However, the World Cup final – frustrating finish and all – was a great way to wrap it up. And to be named Man of the Tournament, that was ridiculous.'

McGrath's last wicket was Russell Arnold, a veteran of 180 One Day Internationals whom he dismissed with the second-last ball of his career. It was not McGrath's greatest ball by any stretch of the imagination – a leg side full toss that Arnold popped off his hip to a diving Gilchrist. While McGrath celebrated, Arnold shook his head in disappointment. He was also retiring, and it was not the finish he wanted for his international career.

'At that stage of the game, we were well behind and it was very dark,' says Arnold. 'I was under the impression he bowled the ball down the leg side on purpose. My shot was more a prod at the ball in self-defence than an attacking one, and unfortunately for me it lobbed in the air and Gilchrist picked it up. I thought it was a strategy. I thought because it was dark, Glenn realised it would be hard for me to pick the ball up so he bowled it in such a manner. I thought it was clever.'

As McGrath wrapped his hands around the trophy amid the madness in the dressing-room, he studied it carefully. He noted the trophy was made from silver and a thin layer of gold. It featured a golden globe supported by three silver columns that were shaped as stumps and bails. He'd heard someone explain once the columns represented the three fundamentals of cricket: bowling, batting and fielding. On this day though, it represented his three winning campaigns: 1999, 2003 and 2007. As he cradled the 11 kilograms of metal and memories in his arms, he allowed his mind to flood with flashbacks from past campaigns and of old team-mates. It struck McGrath as ironic that his final World Cup appearance was against Sri Lanka, since his first World Cup final had ended in defeat to them 11 years earlier in Lahore.

As McGrath recalls, there had been bombings in Sri Lanka and so the Australian and West Indies cricket boards had refused to send their teams there, meaning they'd forfeited the World Cup points. The Sri Lankan government promised to provide all the security they could to ensure their safety, but the Australian Cricket Board was concerned because Ian Healy, Craig McDermott, Shane Warne, Bob Simpson and McGrath had all received death threats before the team left Australia.

'Looking back on it now, the contents of the letter were sick. But I was naive and probably didn't take it as seriously as I should have. I think that growing up in Australia, we develop a false sense of security. Plenty of people, like the police, saw it as a concern, but I was happy to leave it in their hands to deal with. I remember during one previous trip to Sri Lanka, we were at a port and there were two buses. The curtains were drawn across the windows of both vehicles. We climbed on one and the buses went in separate directions. We knew one was a decoy. We knew it was being done for a serious reason but none of us spoke about it. It seemed easier not to have to deal with it at the time.'

Sri Lanka defeated India by default in the first semi-final played before 110,000 fans at Eden Gardens in Kolkata. When India slumped to 8 for 120 in pursuit of Sri Lanka's 8 for 251, some of the crowd bombarded the playing surface with fruit and plastic bottles. The players took shelter in the dressing-room for 20 minutes, but on their return the bombardment resumed. The match referee, Clive Lloyd – who captained the legendary West Indies teams of the 1970s and 80s – awarded the match to the Sri Lankans.

In Mohali, the Australians defeated the West Indies, courtesy of some cool-headed batting by Stuart Law (72) and Michael Bevan (69), and some spin wizardry from Warne, who took four wickets. It was the first time the Windies had ever lost a World Cup semi-final.

In the final, Sri Lanka, who'd only won a combined total of four games in the previous five World Cup tournaments they'd contested, won the toss and sent Australia in to bat. Cricket tragics pointed out they were flying in the face of history, noting that the team batting first had won the previous five finals. Australia finished at 7 for 241, but as night fell they realised why the Sri Lankans had elected to field.

'The dew was incredible,' says McGrath. 'It was impossible to grip the ball and I think the fact we dropped five catches highlighted how tough it was. We were gutted; it was such an empty feeling to lose. There was a view that it was a great result for cricket because the victory would probably mean more to the people of Sri Lanka than it did Australians, but that was no consolation as we tried to come to terms with it. To their credit though, Sri Lanka played well. They also understood the conditions and took advantage of that knowledge.'

The Sri Lankans were champions of the world – and it would take three long years before McGrath and his team-mates could seek redemption. However, they had the shakiest of starts when the 1999 tournament started. They beat Scotland first up but then lost to New Zealand and Pakistan. As McGrath recalls, it felt as if everyone had written them off.

'However, we were so confident of winning it I phoned my dad and told him to put the farm on us. He should've listened. We had to win every game. We beat Bangladesh and then the West Indies [McGrath snared 5 for 14 to set up the victory] and that pitted us against South Africa in the semi-final. Our team meetings throughout the World Cup were always creative and we were encouraged to contribute ideas.

'The night before we played the West Indies I had a thought and while I said it tongue-in-cheek, I was half-serious. I asked, "What would we do if we were in a position against the Windies that we were so far in front? Should we bat slowly?" It had to do with winning points in the Super Sixes. It struck a chord with Steve. He said if we could take the West Indies through the next round with us, we would get two points, but if New Zealand went through we'd get none. Steve and Michael Bevan put the brakes on to slow the scoring down and while they got us home, they took their time. New Zealand hammered Scotland in less than 18 overs, so they got the points and we went through to the Super Sixes with none. It not only set us up to play South Africa, but the fact we had no points also meant we couldn't afford to lose a game because we'd be bundled out.'

South Africa, captained by Hansie Cronje, was the raging favourite to win the World Cup. While the Australians' campaign had started slowly, the Proteas were the pacesetters. They crushed India by four wickets; hammered defending champions Sri Lanka by 89 runs; humiliated England by 122; and thrashed Kenya by seven wickets. The only blemish on their record was a 48-run loss to Zimbabwe before the Super Six phase of the tournament began. The South Africans had no obvious weakness, but at the Aussie team meeting ahead of the crucial Super Six match between the two nations, Warne revealed an observation he'd made which would have an amazing ramification for Australia's World Cup campaign.

'Warnie stood up at the meeting and warned everyone that if Herschelle Gibbs caught them out they were to stand their ground – no matter what,' says McGrath. 'He said Gibbs didn't hold the ball long enough for it to be considered a catch. He'd noticed Gibbs threw the ball straight up in the air to celebrate the second he caught it. His tip was to leave it up to the umpire to make the decision. I think history shows that proved insightful.'

South Africa had set Australia a 271-run chase, of which Gibbs contributed a well-crafted 101. Australia were 3 for 48 when Steve Waugh strode out from the darkness of the dressing-room and on to centre stage. McGrath watched his skipper and couldn't help but think that if he ever needed someone to bat for his life, it'd be Waugh. He seemed unfazed by the job of having to score at 7.5 runs an over and McGrath admired the way his old batting coach picked the runs off one by one.

However, there was a collective gasp from the players in the room when Waugh flicked a Pollock delivery off his pads and it rocketed towards Gibbs at short mid-wicket. The ball went straight into the South African's hands, but *no-one* could believe it when the ball slipped straight out of his grasp because he celebrated prematurely. He went to throw the ball in the air but it dribbled to the ground. Waugh recalled Warne's advice and stood his ground to force the umpires to make the call – they did, and it was in the Australian captain's favour. Legend has it he told the crestfallen South African, 'You've just dropped the World Cup, mate.' In the Australian dressing-room, Warne didn't attempt to hide his elation.

'Warnie was great,' recalls McGrath. 'He was so happy it was funny. He kept saying, "I told you, I told you." And he was right. Steve was on 56 when Gibbs dropped the catch and he made 120 not out from 110 balls – and we got home with just two balls to spare. We won the game and it made it very hard for South Africa to rally in time for our semi-final four days later. It gave us a psychological edge. Though it was a game and a half!'

Australia and South Africa played in the semi-final – and critics agreed it would have been better for cricket if the two teams had been in the final. Australia was dismissed for 213 with Shaun Pollock (5 for 36) and Allan Donald (4 for 32) the destroyers. Warne took three quick wickets against South Africa and when Daryl Cullinan was run out, his team teetered at 4 for 61. Jacques Kallis and Jonty Rhodes each made contributions, but the job of winning the game for South Africa came down to Lance Klusener and Allan Donald.

Damien Fleming bowled the last over of the match, with South Africa needing nine to win. Klusener was on strike. The Australians knew that he hit 80 per cent of his runs through the leg side and wasn't so strong on the off, so Fleming planned to bowl yorkers just outside his off stump. When Klusener belted the first two deliveries to the boundary, Fleming thought to himself, 'That's one hell of a strong weakness.' To put pressure on him, Waugh brought the fielders in. Then there was a missed run-out opportunity – when Darren Lehmann's underarm throw just went past the stumps – and McGrath thought, 'That's it, we've missed our chance.'

But then Klusener hit the ball to mid-off, put his head down and started to sprint. 'It didn't surprise me that Donald didn't back up after what had almost happened the ball before, and he didn't hear the call to run,' says McGrath. 'Mark Waugh fielded the ball and threw it to Fleming, and he rolled the ball along the ground to Gilchrist – it seemed to travel at snail's pace – and Donald was miles out when Gilly ripped up the stumps. The game was a tie and we celebrated like crazy, even though very few of us realised that it meant we'd go into the final!'

A pitched battle had also taken place high in the stands between the Australian and South African players' partners. 'I heard there was a bit of sledging,' laughs McGrath. 'When it looked as if South Africa was going to win, their wives or girlfriends started jumping up and down and would not sit down when the Aussie girls asked them to. It was on, and from what I understand, a few of the South Africans finished the game in tears.'

The lament that the Australia–South Africa semi was not the World Cup decider rang out when Australia won the final against Pakistan by eight wickets. McGrath's contribution was 2 for 13 from nine very tight overs, and the players were honoured with ticker-tape parades around the country.

In 2003 McGrath was laughed at when he suggested in his Indian newspaper column that Australia would not only win the World Cup in South Africa, but they wouldn't drop a game along the way. Little could he have known that Australia would play India in the decider. He credited the calibre of the players in the team for his confidence, though there were two games when the opposition threatened to force-feed him a helping of humble pie.

'We had a few challenges. The game against New Zealand at Port Elizabeth was one, because the pitch was a real turner – it was like a wicket straight from the Subcontinent. It was always going to be a tough game, and Bichel and Bevan saved our bacon with a great stand. England and New Zealand were our two dodgy games, but we got through to the final and once we did that I felt relaxed. I always believed qualifying for the final was more nerve-racking than actually playing in it.'

McGrath, whose early campaign was hampered by a side strain which needed treatment with six cortisone needles, rallied to decimate Namibia by taking 7 for 15. The Africans, who were set 302 for victory, were bundled out for a paltry 45. The record book noted that McGrath's was the best World Cup bowling performance since Winston Davis took 7 for 51 in 1983.

'Andrew Symonds was named Man of the Match against Pakistan and his award was a Pamp solid gold watch made in Switzerland and worth about $3000,' says McGrath. 'When I saw the watch I thought I would *really* love to get one of those, so I couldn't have been happier after Namibia. Trophies and mementos meant a lot to me during my career, because I've found when I looked at them they brought the memories of the games to life. I have a display case at home and I'm proud of what it represents.'

McGrath added a gold Krugerrand to his collection when Australia defeated India in the final at Wanderers. 'We were pretty laid-back and easy-going in the build-up,' he recalls. 'The Indians were very serious and solemn. There was no talk and certainly no laughs. I remember feeling the anticipation build up in the team bus on the morning of the final, but we were confident. The pitch offered good bounce, but I thought Ganguly made the wrong choice when he elected to send us in to bat first. I guess he was hoping the bounce would go out of the pitch as the game progressed and it would become more batsman-friendly. Unfortunately for India, Damien Martyn and Ricky put on 234 runs in the last 30 overs to set India 360 to win.'

McGrath's first over brought the wicket of the great Sachin Tendulkar – caught and bowled for 4. However, the rain clouds – and not India's batsmen – were Australia's greatest concern when they were forced to leave the field during the seventeenth over.

'It was a worry because we had to bowl 25 overs for the final to be classified a game,' says McGrath. 'We were pacing up and down the rooms waiting for the promised clear weather. If we didn't bowl the 25 overs, we'd have to return the following day and start from scratch. Our 359 would have counted for nothing.'

The skies cleared and Australia immediately went on the attack. McGrath, Bichel and Symonds combined to rout India for 234 – and, it seemed, in the nick of time.

'The presentation was conducted against a background of swirling black clouds. It looked like the end of the world,' McGrath recalls. 'We went to the middle of the pitch, draped an Australian flag over it and Gilly led us in our team song. It was special . . . we were the World Champions again.'

McGrath's final hurrah in the West Indies in 2007 was a time for the Australians to celebrate the end of his career as much as their successful defence of a crown the rest of the cricketing world had plotted and planned to knock from their heads. Shane Watson, who'd absorbed all he could from his chats with McGrath during the previous weeks, appreciated the significance of the victory for the paceman who'd become his mentor.

'We were gone for seven weeks and I know he missed home because he has such a beautiful family,' says Watson. 'He really missed Jane, James and Holly. But he wanted to finish as well as he possibly could. Glenn appreciated that it was his chance to have one last crack before going back to what he'd dreamt of for quite a while – his family. He knew the end was coming and he was focused on making his being away from them for such a long time worth their while. I know he wanted it to end on a perfect note before he spent the rest of his life with what I see as his perfect family.'

40

The Sunset

Even then I instinctively understood that the
blithe spirit was rare among humans and that, for
the period of an evening and a day, I had been
part of the human condition at its best.

Bryce Courtenay, *The Power of One*

Following the World Cup triumph and 17 years after McGrath
had left Narromine in such a mad rush he didn't even think
to take a last look over his shoulder, he made a pilgrimage to the
place he still referred to as 'home': *Lagoona*. But as he surveyed
the landscape of his youth he felt disappointed. Drought had
ravaged the countryside – but the deep cracks in the barren
paddocks were more familiar to him than the old homestead.
The new owners had made too many changes to the exterior for
it to feel like his family's spiritual home any more. For quite a
while he'd entertained the idea of buying the property back, but
now the illusion that it was still his home had been shattered. All
McGrath noticed was change – and it stung.

'I had this plan to get it back into the family's hands and
pass it on to the kids,' he says, 'but it had changed too much
for that. It was no longer the place I knew. It was great to return
"home" after the World Cup and to take a look around because

I really needed to do that, but I was also sad to see how much it had changed from how I remembered it.'

McGrath took a last look at *Lagoona* and then hit the highway to return . . . *home* – to Jane and the children back in Sydney. As the countryside rolled by in a blur he thought about the path his life had followed since he'd left the far west to live in a cramped caravan by the shores of Botany Bay.

'I'd never really sat back and thought about what I'd achieved since that day I left Narromine; I just enjoyed living the journey. If someone had have asked me when I was a kid to describe how I'd want my life to turn out, I couldn't have wished for it to have been any better. I've been lucky. You learn what life is about from what you do. Not long after the World Cup it seemed incredible to think I'd played cricket at the top level for so long. Though as I stood looking at *Lagoona,* I wondered what would I have done if I didn't play cricket. I once thought there was no way I could've been a farmer like Dad and Dale, but it struck me that maybe I could've done it. I miss the land a lot more now than when I was 19. I guess I was ready for change all those years ago, but it feels so good to return to the country these days, to return to the fresh air and the openness. It just feels right.'

McGrath, however, didn't dwell on the prophets of doom who told their junior bank teller he was only setting himself up to get knocked down by accepting Steve Rixon's offer to play grade for Sutherland. Instead he returned to their town hailed as a great of modern cricket. But McGrath didn't gloat or puff out his chest, because he saw himself as just another Narromine boy – even when his two nephews joined a queue for him to sign his autograph at a presentation night west of the Black Stump.

McGrath was chuffed, however, to learn the shire's civic fathers had proposed to erect a life-size statue of him in the town's centre. Apart from paying homage to their favourite son's many achievements, they thought it might also lure tourist dollars into the area. News of the bronze statue was greeted with a sense of pride by his family, but they couldn't help but laugh at the idea that pigeons would one day poop on *the* Pigeon.

There were other accolades on McGrath's retirement. In January 2008 he and Jane were appointed Members of the Order of Australia in the Australia Day honours. McGrath was recognised for his contribution to cricket and the McGrath Foundation; Jane was lauded for her outstanding services to community health.

'That was a huge honour and totally unexpected,' says McGrath. 'I was so proud and privileged to have been a member of the Australian cricket team, but the Order of Australia medal topped everything because of what it signified. The Foundation was the result of a lot of hard work by Jane because she wanted to make a difference for women who found themselves in the situation she did. It was courageous and it was compassionate. Jane and I are really proud of the Foundation and of the good it is achieving. It also pleases us no end that so many good people have jumped on board to support us because they also believe in it. It is meaningful. I think all the good things the Foundation represents – helping people, offering hope and support – mirror all the beautiful things I see in Jane.'

Sutherland Council, at the behest of McGrath's old cricket club, renamed Caringbah Oval after him in February 2008. The announcement was made at an emotion-charged testimonial dinner organised by the Sutherland Sharks to celebrate McGrath's career. Shane Warne was the special guest, Alan Jones (the king of breakfast radio in Sydney) was MC, and the function was attended by McGrath's family and friends. Perhaps it was even more special because the room was crammed with the 'Sutho' gang that had adopted him when he arrived from the bush.

'When Steve Rixon turned up to my door and told me about the club's intention to rename the oval, I was stunned. The first thing to come to my mind was: "You can't do that – it's Caringbah Oval!" It's an iconic sporting oval in the Shire and I'm honoured it has my name, especially when I think of the great cricketers who've come out of Sutherland and played for Australia.'

There were also rumblings from Cricket NSW that McGrath would be considered for life membership despite having played fewer than 30 first-class games for his state due to his heavy commitments to the Australian team. CEO Dave Gilbert acknowledges that McGrath's situation was one the board and its members needed to wrestle with sooner rather than later.

'How can you say no to life membership for Glenn McGrath?' says Gilbert. 'His attitude for NSW was the same as when he played for Australia – he never shirked his duty. If anything, he might've been guilty of trying too hard, because when he'd return for NSW he wanted to be as dominant for the state as he was for Australia. There'll be many others who'll also only play a limited number of games for NSW because of national commitments. Brett Lee will take in excess of 300 Test wickets and Michael Clarke seems certain to score 8000 Test runs, but they won't represent the state too often. It is something we as an organisation must address.'

While NSW coach Matthew Mott declared he wanted to recruit McGrath as the state's bowling coach at the beginning of the 2007/08 season and there were suggestions he might become a mentor for Cricket Australia's young guns, McGrath kept true to his promise to stay clear of cricket for a full year. His life was still busy. Warren Craig filled his diary with corporate engagements; he worked tirelessly for the McGrath Foundation; he did all he could to catch up on all the lost time with his young family; and he found his body enjoyed an end to the grind of solid training.

'I wanted a whole year away from cricket so I could spend time with the family. I still worked, but it was so good to see James play cricket, practise his bowling or go to the beach for nippers, and do the Dad things. I love being with Holly – she is such a Daddy's girl and has me wrapped around her little finger . . . and I think she knows it. It was also great to spend time with Jane. Now that I've retired, I've become known as Jane McGrath's husband rather than Glenn McGrath the cricketer, and I couldn't be happier.

'I don't miss playing. I first realised that a few weeks after I returned home from the World Cup and I watched the West Indies–England Test series on television. I did not miss cricket at all. I know that will surprise a lot of people, but I am happy with what I achieved and how I retired. I have no desire now to be out there.'

While Jane describes her husband as a loving and devoted family man, she admits his transition from professional cricketer to full-time father wasn't as smooth as McGrath may have hoped.

'It is great to have Glenn around – we really love it,' she enthuses. 'But it was interesting when he wanted to do some things *his* way. From the kids' point of view, it was a case of, "But we do it this way, Dad." We did things on our own when Glenn was away so, rightly or wrongly, we set our own routines. The kids are mad about Glenn – they love him – but it was a shock to their systems when he wanted to do things differently. That took some getting used to for Glenn and the kids.'

McGrath's old team-mates, Steve Waugh and Ricky Ponting

included, aren't surprised to hear he quickly became Jane's third child, and was often chided for annoying the children.

'They'd better get used to their father tapping them on the shoulder and looking away when they turn around,' laughs Ponting. 'I reckon he did that a dozen times a day to his team-mates; it'll be hard for him to stop – he'll need to do it to someone.'

McGrath was given his chance to annoy a new group of team-mates when he signed a three-year deal with the Delhi Daredevils in the Indian Premier League (IPL). The Twenty20 competition was created by the Board of Control for Cricket in India to capitalise on that nation's insatiable appetite for the modified game. The format is known for its fast-paced, big-hitting excitement – accompanied by rock and roll soundtracks – and the fanatical support it receives translates to Pay TV revenue, big takings at the gates and sponsorship opportunities.

McGrath and Warne were both signed to lucrative deals and, like the rest of the cricketing world, they watched in amazement as the media revealed the amounts of money the competition was generating. The ten-year television rights were sold for US$1 billion and Indian businessmen paid kings' ransoms to buy into the eight franchises. Mumbai, for instance, was snapped up for US$127.27 million. The players were told they could expect to snare hundreds of thousands of dollars through a variety of endorsements and would enjoy top-ups via their franchises. While McGrath has embraced the excitement and hype of the Twenty20 format, he is concerned about the impact it could have on other forms of the game.

'People ask if Twenty20 is the future,' he says. 'It probably is, but we have to wait and see whether it has a positive or negative impact on cricket. It will definitely affect one-day cricket, but it'll be very disappointing if it interferes with Test cricket. I find it sad to think a lot of New Zealanders, including Shane Bond, won't be allowed to play for their country any more because they aligned themselves to the Indian Cricket League [a rebel Twenty20 competition]. It's detrimental to the international game, but when a player can earn much more money in six weeks than they could in 12 months, well, you can understand why they want to join up.'

McGrath received a taste of Twenty20 on 8 January 2008 when he played in a match for NSW against Queensland at the Olympic Stadium. Cricket NSW billed it as both a fundraiser for the McGrath Foundation and an opportunity for SpeedBlitz Blues fans to wish their hero well in retirement. Over 23,000 fans cheered as he was run out for a duck, but rather than storm off the field, McGrath raised his bat in mock triumph and laughed along with the crowd. He was still incredible with the ball in hand despite his months of inactivity. His nagging line and length dismissed Bulls skipper Jimmy Maher cheaply, and his four overs yielded a miserly 11 runs.

Bev, who watched the action from a private box in the grandstand, noted the significance of a 'Steve Smith' playing in the match. The teenager from Sutherland was named Man of the Match after taking 4 for 15 with his leg spin bowling, but seeing his name on the scoreboard took Bev back to that day–night game when Doug Walters had identified her elder son as a rare talent.

'It's funny to think there was a Steve Smith in Glenn's last match, considering Steve Smith [the Test player] played in the Country Cup game at Parkes all those years ago,' she says. 'I can't believe the time has gone so quickly.'

Despite taming the Queensland batsmen with his tight line and length, McGrath describes the hurly-burly pace of the game as a real 'eye-opener'.

'Playing against Queensland was a bit of a reality check,' he says. 'I realised I wouldn't want to play in a game where I'd need to bowl any more than four overs at the one time. I had no desire to be out there playing Tests or one-dayers, but Twenty20 would give me a cricket fix. I knew I'd still be competitive.'

In the IPL, McGrath was one of the standout bowlers. In a competition that brought in American cheerleaders to add even more pizazz to the atmosphere, he demonstrated that he'd lost none of his trademark accuracy despite his year away from the fray. No-one, though, was more surprised at how he dominated a game that was tailor-made for big-hitting batsmen than McGrath himself.

'I was surprised by how quickly I got back into stride,' he says. 'I hadn't bowled a ball since the match against Queensland a few months earlier, so my form was a pleasant surprise. I found playing in the IPL a great experience, but it confirmed why I retired . . . I was so keen to get home to Jane and the kids.'

McGrath's form didn't escape scrutiny in England. He was offered a lucrative deal to 'guest' for three weeks in county cricket, but he had no interest. He'd had enough.

A few days after being warned by Ponting that he was staying in a house close enough to the McGraths' place for Ponting to hit golf balls into their yard, McGrath was surprised to find a couple of balls among the ferns in his garden. He didn't know whether to laugh or get square – though he did think to call his old skipper a 'cheeky little bastard'. He put the balls in his pocket and considered returning them via his driver.

McGrath sat out the back of his waterfront home on sparkling Port Hacking. The sun was deep in its descent over the horizon, its long rays streaked across the sky, lighting it with colours which looked to the retired cricketer as they'd done since he was a boy – like smears of drizzled honey, burnt orange, molten gold and bronze. He was 38 years old, a father of two, a devoted husband and a proud son of the bush. Of the many things he'd learned throughout his life, one of his earliest lessons rang true at this moment: that nature's wonders – sunsets, sunrises, lightning storms – are nutritious for the soul. Twenty years earlier, after slaving in the paddocks as a boy doing a man's job in his father's absence, he had turned his back on such a sight to finish his last chore of the night – bowling at a 44-gallon drum to prepare for the day he'd play for Australia.

McGrath had spent the day with Jane. He'd fished off the jetty with James and entered Holly's fantasy world of palaces, ponies and princesses. After devoting most of his youth to making it in cricket, McGrath put his feet up at last.

The boy who couldn't bowl was happy.

41

The Legend of Glenn McGrath

You take a clean-cut, simple country boy – and I
mean that in the nicest way possible – and turn
him into an absolute superstar. Glenn told me he
could've been working on bridges in the outback
had he gained an apprenticeship, but he was lucky
because he got his chance to come to Sydney. He
lived in a caravan for 13 months and did all the
hard yards, and he never looked back.

Brett Lee, NSW and Australian team-mate

In the years to come, the legend of Glenn Donald McGrath –
the Narromine boy who couldn't bowl – might see him
adopted as the patron saint of all park cricketers told they have
less ability than a fishing rod. As the most successful ever fast
bowler, McGrath proved that determination combined with
the commitment to follow your heart is a powerful force.

McGrath might also be hailed as courageous by future
generations for the way he pushed through the pain and
exhaustion barriers when Australia needed him to take a
breakthrough wicket. Cricket historians might one day identify
his commitment to take the fight to the West Indies in 1995 as
the action that ended the Windies' domination of international

cricket and laid the foundation for Australia's most glorious reign. His partnership with Shane Warne is certain to be remembered, perhaps as the most lethal ever. And just as easily, McGrath could be remembered as the loving family man who, with his wife, Jane, gave their all in the battle to find a cure for breast cancer.

McGrath's one hope is that he won't be remembered for being a 'boring' bowler.

'It's up to others to judge how I'm remembered,' he says. 'However, I'd like to be remembered for playing the game in the right spirit, for getting out on the field and giving it everything I had. Hopefully I'll be remembered not so much for being a boring sort of cricketer who didn't do too much with the ball, but for being an intelligent bowler who had a plan and managed to "think" the batsmen out rather than blast them out. I hope to be remembered for the fact that I loved bowling and I loved every minute I was out on the field and playing.

'I could be remembered as blessed, because apart from being a member of a special group of blokes who mean a lot to me – the Australian cricket team – my life was touched by the many people I befriended or met through a great sport. Yet I received no greater blessing than meeting and marrying Jane, the love of my life. Our greatest achievement has been James and Holly and my life is dedicated to ensuring their happiness.

'I do hope people can take the positives out of what I achieved and see that it is possible to follow their dreams, even though they might seem out of reach or impossible. Dare to dream. Life is boring without dreams. As the kid who pretended he was opening the attack for Australia when I bowled at a 44-gallon drum behind the machinery shed on a farm in the middle of nowhere, I found that with sacrifice, dreams can come true.'

McGrath will be remembered in the game's history as one of the greatest fast bowlers ever to grip a ball. However, the cold hard statistics won't tell the story of the flight of the Pigeon quite like those he played alongside and against.

Jane McGrath's eyebrows knit together when she's asked to reveal the key to her husband's extraordinary success. After a few seconds of deep thought, her face breaks into the same smile McGrath says bedazzled him all those years ago during their chance meeting in a Hong Kong nightclub called Joe Bananas.

'When people ask me what the secret to Glenn's success was, I like to think it was a happy family life,' she says, ignoring her husband's loud sledge for her to 'please tell the truth'.

'While our lives have been affected by cancer, our home life was – is – one of great love and happiness. We learned to take nothing for granted, especially one another, and all the blessings people normally don't notice in their haste to get through the day.'

As someone who didn't have the foggiest idea of the difference between a leg bye and a cover drive the first time she watched McGrath play, Jane saw firsthand the numerous trials and tribulations her soul mate overcame to stake his claim for greatness.

'I know Glenn hopes he isn't remembered as a boring bowler,' she says. 'And while I'll admit to being hopelessly biased, I can't understand how anyone could see him as anything but extraordinary – as a husband, father, cricketer, team-mate and man.

'When I think of everything Glenn and I have endured because of the cancer, I can't help but to think his effort to play cricket at the highest level and to remain focused on competing – and succeeding – was a phenomenal effort, and it is something I'm proud of. While playing for Australia meant so much to Glenn, he never once gave the impression that it was ever more important than me or his family. It's well known there were many times when Glenn put his career on hold to remain at home with me and the children.'

Jane was at home recovering after a short stint in hospital when both she and Glenn were awarded their Australia Day honours. Her recuperation from the surgery also forced her to miss the renaming of Caringbah Oval in her husband's honour, but her pride about it was deep.

'I thought it was marvellous, absolutely fabulous. Glenn has received many awards and acknowledgements throughout his career, but he was so proud the night Steve Rixon knocked on our front door to tell him the news. Though, true to form, Glenn's initial reaction was the ground is Caringbah Oval, and its name couldn't be changed. Sutherland's gesture was very beautiful and very special.

'His achievements mean a lot to me and his family. We were so proud of what he achieved when he was playing and we're equally as proud of him now he's retired. When I'm asked for my favourite memory of Glenn the player, I'm torn between his 8 for 38 at Lord's and his scoring 61 against New Zealand – that innings meant a lot to him and was the end result of a lot of hard work. I am so glad I was there to witness both brilliant moments.'

Jane laughs when she suggests Glenn's busiest days as a bowler are to come. James has taken to cricket and she can see Glenn being recruited as a bowling machine in the many backyard training sessions to come. In between deliveries, Jane says, their daughter, Holly, will demand her time with him; she loves receiving attention from the biggest kid in the house.

For Jane, the happy scenes of father, son and daughter laughing and playing together are perfect.

'Now Glenn is retired and we have more time together, my dream is we grow really old together and that we watch James and Holly grow up. That is our shared dream.

'As for his legacy to cricket, well, he was a great bowler – some say the best fast bowler ever, and that says a lot. What I will say is that Glenn is a champion.

'He's my champion.'

Postscript
After Jane

I would like to think Jane will be remembered as an extraordinary person whose courage and determination humbled me and inspired so many people.

Glenn McGrath

Fate denied Glenn and Jane McGrath the chance to live out their shared dream of a long life together. On Sunday 22 June 2008, with her family around her, Jane lost her battle with cancer. The Australian public demonstrated its deep affection for her with an overwhelming outpouring of grief. For Glenn, the death of his soul mate was devastating.

Jane's funeral took place at the Garrison Church in the Rocks, where nine years earlier she and Glenn had been married. Many of the couple's family and friends who had been present at that happy day assembled again to mourn her loss, and members of the public gathered near the church to pay their own respects. Broadcaster and friend Alan Jones delivered a eulogy, as did Tracy Bevan, who spoke courageously and lovingly about her closest friend. 'I'll miss her every day until I see her again,' she said. After leaving the church, Glenn, James and Holly released three white doves into the clear blue sky.

After farewelling the love of his life, Glenn took the children to his outback property in far-west New South Wales. He'd taken Jane here in 1997 after she was first diagnosed with cancer, and the natural beauty of the land had helped inspire her to fight and beat the disease. Now it was the place where Glenn, James and Holly could remember Jane in their own ways, and slowly come to terms with her death.

'Jane wouldn't have been happy with that,' Glenn says with a smile. 'She was a great mother and very protective of the kids. She thought the bush was a dangerous place, but James and Holly enjoyed their time out there by having wonderful adventures. I have a deep love for the outback and plan to spend more time out there with them.'

They returned to Cronulla three weeks later. Public and corporate donations had flowed to the McGrath Foundation following Jane's death, reflecting the enormous public support for her work. McGrath became chairman of the charity he'd founded with his wife. Recognising his commitment to the cause and his tireless work for the McGrath Foundation, the National Australia Day Council named him as the 2009 New South Wales Australian of the Year.

In December 2008, the Sydney Cricket and Sports Ground Trust announced that the third day of the upcoming SCG Test match against South Africa would be Jane McGrath Day. At the match in early January 2009, the players, commentators and spectators – including prime ministers past and present – all sported pink to show their support, and hundreds of thousands of dollars were raised for the Foundation.

McGrath addressed the crowd at the conclusion of the Test, which Australia won in a tense and close-fought last session.

'It has been an amazing five days,' he said, 'and I stand here now a very, very proud Australian. As we say at the McGrath Foundation, together we can make a difference, and we've definitely achieved that over the last five days.'

Cricket remains an important part of McGrath's life, and in 2009 he will again play in the Indian Premier League. In 2008 – at the age of 38 – he led the Delhi Daredevils' bowling attack, taking the team to the semi-finals, where they lost to the eventual champions, Shane Warne's Rajasthan Royals.

Although life has changed irrevocably for the McGrath family, Glenn is determined that James and Holly never forget their mother's love for them. 'We talk about Mummy all the time,' he says. 'They have chosen a star and we go say hello to Mummy every night.' And Jane lives on every day in her husband's thoughts. 'I want Jane's memory to be a celebration of life,' he says.

Career Highlights

Dec 1989 First-grade debut – Sutherland vs Sydney University – Caringbah Oval.

Jan 1993 First-class debut – NSW vs Tasmania – SCG.
Adam Gilchrist makes his debut in the same match.
29.1-9-79-5 & 13.3-6-29-0

Mar 1993 Sheffield Shield Final – NSW vs Queensland – SCG.
NSW wins by eight wickets.
24.5-5-64-4 & 18-5-28-3
Fourth in the first-class season bowling averages – 25 wickets at 23.92

Nov 1993 Test debut – First Test, Australia vs New Zealand – WACA Ground.
Becomes the 358th Test cricketer for Australia.
39-12-92-2 & 16-6-50-1

Dec 1993 One Day International debut – Australia vs South Africa – MCG.
Becomes the 113th ODI cricketer for Australia.
8.4-1-28-0

Apr 1995 Man of the Match – First Test, West Indies vs Australia – Bridgetown.
12.1-1-46-3 & 22-6-68-5

Dec 1995 Man of the Match – Second Test, Australia vs
Sri Lanka – MCG.
23.4-9-40-5 & 33.5-6-92-2

Mar 1996 World Cup Final – Sri Lanka vs Australia – Lahore.
Sri Lanka wins by seven wickets.
8.2-1-28-0

Mar 1996 Man of the Match – First-grade Final, Bankstown vs
Sutherland – Bankstown Oval.
17-5-28-5 & 23-5-72-3

Nov 1996 Named an ABC McGilvray Medallist for 1996 as
one of Australia's four outstanding players during
the period November 1995 to March 1996.

Dec 1996 Man of the Match – Second Test, Australia vs West
Indies – SCG.
31-9-82-4 & 17-7-36-3

Dec 1996 Takes 100th Test wicket – Third Test, Australia vs
West Indies – MCG.
Robert Samuels lbw b McGrath.

Feb 1997 Man of the Series – Australia vs West Indies in
Australia.
5 Tests – 26 wickets for 453 – average 17.42

Jun 1997 Man of the Match – Second Test, England vs
Australia – Lord's.
20.3-8-38-8 & 20-5-65-1

Aug 1997 Man of the Series – England vs Australia in
England.
6 Tests – 36 wickets for 701 runs – average 19.47

Nov 1997 Named an ABC McGilvray Medallist for 1997 as
one of Australia's four outstanding players during
the period August 1996 to August 1997.

Jan 1998 Named as one of the five Wisden Cricketers of the
Year for 1997.

Nov 1998   Man of the Match – First Test, Australia vs England
– Gabba.
34.2-11-85-6 & 16-6-30-1

Jan 1999   Takes 200th Test wicket – Fifth Test, Australia vs
England – SCG.
Alec Stewart c Warne b McGrath.

Jan 1999   Takes 100th ODI wicket – Australia vs England –
MCG.

Mar 1999   Man of the Match – First Test, West Indies vs
Australia – Port-of-Spain, Trinidad.
14-3-50-5 & 10-3-28-5 and 39 & 4*

Jun 1999   World Cup Final – Australia vs Pakistan – Lord's.
Australia wins by eight wickets.
9-3-13-2

Oct 1999   Plays 100th ODI – Australia vs Zimbabwe –
Bulawayo.
6.4-0-21-1

Nov 1999   Named as Wisden's Australian Cricketer of the Year
for 1999.

Nov 1999   Named an ABC McGilvray Medallist for 1999 as
one of Australia's four outstanding players during
the period September 1998 to June 1999.

Jan 2000   Named in the NSW Blues Living Legends XII,
selected from all living players who have represented
NSW.

Jan 2000   Man of the Match – Third Test, Australia vs India –
SCG.
18.5-7-48-5 & 17-1-55-5

Jan 2000 Named inaugural Allan Border Medallist as Australian Cricketer of the Year – awarded to the player who receives the most votes from a voting academy of players, umpires and media. Glenn received the most player votes and the most umpire/media votes – 97 in total – to win from Steve Waugh (87) and Ricky Ponting (77).
Also named as Test Player of the Year, with 14 votes, from Ricky Ponting and Steve Waugh (both 12).

Jul 2000 Named International Cricketer of the Year 2000 – nominees are players whose consistently excellent performances have led to high placing in the PricewaterhouseCoopers Cricket Ratings for Test and One Day International cricket over the previous year.

Jul 2000 Playing for Worcestershire in English county cricket, scores maiden first-class half-century with 55 vs Nottinghamshire.

Sep 2000 Finishes English county season as the leading first-class wicket-taker (80 wickets at 13.21), with the best average and strike-rate of bowlers with over 40 wickets. In the Sunday League, takes 30 wickets at 8.13 – third-highest wicket-taker and best average and best economy rate of all bowlers. Named Bowler of the Year.

Nov 2000 Named an ABC McGilvray Medallist for 2000 as one of Australia's four outstanding players during the period August 1999 to April 2000.

Nov 2000 Man of the Match – First Test, Australia vs West Indies – Gabba.
20-12-17-6 & 13-9-10-4

Dec 2000   Takes 300th Test wicket – Second Test, Australia vs West Indies – WACA Ground.
Brian Lara c MacGill b McGrath.
Becomes the tenth Australian player to take a hat-trick in Test cricket.
Sherwin Campbell, Brian Lara, Jimmy Adams.

Jan 2001   Man of the Series – 2000/01 Australia vs West Indies in Australia.
5 Tests – 21 wickets for 359 runs – average 17.09

Feb 2001   Named One Day International Player of the Year, with 18 votes, from Damien Martyn and Mark Waugh (16).
Also finishes fifth in the Allan Border Medal with 57 votes, behind Steve Waugh (63), Mark Waugh (62), Brett Lee (61) and Adam Gilchrist (58).

Mar 2001   Australia scores world-record sixteenth consecutive Test victory – First Test, Australia vs India – Mumbai.

Mar 2001   Takes 200th ODI wicket – Australia vs India – Indore.

Jul 2001   Man of the Match – Second Test, Australia vs England – Lord's.
24-9-54-5 & 19-4-60-3

Aug 2001   Man of the Series – 2001 England vs Australia in England.
5 Tests – 32 wickets for 542 runs – average 16.94.

Nov 2001   Named an ABC McGilvray Medallist for 2001 as one of Australia's four outstanding players during the period September 2000 to August 2001.

May 2002   Australian Team named as Best Team at Laureus World Sports Awards.

Oct 2002   Takes 400th Test wicket – Third Test, Australia vs Pakistan – Sharjah.
Waqar Younis lbw b McGrath.

Feb 2003   Best figures by an Australian in ODIs – World Cup vs Namibia – Potchefstroom.
7-4-15-7

Mar 2003   World Cup Final – Australia vs India – Wanderers. Australia wins by 125 runs.
8.2-0-52-3

Jul 2004   Man of the Match – First Test, Australia vs Sri Lanka – Darwin.
15-4-37-5 & 16-9-24-2

Oct 2004   Plays 100th Test – Third Test, Australia vs India – Nagpur.
25-13-27-3 & 16-1-79-2

Nov 2004   Scores maiden Test half-century – First Test, Australia vs New Zealand – Gabba.
61 runs from 92 balls, with 5 fours and 1 six.
Record score for Australia by a number 11 batsman.
Tenth-wicket partnership of 116 with Jason Gillespie.

Nov 2004   Man of the Series – 2004/05 Australia vs New Zealand in Australia.
2 Tests – 9 wickets for 184 runs – average 20.44

Dec 2004   Achieves best bowling figures in Tests – First Test, Australia vs Pakistan – WACA Ground.
16-8-24-8

Feb 2005   Takes 300th ODI wicket in 200th ODI, Australia vs Pakistan – MCG.

Jul 2005   Takes 500th Test wicket – First Test, England vs Australia – Lord's.
Marcus Trescothick c Langer b McGrath
Career record at Lord's:
3 Tests – 26 wickets for 299 runs – average 11.50

Sep 2005   Plays last Test in England – Fifth Test, England vs Australia, The Oval.
Career record in England:
14 Tests – 87 wickets for 1683 runs – average 19.34

Nov 2006   Resumes Test career after ten-month break – First Test, Australia vs England – Gabba.
23.1-8-50-6 & 19-3-53-1

Dec 2006   Announces retirement from Test cricket at the conclusion of the Fifth Test at the SCG, and retirement from all cricket after the 2007 World Cup.

Jan 2007   Plays 124th and last Test – Fifth Test, Australia vs England – SCG.
Takes a wicket with final ball.
29-8-67-3 & 21-11-38-3

Mar 2007   Breaks Wasim Akram's record of 55 wickets for most wickets taken in World Cups – Australia vs Bangladesh – Antigua.

Apr 2007   Plays 250th and last ODI – World Cup Final, Australia vs Sri Lanka – Kensington Oval.
Takes a wicket with second-last ball in ODIs.
Australia wins by 53 runs.
7-0-31-1
Breaks record for most wickets taken at a single World Cup:
11 matches – 26 wickets for 357 runs – average 13.73
Named Player of the Tournament.

With thanks to Tom Iceton of the Sutherland Cricket Club.

Statistics

BATTING

	Matches	Innings	NO	HS	Runs
Tests	124	138	51	61	641
ODIs	250	68	38	11	115
First-class	189	193	67	61	977
First-grade	53	30	11	20	129

BOWLING

	Overs	Maidens	Runs	Wickets	Average
Tests	4874.4	1470	12186	563	21.64
ODIs	2161.4	279	8389	381	22.02
First-class	6959.5	2118	17414	835	20.85
First-grade	940.0	260	2301	133	17.30

With thanks to Tom Iceton of the Sutherland Cricket Club.

Average	100s	50s	Catches
7.36	–	1	38
3.83	–	–	37
7.75	–	2	54
6.79	–	–	14

Best	5wI	10wM	S/R	Economy
8-24	29	3	52.0	2.50
7-15	7	–	34.2	3.89
8-24	42	7	50.0	2.50
7-47	11	–	42.4	2.45

Acknowledgements

I would like to express my gratitude to a long list of friends and acquaintances for their willingness to contribute their thoughts and anecdotes to *Line and Strength*.

Firstly, all my love and thanks to my family: Jane, James and Holly; my mum, Beverley; my dad, Kevin; and my siblings, Dale and Donna. My appreciation also extends to the following people: my manager, Warren Craig; my personal trainer, Kevin Chevell; Sutherland Sharks stalwarts Steve Rixon and Tom Iceton; my former captains, team-mates and support staff, including Allan Border, Mark Taylor, Steve Waugh, Ricky Ponting, Shane Warne, Jason Gillespie, Justin Langer, Adam Gilchrist, Stuart Clark, Nathan Bracken, Mark Waugh, Simon Katich, Shane Watson, Phil Jaques, Dom Thornley, Brad Haddin, Michael Hussey, Brett Lee, Trevor Bayliss, Greg Matthews, Daniel Smith, Steve Small, John Buchanan, Pat Farhart, Jock Campbell and Alex Kontouris; former Test players, including the late David Hookes, Rodney Marsh, Doug Walters, Len Pascoe, Geoff Lawson, John Dyson and David Gilbert; my respected opponents Graham Thorpe, Michael Atherton and Alec Stewart (England), the great Courtney Walsh (West Indies), Shoaib Akhtar (Pakistan), Russell Arnold (Sri Lanka), Dene Hills (Tasmania) and Tony Fort (Northern Districts, Sydney).

I offer a very special thanks, too, to the great Dennis Lillee for his wonderful and thoughtful foreword. Your sentiments are very humbling, Dennis, and add to the incredible debt I owe you. My gratitude extends to Narromine's Melinda Gainsford-Taylor, her father, Brian, and rugby league international David Gillespie. To Tracy Bevan, Jane's dearest friend, I thank you for so much, not least for your insights that appear in this book.

Daniel thanks the following people for their support: his mum, Carol; brothers Richard and Nick; Daniel Scully; Bernie McCarthy; Adam Cox; Karen Grega; Caron LeFever; Peter Gearin; Scott Longmuir; Rob Horton; Ginger Winslow; Ian Heads; Ern McQuillan; Jason Thompson; and John Polly. He also acknowledges a long list of journalists and authors from whose work he sourced information.

To the Random House gang, especially the wonderful Meredith Curnow and Julian Welch, I thank you for displaying a much-welcomed and rare faith in – and passion for – this project. A special mention for a job well done to Jane Gleeson-White – surely the D. K. Lillee of book editors.

And last but not least, a big hug from Daniel for the ever-patient Camille.